What people are saying about
Insatiable Hunger

This is not the Canadian History I was taught at school back in the sixties. Then, it was all about which European 'discovered' which river or 'founded' which settlement and how they fought with each other over 'ownership' of the country. Graham gives us a very different history, seen from the perspectives of both the incomers and the original inhabitants. He makes the point that the rivers had supported a considerable indigenous population through forest stewardship and agriculture for millennia before the Europeans arrived in any numbers. He describes the cultural system of the indigenous tribes as being a gift culture. In contrast, the Europeans brought their culture of ownership, entitlement and hierarchy.

Graham takes us from early encounters between the two cultures in 1534 through to 1812. He tells the story as it unfolded in Europe, where religious wars led people to seek a new world.

"Driven by these religious priorities, they sought new homes. The French and the English both found those homes in northeastern North America. The French attempted to expand Christendom while the English found a home for the reformists, the Protestants. Both discovered that the space they sought was already inhabited and that the people here had no tradition of or need for Christianity."

In parallel, he describes what happened in the new world, as the arrivals brought with them new and deadly diseases as well as their alien religious and political convictions. The story is almost unbearable to read, particularly now that we know more about the events that followed.

In a moving final chapter Graham suggests the lessons we should learn from this story in a world now subject to viral pandemics and global warming. This book was 12 years in the writing and the research and thought that Graham put into it is evident. The book contains a wealth of contemporary maps and engravings and an extensive bibliography of works consulted. His writing style is engaging and it is easy to get swept into the unfolding story.

I would recommend this book to anyone with an interest in Canadian history, the impact of colonisation on indigenous people or concern about the sustainability of our world.

Professor Elisabeth Paice, OBE

I must confess I am not a fan of what is known as non-fiction. Everything is tied to story for me. That aside, this is an important work. It struggles for truth and accuracy in unfolding the story of Canada. I am not a fan of Canada. Canada is the name of the empire that Britain gave our homelands to, but this is clear in the book. What is not clear is what do we do about it. Reconciliation begins with truth and in this case, it is really our homeland, and nothing can be decided without us. We must become the authors of a new story and I think the writer is taking us in that direction, bravely, doggedly and with grim determination.

Lee Maracle
Award-winning poet, novelist, and teacher.
Currently a teacher and Mentor for Indigenous Students at the University of Toronto and a cultural instructor at the Traditional Cultural Director for the Indigenous Theatre School.

———◆———

Twelve years in the making, Joseph Graham's Insatiable Hunger makes no excuses for the blind ravages of the Euro-Christian invasion of North America. Grasping the distinction between the Indigenous American gift economy, with its emphasis on nature-connected sustainability, and the Euro-Christian market economy, with its emphasis on wealth accumulation at any cost (to others), Graham wends his way through the meta-history of European colonization, 1535-1814. He places it in the context of, on the one hand, the lack of any Indigenous need for Europeans in the Americas, and on the other hand, the invading Europeans' desire to escape Christianity's belligerent factions at home, even as they continued their internecine wars of all against all in America. Having escaped Christianity at home, European began imposing it on Indigenes. Locked in their cultural bubble, disdaining Indigenous societies, the French, Spanish, Dutch, Swedes, and British invaders then pushed relentlessly inland, spreading lethal diseases visiting mortality rates on Indigenous nations that fell below population sustainability. What disease and siege did not take, liquor did. Throughout, Graham's lingering question is how the damage is repaired, as he urges moving from hierarchical markets to egalitarian gift relations. Eminently readable, Graham's clear and unpretentious yet documented prose respects Indigenous stories as much as Euro-Christian stories in contrasting Indigenous female-male co-valence with European male dominance.

Barbara Alice Mann, Ph.D.,
Professor of Humanities at Jesup Scott Honors College
Author of numerous books, including *Spirits of Blood, Spirits of Breath, The Twinned Cosmos of Indigenous America* (2016).

Insatiable Hunger

Colonial Encounters in Context

Joseph W. Graham

BLACK
ROSE
BOOKS

Montréal/Chicago/London

Black Rose Books No. VV426

Library and Archives Canada Cataloguing in Publication
Insatiable hunger : colonial encounters in context / Joseph W. Graham.
Names: Graham, Joseph W., author.
Description: Includes bibliographical references and index.
Identifiers: Canadiana (print) 20210193166 | Canadiana (ebook) 20210193239 | ISBN 9781551647746 (softcover) | ISBN 9781551647760 (hardcover) | ISBN 9781551647784 (PDF)
Subjects: LCSH: Indigenous peoples—Colonization—Canada. | LCSH: Indigenous peoples—Colonization—United States. | LCSH: Indians of North America—First contact with Europeans. | LCSH: War—Religious aspects—Christianity. | LCSH: Europe—History.
Classification: LCC E59.F53 G73 2021 | DDC 970.004/97—dc23

C.P.35788 Succ. Léo-Pariseau
Montréal, QC, H2X 0A4
Explore our books and subscribe to our newsletter:
blackrosebooks.com

ORDERING INFORMATION

CANADA
University of Toronto Press
5201 Dufferin Street
Toronto, ON M3H 5T8
1-800-565-9523
utpbooks@utpress.utoronto.ca

USA/INTERNATIONAL
University of Chicago Press
Chicago Distribution Center
11030 South Langley Avenue
Chicago, IL 60628
(800) 621-2736 (USA)
(773) 702-7000 (International)
orders@press.uchicago.edu

UK/IRELAND
Central Books
50 Freshwater Road
Chadwell Heath, London RM8 1RX
+44 (0) 20 8525 8800
contactus@centralbooks.com

Cover and book design: Rita Bauer, Silver Lining, Montreal

Cover features the public domain images:
Boisseau, Jean, Active. Description de la Nouvelle France, ou, sont remarquées les diverses habitations des françois, depuis la première descouverte jusques à present, receuillie et dressée sur diverses relations modernes. [Paris: Chez Iean Boisseau, enlumineur du Roy pour les cartes géographiques, 1643] Map. <https://www.loc.gov/item/91683582/>; and Natives worshipping erected column. 1562. State Archives of Florida, Florida Memory. <https://www.floridamemory.com/items/show/4352>.

For my grandchildren

Jacob, Addison and Ozara

and

for their grandchildren

God blessed them and God said to them:
"Be fertile, and increase, fill the earth, and master it;
and rule the fish of the sea, the birds of the sky,
and all the living things that creep on earth."

God said:
"See, I give you every seed-bearing plant
that is upon the earth,
and every tree that has seed-bearing fruit;
they shall be yours for food."

Genesis 1: 28–29

When the last tree is cut, the last fish is caught,
and the last river is polluted;
when to breathe the air is sickening,
you will realize, too late, that wealth is not in bank accounts
and that you can't eat money.

Alanis Obomsawin

CONTENTS

THE BREAKDOWN BEGINS 1613-1701

A MONSTER REPLICATES 1709-1760

BRITISH HEGEMONY 1763-1814

INTRODUCTION

After over a thousand years of slowly steeping itself in the dogma of Catholicism, Europe began to fragment during the Reformation. All of the players, deeply Christianized, sharing unshakeable tenets, struggled over the sharing of power. New religious ideals shook the establishments, leading to wars. Driven by these religious priorities, they sought new homes. The French and the English both found those homes in northeastern North America. The French attempted to expand Christendom while the English found a home for the reformists, the Protestants. Both discovered that the space they sought was already inhabited and that the people here had no tradition of or need for Christianity.

From the beginning, the people who were here maintained a totally different belief system in the face of an onslaught of disease and masses of newcomers. One of the first agreements between the two different civilizations was called the Two Row Wampum. It consisted of a belt of white beads with two parallel lines of purple running on opposite sides of the centre. It commemorated an understanding that these two purple lines represented the two very different civilizations, travelling together, respectful of each other and not interfering in each other's jurisdiction. The agreement, between the Dutch and the Mohawk of the Five Nations, established how they could share and co-exist.

Over time, one of those purple lines has become thinner, while the other has become much thicker. Somehow, though, both have continued, mostly running parallel, but the values do not overlap. One is a sustaining culture, while the other is a consuming culture. One belongs to the world. The other presumes to own the world.

Our conceit in Western society is that we have progressed through time, that modern civilization is the result of an evolutionary process bringing us an ever more technological and perfect world, a culture determined to reconstruct "nature." But civilizations, including ours, come and go. Rather than having evolved, I see our civilization as analogous to the growth of a plant, starting small and growing at first geometrically and then exponentially to enormous size and impact. There are many ways of organizing societies, but all must conform to the basic rules of our modern market economy. If they don't, they are conveniently dismissed through classifications such as Indigenous. Looking holistically, from that Indigenous side and from modern thinkers like James Lovelock, we see that our world is a symbiotic system in which we play an important role, a role of stewardship. The market economy perceives the whole world as potential products. Spaced in time between the "great" civilizations of history with their expansionist ways, people lived within their means, in a symbiotic way. Today, we are sure of our superior status as a civilization and when we look back, we are blind to earlier sustaining communities that lived lightly on the land for countless thousands of years. Even when we do glimpse these communities, we dismiss them as "primitive" or "savage," failing to see that ancient anomalous structures like Stonehenge or other unexplained abandoned artifacts would have been preceded and succeeded by long periods of the sustaining form of human social organization. I have come to understand that these sustaining communities are as thoroughly modern as any other and achieve the highest standard of social order by being able to share as a community even onto death.[1] By contrast, something happened, perhaps during the evolution of the herding-based cultures of Eurasia that began a spiral of power through consumption, reaching into our times as an endgame that threatens our continued existence. It is thanks to this way of living that the first Europeans who came to our northeastern region of North America found the Anishinaabe and Iroquoian communities, found rivers teeming with fish, skies blackened with clouds of birds, and found a sustaining forest from the Atlantic Coast to the Great Lakes with interspersed farming communities. Belittling nature as something over which an omnipotent personal god had given them dominion, they dismissed the humans they encountered as simply a part of nature. This was somehow seen as a primitive rather than as an equally modern form of society.

One must view the world from where one is, and I live happily in the Laurentian hills north of Montreal. I am not of Indigenous descent but from the European stock that are called settlers in the context of the people who were already here. Like many before me, I seek to understand who I am, how I belong here, and what my responsibilities for "here" entail. Acknowledging my Catholic upbringing, the strong Sephardi-Jewish influence in my married life, and my life-long passion for written history, I have come to appreciate the shortcomings of this mixed heritage and to appreciate history whether written in a European script, presented through Oral Tradition, or registered in the physical world, the rocks, the running water, the soil, and the vegetation. In this work, which has taken me well over twelve years to think through and express, I try always to see the world from here, from the Laurentian hills where I live, because without a "here" it is hard to maintain a perspective. It is necessary, not just to give more space to understanding sustaining Indigenous communities, but also to look objectively at the deeply troubled history of the people who first came from Europe. The European Wars of Religion led in large part to the European settlement of America, and looking at those currents will, I hope, explain the foundation upon which our modern society and economy sits.

How different the Laurentian hills were for the first European-descended colonists who explored and settled here. Our immediate geographical predecessors, the Anishinaabe, have lived in the surrounding forests for millennia, although today they have been segregated onto reserves or barely tolerated in cities and large unceded regions. There is no sure way of knowing whether the Anishinaabe or some other original people lived here in Biblical times, but one or another did. They used the rivers as we today use roads and they developed trails through the woods, set up homesteads, fished, hunted—including monitoring and culling — harvested fruit, fabricated clothing, canoes, and preserved food and other products to contribute to the greater communities of their gift economy. They lived in what settlers dismiss as a ruthless harmony with nature, but settler society dwells on the "ruthless" element and does not see the harmony. In the sustaining communities, there is respect for the other creatures as elder siblings, each with similar rights and powers, each with a specialty, sharing the natural environment. In many such communities, their role, which could be called stewardship, even extends a sense of being, of personhood, to some of what is classified scientifically as inanimate. Their fundamental values have not changed.

Around a thousand years before the Europeans arrived, at the time the Roman Empire had finally fallen, a sister people developed complex horticultural communities, bringing ancient southern methods of agriculture north, eventually to the Great Lakes and Laurentian basin. We call these farming people the Iroquoian, but the horticultural communities were not limited to the Iroquoian-speaking people. They were also found among some Anishinaabe, or Algonquian-speaking people. Their skills came from generations of women selecting seeds of maize and other crops over nine to ten thousand years.[2] Their techniques, mastered in what is now Mexico, had migrated here and their horticultural skills allowed them to grow crops they could share. They also accepted nature's "ruthless harmony," respecting the other creatures' space. At the time of Jacques Cartier and the early European explorers, these Iroquoian and Anishinaabe people lived in similarly advanced societies and were healthier and of greater stature than the European visitors. Their nature was symbiotic, living in the world with its natural systems and becoming a respectful part of them, influencing changes that could conserve their sustaining role. Their primary ethic of sharing manifests itself in a society based on giving. This is not to imply that nothing ever went wrong or that there was never any injustice, but simply to contrast it with the personal-property-based market economy we have today.

The first European-descended settlers moved north of St. Sauveur a mere 170 years ago. They used the North River where they could. After all, they had learned to navigate it in canoes and with knowledge acquired from the Anishinaabe. They even learned the rhythm of paddling songs from them, used to maintain their tempo as they moved, sometimes laboriously, upstream. Augustin-Norbert Morin, the Minister of Colonization who established the first settlement north of the seigneuries in present-day Ste. Adele, prided himself in the songs he sang when he paddled up that river in the 1840s. We still have the words to some of those songs. But his colonists could not navigate the river to the north of Ste. Adele. The elevation increased rapidly, and the river was turbulent with waterfalls and rocks. Fortunately for them, they found a trail, a road, that cut over and around a high mountain. The road passed through the woods, travelled and maintained by the residents of that mountain and their ancestors through a forest land they had traversed and sustained for uncounted centuries, hunting and trapping, sometimes moving on, occasionally staying longer. If one of them had been asked to draw a map in the sand, their pathway would have followed the river where possible and then their trails, roads through the woods, without distinction.[3] According to the nineteenth-century historian Benjamin-Antoine Testard de Montigny, the settlers encountered a single man, an "Iroquois Savage" named Commandeur, who camped there, above Ste. Adele. Subsequent research[4] shows there were several families present—savages, according to the French colonists—and so the colonists called Commandeurs' mountain home Mont Sauvage. It is still called that today, although the families are absent. Commandeur is not an Iroquoian name but an Anishinaabe (Algonquin) one,[5] and we now know that the family was both. Iroquoian and Algonquian Nations figured among the sustainable communities. Both lived respectfully on the land, accepting their roles in Mother Earth. The Iroquoians, the current name for a cultural-linguistic grouping, were largely agricultural, not herders but horticulturalists. The Algonquians, the current name for another cultural-linguistic grouping, were largely hunter-gatherers and manufacturers, also not herders. Both groups of Nations respected each other. They also respected the independent jurisdiction of individuals and other creatures, all having inherent rights, each to its own nature.

In their world, the Anishinaabe knew of the Little People, hidden, mystical, called the Pukwudgie and other names. At full height, they stood no higher than your knee and they might be right beside you in the smell of flowers, but they could choose to be invisible. They might also appear as dangerous predators and their powers made people afraid of them, but they were only little people. The Commandeur family no doubt knew of them, may have even had encounters that they could have shared with us, but instead, the Commandeurs faded into the woods, becoming like the Little People themselves, powerful and scary to the new settlers in their seeming invisibility as they moved farther away.

The name Mont Sauvage is a reminder of the existence of these people whose symbiotic relationship to the world around them has been replaced with speeding cars and concrete homes filled with giant television screens and internet connections, a modern settler society sharing information and virtual mythologies, personality cults and world-class sports teams, protected, well-fed, and comfortable, living in a universe that changes and re-invents itself like a kaleidoscope. Young and vigorous, seeming capable of adapting to any challenge, willing to accept all people into their system provided they take a number—but these modern people are recent arrivals and part of a culture that has little sustainability and is losing its sense of local communities, not really connected to the nature of here—unproven in that sense. Having grown up here, I know firsthand a sense of alienation, of not understanding a place for myself in the natural world. The ancient Anishinaabe culture more closely resembles the sustaining communities of the long ages of humankind, stewards who lived in the land and belonged to it with no sense of alienation.

The Commandeur family who lived on Mont Sauvage were from the sustaining communities, sustaining not simply themselves, but their environment, looking generations forward.

I fear that our advanced civilization, in which everything is ownable, is not a sustainable or sustaining model. Both the Algonquian and Iroquoian peoples share precautionary tales of the kind of dangerous greed that threatens our world today, an insatiable hunger that simply cannot be satisfied, seen both in the stories of the Windigo and of Adodaroh described below. When confronted with the reality of needy Europeans, they shared their lives and space, respecting their ethical priorities of giving, sharing. Neither of their precautionary tales was strong enough to save them from the imminent danger of the ownable, product-driven market economy we have become.

In this book, you will read stories that I have learned over the years, stories of the European Wars of Religion, the hierarchies, and the culture that grew out of an insatiable need to possess, to control, to consume, to the point that even women were property. I have tried to show how these concepts came to burden a sustaining culture that was governed by a different ethic, an obligation to share.

Today, we are presented with the concept and challenge of reconciliation with the sustaining communities that nursed the settler communities when they first arrived and that were obliged to watch in horror as the newcomers consumed all that their hosts had maintained.

We have ninety-four Calls to Action, developed through the Truth and Reconciliation Commission of Canada and based on the United Nations Declaration on the Rights of Indigenous Peoples and the United Nations Joinet-Orentlicher Principles.[6] These Calls are addressed to this market-driven culture we have become. The Calls tell us to rethink many aspects of our society, to address our educational curricula so that the story behind the problems we have today and the means of dealing with them can be taught to our children. We are called upon to make good on broken promises. We are asked to learn and teach these stories and to re-examine foundational stories and knowledge of both sustaining communities and market-driven societies. The path to reconciliation is learning to understand, to share, to live for each other.

CONTACT
1534-1541

What we call Contact describes the first recognized trips, where the explorers staked claims on land that had no Christian residents and therefore was considered uninhabited.

CHAPTER 1

First Encounter

Jacques Cartier was not the first European to explore the mouth of the St. Lawrence River, but he documented his three visits in detail. His first visit describes a paradise completely foreign to his experience.

A rriving off the coast of Newfoundland on May 10, 1534, Jacques Cartier guided his two ships north to the coast of Labrador and then south between Labrador and Newfoundland, describing the barren shorelines that he saw from his ship as the "Land of Cain." He sailed next to the Magdalen Islands, to Prince Edward Island, into the Baie des Chaleurs, and along the coast of the Gaspé Peninsula.

The first time he and his crew saw people was when they were cruising off the east coast of Prince Edward Island[7] looking for a harbour but seeing only the coastal sandhills. Spotting a stream, they lowered a small boat and rowed a ways. Beyond them, they saw several canoes full of people and hailed them, but the wind carried their voices away. They got no response, so they returned to the ship.[8] There is something haunting about this missed encounter, as though a closed window separated them, as though they were not yet meant to meet. Sailing on through the night, they found themselves caught in a storm early the next morning, July 1st, the harsh coast offering no protection. They reefed the sails and by midday the weather had calmed. That was when they noticed a man following them, waving, and signalling them from the shore. When they turned toward him, the man fled. Still unready for a direct encounter, they saw each other and knew the other was there. It was the second moment where Cartier and the Indigenous Peoples missed making contact.

They continued along the coast for another ten miles in search of a harbour, venturing ashore at several different places. Cartier's log records what they experienced: the quality and beauty of the forest, with its rich, fragrant summer air and treeless areas with two colours of currants, strawberries, peas, and a wild wheat that resembled rye growing in flat, fertile fields that looked "to have been sown and cultivated." The peas were likely beans, and the wild wheat was maize. At the beginning of July, before they head out, many of the grains look similar. We know that the Three Sisters companion-planting of the Indigenous North Americans consisted of maize, or corn, beans, and squash[9]—a garden at the edge of a vast horticultural civilization. It passed like a picture in an album that was noted as the page was turned.

Cartier and his crew subsequently sailed along the coast of the Gaspé Peninsula to Cap d'Espoir, where a little exploration allowed them to locate a place they called St. Martin. They made a base there for the next week. Once at anchor, they began to explore with a small boat and soon came upon forty or fifty canoes filled with people making a great deal of noise, encouraging them to land and showing them furs, indicating a desire to trade. They felt too vulnerable, having only one boat, and turned back to open water. There were canoes there too, and soon seven canoes crowded around their boat, making signs of happiness and showing friendship, calling to them. Cartier's crew indicated that they wanted the canoeists to go away. Finally, they fired two cannon shots over the people's heads and drove them away, but only for a moment. When they returned, Cartier's crew threw burning torches, called lanses à feu, at them. They withdrew.

The next day, the canoeists returned to where Cartier's people had withdrawn. They kept a respectable distance but indicated again their good intentions. This time, two Frenchmen were sent to approach them with gifts of hatchets and other iron tools as well as a bright red cap. Soon the people were dancing around them, doing handstands on the water's edge, and expressing their joy. By the time the meeting was finished, their hosts left in great happiness, stark naked, having traded everything they had for treasures of iron and other small European items. They indicated they would return soon with more goods to exchange.

This whole happy occasion repeated itself a few days later when Cartier used small boats to explore the Baie des Chaleurs. On this second visit, the people, a different group with greater marketing skills, placed cooked seal meat on boards, indicating their guests should eat, and withdrew. There were around three hundred of them—men, women, and children. Once the French were comfortable that they would not be hurt, their hosts approached them dancing and singing, rubbing the crew's arms affectionately and showing other signs of reassurance. Again, by the time the exchange was over, they left naked and happy, carrying pots, trinkets, and metal tools. Cartier noted, as he had done before, that the products he had received were of little value but added that these people could be easily converted to the Catholic faith.

Cartier and his crew had touched the rim of a large civilization that had no need for the Catholic faith. They had their own beliefs and they had given value for what they received, satisfied no doubt that the exchange had been fair. They were a part of a culture that saw giving as a form of expression and received in the same spirit; a society where their measure was the stature achieved through sharing.

Our institutionalized perspective, inherited from Europe, assumes that there was no contact between the Americas and the rest of the world before the time of Columbus, or at least before the Vikings. However, over thousands of years, it seems improbable. Where there was contact, stories would have travelled in both directions.

The star patterns in the sky, the constellations, told stories that the Elders shared from time immemorial. The Iroquoian story of three hunters who chased a bear up a tree, wounding it and witnessing it bleed onto the leaves before it saved itself by jumping into the sky, is a story that other peoples have told differently, not just in the Iroquoian family of Nations but all over the world. The three hunters leapt in pursuit. We can still see them, in the northern sky, forever chasing the bear as they turn around the stationary North Star. Every year, the forest recalls the event. The bear's blood appears again, splashed on the autumn leaves.

Similar stories have enriched European culture and the constellation of the Great Bear, Ursa Major, and her son, Ursa Minor, have come down to us through Greek and Roman mythology. The Milky Way, that large band of stars and galaxies so close together and fine that it almost seems to flow through the sky, is also the path that the spirits of the dead take to get to Aataentsic, the founding mother, and to her grandson Iouskeha in Wendat culture.[10] Upon death, each human has two spirits, one that stays by the bones and one that travels to the stars. These spirits live in celestial villages that correspond to earthly ones. There they can continue doing all they enjoyed doing here in life. Among the many different cultures of the Americas, there are many different stories. They belong to the teller, to the Elders, to the ancestors. Stories are valued possessions.

Northern people knew that the North Star is the only stable light in the heavens. Everything rotates around this one central point. In our time, while we theoretically know much more about the night sky and the movements of the stars, we live under roofs; even when outside, we can see the sky only through a veil of reflected light and smog that does not afford us the same clear view our ancestors had. Stories about our sky come to us from some ancient cultures; given our country's current predominantly European background, too few of us know the stories that were told around the home fires of our Indigenous Peoples.

The Mi'kmaq, Passamaquoddy, Iroquois, Delaware, and Fox all tell sky stories about a bear, stories that relate to the Big Dipper and the North Star. The Mistassini Cree tell how the North Star was set in place during a quarrel. The people of an earlier world quarrelled with North Star, who was one of them. They plotted to kill him. He fled into the sky where he'd be out of their reach. When they saw where he was, and that he was out of their reach, they decided to leave him there as a marker for night travellers.

The Farmer's Almanac based its lunar calendar on Algonquian descriptions of the full moon—Algonquian months. June is the Strawberry Moon, followed by the Moon of the Buck as its young antlers become apparent. It is also known as the Thunder Moon in recognition of the thunderstorms during the early part of the summer. The Navaho tell of Revolving Man, the constellation of the Big Dipper, and Revolving

Woman, Cassiopeia, both turning around the home fire, the North Star.

The Algonquian also call the Milky Way the spirit path and see it as the trail taken by the dead as they travel to a place that we cannot know. Each star of the spitit path is a home fire of the departed; each night, while they sit around it telling stories on their long pilgrimage, they look down upon us and see our home fires.

The Algonquian people tell stories about the night sky and share Traditional Stories associated with the constellations. We have learned that they called the full moon of January the Wolf Moon because the wolves howled in hunger around their snowy encampments. They tell stories of the wise woman Kisisok8e[11] who explained the colours in the sunset and the bear's head in the sky that indicated the seasons.

Much of this is unknown to most Canadians, and some of the stories have been embellished with European contact but even the most critical historians acknowledge that there are similarities between the European stories and the North American ones. Some of these stories may even have the same origins. The human presence in the Americas is so old that a story first told here could have travelled back to Europe and Asia, shared among the circumpolar peoples or in other ways beyond our memory, and may have inspired some of the European classical myths. Evidence of the presence of ancestral Algonquin, even in the northern part of our territory, predates the classical European cultures, dating back to the time of the building of the pyramids, a time before the creation of the alphabet. Some modern theorists propose that these most ancient stories come from a still older culture that we all descend from.[12] In the long absence from each other, Europe and the Americas had developed very differently. As Cartier continued exploring this strange new world, he would show his lack of comprehension of common respect. The window that his hosts opened would soon slam shut against him.

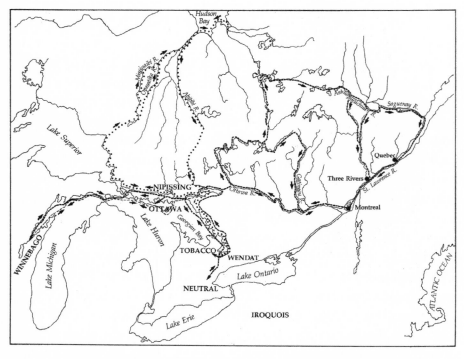

The Wendat Nations lived closely around Lake Simcoe and Georgian Bay.
They were a part of a larger group of exchange that included
the Algonquian and other Iroquoian Nations.

CHAPTER 2

The Great Law of Peace

At the time of the Wars of Religion in France, the centre of trade for the
Algonquian people living in the Laurentian hills was to the west, towards
the Ottawa River and beyond. They were the Wendat, Iroquoian Nations
that the French called the Huron.

The great Wendat Nations that lived tightly around Lake Simcoe, north of Lake Ontario, and on Lake Huron's Georgian Bay were the centre for a huge cosmopolitan trading culture surrounded by Algonquian peoples. They were the easternmost of the Wendat neighbourhood, Iroquoian people who were agricultural and had centres that spread to the west, north, and south of Lake Erie. To the south of Lake Ontario, all the way back to Montreal and along the St. Lawrence River, were five other Iroquoian Nations, the Five Nations of the Haudenosaunee. In their most ancient history, the Attiwandaronk, Kahqua,[13] or Neutral Nation, situated north of Lake Erie, held a special place, but other Iroquoian Nations figured in some form into the Foundational Story of the Great Law of Peace told by the Five Nations of the Haudenosaunee.[14]

Almost a thousand years ago, before the time of the Crusades in Europe, there was intense infighting among the five Haudenosaunee Nations. A strongman named Adodaroh,[15] with snakes in his hair and the severed heads of snakes on the ends of his fingers, was terrorizing the people. The descriptions of this antagonist try to evoke the most horrible of social monsters imaginable, creating a baseline of social disintegration and chaos in the minds of those learning the story. Adodaroh had a following of like-minded, aggressive people who were destroying all of society through their actions and wars. They would stop at nothing, taking all for themselves. They even practised cannibalism, not to honour, but simply to eat. He was described as the most horrid monster imaginable,

with an insatiable hunger ready to consume everything. One of his followers was Aiewáhtha, whose name also takes the form of Hiawatha. He
had just lost his family to the wars and could think only of revenge. Having killed an enemy, he determined to eat him, dragging his prize back
to his empty home.

The prophet Deganwidah,[16] born a Wendat on the Bay of Quinte to
the north of Lake Ontario, felt he had to bring a message of peace to the
warring Nations, so he crossed the waters and happened upon Aiewáhtha
who was approaching his home, dragging the dead enemy. Deganwidah
climbed carefully up onto the roof of Aiewáhtha's home and peered down
through the smoke hole. As Aiewáhtha prepared his cooking pot, he saw
Deganwidah's reflection in the pot full of water. Thinking the peaceful
face was his own reflection, he smiled with pleasure, and Deganwidah,
sensing that he had an opportunity to approach the warrior, climbed back
down and came to talk with him. After a long discussion, Deganwidah
offered to conduct a condolence ceremony for Aiewáhtha's loss. Aiewáhtha accepted. Deganwidah told him of his mission to stop the wars and
to help the Five Nations unite in peace. Deganwidah explained that he
consulted Jigonsaseh,[17] leader of the Neutral/Kahqua, a greatly respected
sister Nation that was also a part of the maize culture, and that she told
Deganwidah that the women must be acknowledged as the farmers and
that families would descend through the mother's line and continue to
live in the mother's home. Deganwidah accepted her wisdom. He further
encouraged Aiewáhtha to stop eating human flesh and to substitute deer
in its place. The three of them, Jigonsaseh, Aiewáhtha, and Deganwidah,
shared their vision with the people. There was a custom among the
women to make sure all the warriors were fed outside of the villages, re-
gardless of whose side they were on. The women would feed them to keep
the fighting away from the villages. Jigonsaseh told the women not simply
to feed them, but also to talk with the warriors, to encourage them to join
Deganwidah and Aiewáhtha. Deganwidah elaborated the Great Law of
Peace including matrilineal descent, women's collective responsibility for
agricultural land, the condolence ceremonies to mourn the loss of family
members and leaders as well as the political structure of the Five Nations
Confederacy. Deganwidah envisioned fifty worthy men, chosen by the

clan mothers, making decisions at the Council Fire, a governing body. He even gave them their names, which he decreed would return to the clan mothers when they died so that the women could give the same name to a worthy successor, as long as it was not that man's son. The women could also recall a leader if they lost confidence in him. Their political structure contrasts sharply with the male-dominated early European democracies. It acknowledged different, equal jurisdictions of men and women. Among the important agreements formalized in the law with Wampum Belts and other symbolic items was the concept of "A Dish with One Spoon," meaning that in times of need, resources would be shared and that no people would take more from nature than could be sustained. This was a concept that was not unique to the Great Law of Peace but was evident in many treaties among other Nations as well.[18] The Great Law of Peace is associated with a great pine tree, known as the Tree of Peace, situated on Onondaga territory in the middle of the Five Nations of the Haudenosaunee, and the five needles of the pine's coniferous leaf represent those Five Nations. In this telling, it started in the agricultural period, the time when the women began growing corn and were able to feed the people from their crops.[19]

Ancient Iroquoian culture respected complex rules to avoid consanguinity even when not at war, but during war, taking warriors as prisoners was an effective, if perhaps not premeditated, means of the genetic exchange that was essential between Nations. The Eurasian model of this exchange involved forcing women into submission, often through rape and slavery, thereby also achieving an unpremeditated genetic exchange among nations.[20] It does not matter if these strategies were conscious and planned for the purpose they achieved, but the Eurasian model contributed to the lower status of women that categorized them as the property of men.

The Five Nations, the Wendat, and the other Iroquoian Nations all experienced greater or lesser degrees of fighting, especially among the younger men, warriors who had little other means of improving their status. With less dependency on trade with Algonquian Nations than the Wendat had, these wars may have been more intense in societies like the Five Nations that ultimately formed the Haudenosaunee Confederacy.

Once all the warriors decided to support the Great Law of Peace, they approached Adodaroh together and, with Aiewáhtha as the spokesperson, asked him to join them as their leader, to accept the Great Law of Peace that Deganwidah proposed. Aiewáhtha is said to have brushed the snakes out of Adodaroh's hair, untangling it, bringing him calm and reason and allowing him the space to make the decision to join—and lead—them. It is remarkable that in this foundational story, the murderous dictator is not killed, but rehabilitated.

CHAPTER 3
Herding and Male Dominance

*From a European perspective, the natural hierarchy of male dominance
was an accepted fact of the human species. Many Indigenous American
societies suggest otherwise, and anthropologists have sought its advent
in Euro-Asian social evolution.*

The Judeo-Christian culture is patriarchal, but in Jewish tradition, identity as a Jew comes through the matrilineal line. Many studies have explored the origins of patriarchy, indicating that it was a choice made through social evolution. One argument for its origin, through herding cultures, can be found in a document written by Dr. Anke Becker of Harvard University. In it, she describes how and why a herding culture, as distinct from cultures of farming and animal husbandry, favoured the evolution of male dominance. The males lived and slept with the herd, returning from time to time to the camp where the women looked after the children. Depending upon the movements of the herds on marginal land, the women's opportunity to diversify or develop property was reduced, leaving them more dependant upon their men. Long absences of the male also favoured female genital mutilation and infibulation as a means of reducing female sexuality with the intention of ensuring patrimony.[21]

The social structure that formed in such a herding culture could also lead to a hierarchical social pattern, developed as a defence system for a mobile, vulnerable asset. The men worked together to deal with predators, both human and animal, leading to a hierarchy of power. Hierarchy ultimately leads to a single leader. The herding culture is described in the foundational stories of the Bible. One of the earliest stories is of Cain and Abel, two brothers exploring their favour with God. Abel, the herder, burned an offering of meat, a lamb, that was well received by the Lord,

19

while Cain, the farmer, saw his sacrifice of the best fruit of his crop rejected. Cain killed Abel and became a pariah, rejected by all.

Adam and Eve gave birth to Seth to replace Abel, and in the time of Seth's son, Enosh, people began to call the Lord by name. Enosh's descendant Enoch is described as having "walked with God," and when he died, God took him.[22]

These stories were parts of the Oral History of a herding people and were eventually written down, becoming part of the Book of Genesis in the Bible. Could the story, with its mystic interpretations of finding fulfillment in walking with God also be describing a social hierarchy? Established in a herding society, the farmer is excluded. Over time, it becomes possible for the shepherd to accept an overlord to help him protect his flock. Enoch walked with the Lord. Can he also accept that, just like he with his flock, his lord must retain the power of life and death over him in the process of their collective defence? In this herding hierarchy, the expression "The Lord is my Shepherd..." takes on a hierarchical significance. The Lord, at least in the Abrahamic tradition, has grown into an infallible personal God who guides His people, a concept that gives His people absolute licence, and has created a cult that devolved into Christianity and Islam. This cult thinking underpins our modern legal systems and even our market economy. It is a sentiment that is simply foreign to a culture that has no experience with herding and ownership. It is ultimately incompatible with a symbiotic world environment where infallibility does not belong to God or to man.

Cain does not go away. A marked man, he is still a farmer, and in time he is associated with cities, the centres of early agriculture. James Scott, professor at Yale University and author of Against the Grain: A Deep History of the Earliest States, argues how great the resistance was to farming,[23] reaffirming its low status in that social hierarchy. Herding and agriculture developed together in areas where small herd animals could be contained and selected.[24] Cain's and Abel's descendants are complements in the Biblical story of early herding and agricultural societies that gave rise to the patriarchal paradigm that reinforced the concept of a One True God, the Lord at the top of the hierarchy.

CHAPTER 4

Eurasian Versus American Agriculture

It is popular today to describe the superior diet of the hunter-gatherers, but herding does not come into the argument in terms of how it may have modified the social structure and diet where agricultural societies were exposed to it.

W hen Charles Darwin proposed the concept of the survival of the fittest, he did not state that the fittest is necessarily the best in any moral sense. The two should not be confused. The fittest relates to a specific adaptation. The herders lived with their flocks and became exposed to their diseases, the survivors developing resistance. This resistance was shared with their offspring by those who survived the diseases and, over time, these descendants were the fittest in resisting the diseases of animals. Agricultural centres would also develop their own resistance to diseases. Their interaction, whether in battle or trade, would provide an unwitting opportunity to spread contagion, and again there would be the survivors. By Darwinian rules, thanks to resistance developed to transspecies diseases, the survivors and their descendants were the fittest.

By contrast, the Americas had virtually no herding cultures and, therefore, no exposure to the diseases that come with them. Their societies traded and fought, and surely became resistant to diseases as well, but the nature of most of their agricultural, horticultural societies did not involve herding. Their trade was with thinly populated rural peoples who hunted and fabricated products for trade but did not share their home space intimately with herd animals. This led to a much different biome, one that would prove itself highly vulnerable to the Europeans. Even today, the few remaining isolated societies in the world are highly allergic to modern people.

Corn, or maize, required human intervention to develop and to adapt the varieties that fed people from Central America to the Great Lakes.

In their milieu, the Indigenous Peoples of the Americas each respected separate jurisdictions. The farmer-horticulturalists were resilient, thanks to food redundancies such as many varieties of seed for the same species of corn, squash, potato, and so on. They used a process that allowed them to selectively breed plants that suited their changing needs by choosing seeds from those that strongly displayed the desired characteristics, allowing them to grow crops such as the Three Sisters—corn, squash, and beans—adapted to different climates from Mexico to the Great Lakes. Crop rotation was essential to the health of the soil and fields were cultivated over a long rotation cycle that could spread over a century, leaving little opportunity for specific diseases to develop. This may also have contributed to the people's advanced ability to adapt. They were the world leaders in horticulture, and we owe to their development about half of all the plant edibles that we now consume.[25] Among these are tomatoes, potatoes, chocolate... the list is long and varied, including such things as the African staple manioc. They had myriad small cultural units, all separate, with a multitude of languages and stories. As an example, California alone boasted hundreds of communities and a hundred different language groups. Their variety was their strength, their resilience. Their fitness and greater size were a wonder to the first Europeans who came. Their respect for other species, not herding but culling, and their extensive use of fish gave them a diet that maintained attributes of the hunter-gatherer diet praised today. All this good health and adaptability did not make them fit to survive the trans-species diseases such as measles and mumps that descendants of the herders brought with them. For similar reasons, they were very vulnerable to smallpox.

Ultimately, the gender roles in the Eurasian cultures tended to be balanced in favour of the male, with the female living a subordinate role. Her value was to her man's family, and what she could provide were children and loyalty. In difficult times, the family would need more children, solving resource shortcomings with an increased workforce, but creating a larger problem over time with an increased population to feed. By contrast, most of the Indigenous Americans respected the separate jurisdictions of men and women and, therefore, the agency of a woman over her own body. In the Great Law of Peace, Jigonsaseh's conditional support assured the independent jurisdiction of women and their control of agriculture. Further, practising means of birth control through herbs and plants such as blue cohosh did not carry a stigma. Since women were the farmers, getting pregnant when the need for farm work increased would offer no relief for the tasks at hand. Among the consequences of these differences, children who were born were children who, in themselves, were wanted, and population control, tied to the supply of resources that could sustain it, was the domain of women.

Among the missing herd animals in the Americas was the horse. The Eurasian societies had learned to use the horse in work and war. It enabled an attacking force to travel faster than the news of its approach, allowing the attacker to storm and slaughter an enemy. This, combined with the hierarchical nature of the herding society, led to a powerful fighting unit, which could have led to an escalation of weaponry. The wars themselves were often dictated by the need for territory to accommodate an expanded population, and, therefore, it was not enough to subdue the enemy, but it was sometimes necessary to kill the people, to free the land for the aggressor's use. By contrast, pre-contact American armies did not rely on surprise the same way as they could move no faster than the news of their advance. They relied on numbers, intimidation, and negotiation, developing empires of influence and tribute rather than territory.[26] Since they had no herds to protect, they were not fighting over a vulnerable, mobile asset, but over influence and recognition, expressed through gifts of respect, and over honour, as in blood feuds.

When the two different civilizations came together, most of these things suddenly didn't matter, because there was one that dominated: The people of the Americas had no resistance to all those diseases of the herding cultures.

CHAPTER 5

Off to a Bad Start
Cartier and the Laurentian Iroquoians

Certainly not intentionally, Jacques Cartier's detailed records show the reader of our time how little he understood and ill-equipped he was to deal with the unique world he visited.

Jacques Cartier's perambulations continued. He and his crew travelled to Percé Rock where they encountered a huge storm, forcing them to take refuge between the shoreline of Percé and the island of Bonavista. The storm gathered strength, forcing them to take shelter in the Baie de Gaspé. While the ships were at anchor, they used their boats to explore the bay, seeking a natural harbour. They were forced to stay there for over a week and during that time, around July 16, 1534, they discovered another fleet of canoes full of men, women, and children who were fishing for mackerel with nets. This time, neither party seemed too nervous and they moved freely among each other on shore and around the ships. These were different people who, according to Cartier, shamelessly wore nothing but a small skin covering their loins, using other skins as scarves and shawls when needed. Cartier noted they had a different way of carrying themselves from the others he had met. Their hair was cut to form only a band in the middle with a long lock of hair growing from the top of their heads hanging behind them like a horse's tail, held to their heads with leather cords. They slept on the ground under their overturned canoes and ate their food barely warmed. Cartier and his men could wander freely among them, examining their customs and learning about their habits. They ate some meat but also had huge amounts of mackerel, fruits, and vegetables. Cartier's notes described maize as being like large peas similar to what he had seen in Brazil, where he had travelled years earlier on the ship of an Italian explorer. He did not say they made bread from it, but he did say that they ate it like bread. Observing that they were travelling far from home, he noted they had plums dried to prunes, pears, apples, figs, nuts, and other small fruits. Yet he also wrote, "They can with truth be called savages, as there are no people poorer than these in the world, and I believe they do not possess anything to the value of five pennies, apart from their canoes and nets."[27]

On the morning of the 24th of July, Cartier and his crew built a large crucifix, ten metres tall, on which they placed a shield with three fleurs-de-lys and an inscription carved in large letters above it saying *"Vive le Roy de France."* The people watched the process with a certain intensity, and when the work was finished, the Frenchmen all knelt before the cross, holding hands. Then they made signs, pointing to heaven, signalling their religious convictions.

Later in the day, a Chief, wearing a robe made of black bear hide, came to the ship where Cartier was. He was in a canoe with his three sons, and he made a long speech, clearly about the cross, imitating its shape with his fingers. He spread his arm, sweeping around, indicating he was talking about the whole region and seemed to be indicating that Cartier should have requested permission before erecting the cross.

When he finished his discourse, Cartier held up a lovely axe, indicating that he would exchange it for the bearskin. In the meantime, he had given his men instructions that, as the canoe came closer, they were to board it and force the passengers onto the ship. Cartier made reassuring signs of affection to calm the astonished men. He next invited them to feast with him and they were plied with French food, most likely the same mackerel the people had caught in their hemp nets but prepared differently. He offered them drink as well, and although he does not state it, the offering was most likely wine. While they ate, Cartier tried to explain that the cross was intended only as a sign so that their ships could return to this same place when they next came. He didn't trouble to explain to them the Doctrine of Discovery, a papal bull published in June 1452 that gave Cartier the right to declare the territory a property of the Catholic king of France provided that it was uninhabited by members of the Catholic faith. Instead, he conveyed to them that he would take two of the Chief's sons with him, but they would come back again in a year. He gave the sons French attire including red caps and placed a brass chain around each of their necks, which, he wrote, "pleased them immensely." As he escorted the others back to their canoe, he gave each of them a hatchet and two knives. Later, other canoes came to the ship bringing fish for the two brothers.

Exactly what they all understood of the events of the day is subject to speculation. We know now that the people were Laurentian Iroquoian, and that they had a tradition of exchanging a willing young man with allies, keeping one of theirs to make it mutual, but we don't know if the sons felt captured. The next morning the French ships caught a favourable wind and sailed away.[28]

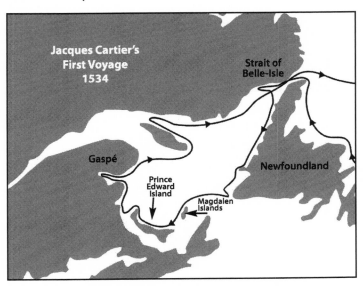

Jacques Cartier missed the St. Lawrence River on his first visit. Upon his return in 1535, Taignoagny and Domagaya led him to their home at Stadacona near modern-day Quebec City.

On Cartier's second voyage, in 1535, he returned with the two young men he had taken with him the previous year, Taignoagny and Domagaya. They now spoke French, and thanks to them, Cartier discovered the St. Lawrence River. They guided him past Gaspé, up the St. Lawrence, entering an area that Cartier had missed completely on his previous voyage. Their father, they had explained, was Donnacona, the man wearing the black bear robe the preceding year. Stadacona, their home, was located near present-day Quebec City, but the family was strongly linked to the agriculturally rich Île d'Orléans. The ships stopped there on the way through, enjoying a meal of bread made from maize and "several large melons."[29]

Donnacona was a colourful storyteller who shared tales of a great culture to the west, or perhaps the north, called the Saguenay. He told many stories, as though testing European gullibility, including describing a people who lived on a strictly liquid diet and had no anus. Cartier also learned that they traded with Nations to the South for oranges, Nations who he was told were very warlike. Communications with the sons became increasingly difficult though, with Taignoagny and Domagaya's reticence and cool withdrawal from the French once they were home. Cartier's mission was "to discover certain islands and lands where it is said that a great quantity of gold and other precious things are to be found." It was also hoped that he would stumble upon a passage to China.

The brothers' aloofness may have been boiling under the surface ever since their abduction the previous year but may also have resulted from Cartier's firm refusal to give up his intentions of travelling to Hochelaga, one of the exotic places they had described to him. They indicated their terms, to be the trading intermediaries with Hochelaga, and they did everything reasonable to establish a decent trade relationship with Cartier, but the French sea captain had no diplomatic skills and sowed distrust among the people he met. The Stadaconans tried to discourage him from making the trip, including having three men dress up as spirits and share a message of warning. They visited the crew with a large number of people, performed a dance, and then Donnacona, holding a ten- or twelve-year-old girl by the hand, made a long speech. He then presented the girl to Cartier as a gift and repeated the performance, giving him also two boys. Taignoagny then reiterated that he should give up his plans, but Cartier told him that if the gifts were to discourage him from going, then they had best take them back. The two brothers insisted the children were given freely, but ultimately both brothers refused to accompany Cartier, leaving him without a translator.

Cartier's log describes Hochelaga, how the longhouses were built,

The inside of a longhouse, as envisaged by Bonnie Shemie.

and how the palisade formed three rings around the town. Upon his arrival, Cartier was greeted as though he were expected, with formalities performed before he was escorted into the village. There was only one way in, which involved following a spiral between the walls. When they were finally inside, they saw about fifty longhouses, each fifty steps long and twelve to fifteen wide, covered with sewn bark.[30] Huge fields would have been needed for the crops for the more than a thousand people who greeted Cartier's party. Inside the longhouses, they could see that it was a series of residences and that there were lofts filled with the maize grain.

In the middle of the longhouses there was a large square area that looked like a communal room. Women came there, some carrying children. They rubbed the Frenchmen's faces, arms, and elsewhere that they could touch, greeting them warmly. Then they indicated it would please them if the crewmembers would touch the children. After that, they brought mats for the men to sit on, and then an older man was carried in and placed before them. They addressed him with the same title Cartier had heard used when addressing Donnacona, "Agouhanna." Cartier records this as meaning king or chief and mentions the man wore a red crown made from the skin of a hedgehog. They had no interpreter but the reception was warm and the people offered food and organized a ceremony of welcome. Then, in Cartier's interpretation, they presented their sick to be cured, including Agouhanna, whom Cartier massaged, and he read from the Bible for a long time to bless them.

That same day, Cartier managed to walk to the top of Mount Royal, the name he gave to the mountain in the centre of the Island of Montreal, and he described large expanses of agricultural lands. They could see as far as the rapids, over open country. His guides pointed to three sets of rapids and described through gestures that beyond lay a place where he could find the precious metals that he sought.

Cartier stayed in Hochelaga for only one day. He learned that there were waterways beyond and a further country that was very wealthy, but that the passage was blocked to his ships by rapids. Upon his return to Stadacona, he found the men he had left behind erecting a fort to protect themselves from Donnacona's people. The French had lost the trust of their hosts and feared they would be attacked. Cartier had planned to stay for the winter, and he worked to re-establish the relationship. Donnacona's sons had lost confidence in the intentions of the French, but they were still willing to listen and try. They proved this during the hard winter that followed by sharing their medicinal expertise to save the French from scurvy, demonstrating their civility. Even upon learning the method, Cartier acted warily, explaining to Domagaya as he sent for the medicine that he needed it only to help a sick servant. He had already requisitioned his few healthy men to make excessive noise working in one of the ships, telling the Stadaconans that they were making the ship ready for their return. The noise was to hide the silence that resulted from a loss of one-third of his men to the disease. He was clearly afraid at every juncture that he could not trust his hosts. At one point, the girl who had been given to Cartier ran away. The brothers insisted they would find her and bring her back. She accepted to return but told her people that she had been beaten and mistreated.

Early in the spring, Donnacona and Taignoagny left on an extended hunting trip and Cartier was suspicious that they were planning some mischief. When they returned, they came with a huge number of people, and their houses were full. Cartier was anxious and interpreted every minor event as ominous. It is likely that the new people were from an outlying village and probably were simply curious. There was no reason to assume the new people harboured hostile intent, but Cartier sent his servant, a man named Charles Guyot, whom the Stadaconans had come to trust, to bring a gift to Donnacona and try to find out more. Taignoagny gave him a message for Cartier that, if the French would be willing to take a man named Agouhanna back to France, the man would be delivered to them. This word, Agouhanna, appears in several places, once as a title for the old man at Hochelaga, again as a title for Donnacona, and now as the name of the new player. It is, therefore, assumed that he was a Chief. Cartier nevertheless interpreted Taignoagny's proposal as a desire to eliminate a competing Chief who was threatening Donnacona's rule. Instead of trying to understand further, Cartier hatched a plot whereby he invited Donnacona, his sons, and others to celebrate Holy Cross Day on May 3. He had his men erect a cross ten metres high, with a wooden shield on it inscribed with the words *Franciscus Primus Dei Gratia Francorum Reonat* (Long Live François I by God's grace King of France). If Cartier wished to reassure them of his goodwill by using a religious ceremony with which they had some familiarity by this time, it worked up to a point. Donnacona, his sons, and other men came, but, by Cartier's description, nervously. Taignoagny even warned them to not enter the ship and encouraged the women accompanying them to leave. Then he more aggressively tried to discourage his father from entering the fort but Cartier, understanding that there was resistance, had his men seize them. The other men still outside fled as though trying to save themselves. It is likely that the Stadaconans had no malicious intent and were shocked by Cartier's actions.

All night long, the people howled "ceaselessly like wolves"[31] shouting Agouhanna. By noon the next day, the crew witnessed a larger gathering than they had ever seen. Worried, Cartier told Donnacona he would be going to meet the king of France, and he could relate to Cartier's great leader all the wonders of his world. He would be given a large present in recognition and would be returned in ten to twelve months. He gave Donnacona a raised position where he could be seen by his people and Donnacona made a long speech, reassuring them, after which they were mollified. Cartier encouraged Donnacona to invite the leaders on board, so they could talk more easily, and they came, all praising Cartier. They also brought twenty-four necklaces along with Wampum. Cartier offered Donnacona several gifts that included brass pans, hatchets, knives, and beads, which Donnacona gave to the care of the women to be given to the wives and children of those who were leaving. The next day, the women brought Donnacona and his Stadaconan companions food for the journey. Altogether, Cartier had ten hostages with him.[32]

Cartier's third and last voyage, in 1541, followed the beginning of a period of persecution of the "heretics" that would set the stage for the Wars of Religion in France. From as early as his first voyage, King François I had begun to attack any sign of what he considered disrespect for the Catholic Church. During the 1540s, this took the form of a massacre of Protestant Waldenses of the valleys of the Alps, Christian followers of Pierre Valdes, a wealthy man who gave to the poor and who preached around 1170. It also coincided with the escape of Jean Calvin, the founder of Calvinism, from persecution in his native France. He fled to Switzerland in 1545. On that last trip, the French king had assigned Cartier to the command of Jean-François de La Rocque de Roberval, a Protestant who had the means to finance the establishment of a permanent colony.

Upon Cartier's return to Stadacona in late August of 1541, Cartier reported that Donnacona had passed away and the others had declined to leave France because they had become large landowners. In truth, nine were dead and the only survivor at that point was a child, a girl who was the youngest of the group. Cartier, initially welcomed, soon found that the Stadaconans distrusted him. His men built a fort further east at Charlesbourg-Royal, near present-day Quebec City, but the Stadaconans travelled there anyway, keeping it under siege the whole winter and killing thirty-five Frenchmen. In the spring, Cartier abandoned the fort and headed back down the St. Lawrence.

Cartier, who was the expert on the St. Lawrence Valley, now had to report to Roberval, who would take over the process of establishing a permanent presence at Charlesbourg-Royal. He was not forthcoming about the state of his relations with the Stadaconans. Roberval was travelling with settlers and all the makings of a colony and was due to arrive that spring. Cartier met Roberval's contingent at the port of St. Jehan (St.

John's, Newfoundland). Roberval insisted that Cartier return to Stada-cona to found the colony the king had authorized Roberval to establish. Cartier put to sea and returned to France, disobeying direct orders, making it impossible for Roberval to succeed. Roberval nevertheless proceeded to Charlesbourg-Royal but was forced to abandon his colony and return to France within a few months.

No Frenchman succeeded in creating a colony in the St. Lawrence Valley during the balance of the 1500s, and by the time Samuel de Champlain arrived in the early 1600s, the "St. Lawrence Iroquois," as Champlain classified them, had disappeared.

What happened to the people Cartier met is the subject of a lot of speculation. One explanation is that Cartier's presence had spread European diseases among his hosts, reducing their numbers and leaving a vacuum to be filled by the Innu, a people Champlain called the Montagnais, and the Algonquin. It is worth noting that Cartier felt the people of Hochelaga who greeted him were sick, hoping for cures. Even the Chief was sick. He may have simply misunderstood their welcome. Is it possible that some other source of illness had already struck them? As farmers, the Hochelaga people were valuable to their woodland neighbours but if their society was collapsing under the weight of illness, their vulnerability would also have left them exposed.

Another theory is that Hochelaga and Stadacona were at the northern limit of the Mohawk who are associated with regions south of Lake Champlain.[33] Iroquoian agricultural techniques involved farming intensely for about fifteen years and then leaving the fields to go back to nature for five times that long, about seventy-five years. Cartier's visit coincided with a temperature drop during the period described as the Little Ice Age,[34] and it may have encouraged horticultural societies such as these Iroquoians to scale back the territory they were farming. Also, Iroquoian presence in the St. Lawrence Valley may simply have been following its intermittent rhythm, leaving the site of Hochelaga dormant.

There is archeological evidence of other farming communities along the St. Lawrence. There is also mention in Cartier's notes that Donnacona's people had fields on the island of Orléans, indicating that the agricultural practice was not uncommon among them.

In 1539, the Spanish explorer Hernando de Soto travelled from Florida through Georgia, the Carolinas, Tennessee, Alabama, Mississippi, Arkansas, Texas, and Louisiana with six hundred soldiers, two hundred horses, and three hundred pigs. A violent, fearless man, he sought only gold and doomed most of his party to a horrible end. The few Spanish survivors described a densely populated countryside where often three towns at a time could be seen from the higher prospects. They raided the towns for what they needed, depending mostly on the pigs as a food source, but the pigs could have carried with them diseases that destroyed the people who lived there.

A century and a half later, René-Robert Cavalier de La Salle travelled through the same territory and found it virtually empty. Estimates are that 96 percent of the population died soon after the De Soto visit, and the population dropped further after that.[35] This massive area abandoned through a precipitous drop in population could have contributed to the Little Ice Age as the forests grew rapidly back on their farmland, acting as a carbon sink.[36] The Nations to the north would have been able to spill somewhat beyond their southern borders, and this, coupled with the colder weather, could also help to explain the temporary displacement of the Iroquoian people from the St. Lawrence Valley.

When Champlain arrived some sixty-five years later, he met different people, not the Iroquoian whom Cartier had met. Their absence noted, the area was considered a no-man's land.[37] The Innu, an Algonquian people, slowly introduced Champlain to a large series of Nations. No absence was noted by them, but there was animosity between them and the Mohawk who were present on the St. Lawrence River even without agricultural bases. They considered it to be in the northern part of their region of occupation.

We will never know if a Laurentian Iroquoian people died of disease, moved to join the Mohawk, or joined other neighbouring peoples for other reasons, but having been reported as present by Cartier, they were seen as no longer there in Champlain's time. It is true that Hochelaga and Stadacona were gone, but the Mohawk were very much present, as Champlain was to learn.

Jacques Cartier sought riches in the St. Lawrence Valley for King François of France. During that same period, two separate movements became the foundations of Protestantism. One, in the German states, is identified with Martin Luther, the other, in France, with Jean Calvin.

When Jean Calvin first left France for the greater security of Geneva in 1541, the French Protestants continued to fight for religious freedom, for a more localized and autonomous form of social adminis-tration. They were called the Huguenots and Jean Calvin remained their spiritual advisor. To understand what drove the Wars of Religion, it is helpful to consider the role the Church filled. Composed of priests, brothers, and nuns in the service of God, caring for the immortal souls of His people, they also provided health and social services, education, and the registry of births, deaths, and marriages. The Catholic service in-cluded the Sacraments, such as Baptism, Holy Communion, Marriage, Confession, and Absolution. Filled with symbolism and a medium of communication with God, they served to bring each individual closer to God and into the administration of the Catholic Church, where records were kept. These services were useful to the civil rulers, whose lives were also subject to the processes. It was so effective that after a thousand years, the Catholic Church had changed the social organization of Europeans, even the way they thought. It had eliminated all competing hierarchies such as clans and local religions. It also sold Indulgences. This allowed the wealthy to buy their way into the heaven promised in the afterlife. As an example of its impact, by the time of the Reformation it had become the single largest property owner in Europe, owning half of Germany.[38] Whatever else they may have argued about, every one of the members of this huge cult accepted the same basic premise, that there was only one God, and He had given them Christianity and with it, dominion over His world.

The Roman Catholic Church governed through a central administration, and even the kings were its subjects. Satisfied that they all agreed on the basics, though, the administrators eventually overplayed their hand. Whether it was a consequence of Indulgences, or a sincere concern among the more aware that the needy were being left behind, or a belief that papacy had become too doctrinaire, or that new knowledge was permitting people to develop more local methods of administration, cracks began to form.

The twinned kingdoms of Aragon and Castille, favoured by the papacy, had extended Catholic authority over the whole of the Iberian Peninsula, pushing out the Muslims and the Jews. With their newfound wealth, they had crossed the ocean and absorbed the great country of the Aztecs in Central America, Christianizing them as well. Other European kingdoms saw the wealth Spain accumulated in the process. No doubt that, too, influenced the spread of tensions through Christendom. Poorer outlying kingdoms knew of the wealth that travelled in the merchant vessels and brigands were tempted by them.

CHAPTER 6

England Leaves the Catholic Fold

With Luther gaining followers in the Holy Roman Empire, Calvinism growing in France, and Geneva courting Jean Calvin, King Henry VIII believed he could move against the Catholic Church with impunity.

Before the reign of Henry VIII, the rulers of England began to prey upon the common lands, incorporating them into their private holdings. This was accomplished through the Enclosure Laws and through a process called engrossing. Common lands were redefined and enclosed, used for grazing sheep. At the same time, smaller holdings were brought together under one family, causing evictions.[39] A consequence of these changes was a growing landless population.

In 1533, Henry VIII broke from the Catholic Church over his right to divorce Catherine of Aragon, aunt of the Holy Roman Emperor, Charles V. The break resulted in the king's excommunication from the Catholic Church and alienation from the Continent. It also gave King Henry ownership of the Church's extensive properties in England. His right-hand man, Thomas Cromwell, Earl of Essex, promptly dismantled and distributed these lands for the king's benefit as well as for his own and his friends. The new wealth enabled the king to create a navy, albeit made largely of pirates who traded in slaves and attacked Catholic ships on the high seas.

This break of the English kingdom from the Catholic Church put them on the side of the Protestant reform movement that was beginning on the Continent. This does not mean that the English king was a reformer. Leaving the Catholic Church caused huge social tremors exacerbated by Cromwell's propaganda campaign against the Church. It also added to the landless underclass, leaving thousands of vagrants or vagabonds wandering the streets. The king passed vagabond laws that, according to historian Jasper Ridley, resulted in as many as 72,000 hangings.[40] Taking apart a country's religion and social infrastructure proved to be a lot easier than putting it back together.

When Henry VIII of England died in 1547, his ten-year-old son and successor, Edward VI, a terminally ill adolescent, tried to maintain the legacy of his father. Taking the self-serving advice of the Duke of Northumberland, he named his Protestant cousin, the 17-year-old Lady Jane Grey, as his successor. She was Northumberland's daughter-in-law. Edward's elder half-sister Mary, a devoted Catholic and the daughter of Catherine of Aragon, Henry's first wife, rejected the decision, even before Edward's death. The naming of Lady Jane, fifth in line to the throne, upset the people. Tradition was not respected. Mary was first in line to the throne. In 1553, Queen Jane was deposed after only nine days but, at least in the beginning, the deposal was peaceful. Mary became queen.

Mary has been portrayed as both a terror and a kind queen. She was concerned for the poor and even walked among her people incognito to assess their wellbeing. Taking the steps she did to turn the clock back and make England Catholic again, she followed the advice of her cousin, the Holy Roman Emperor Charles V. Once her main decisions were set in motion, the consequences were beyond her power to control. The emperor's guidance led to her marriage to his very Catholic son, Philip. It took place only ten months after her coronation. Two years later, when the emperor abdicated and his son became King Philip of Spain, the royal couple was styled in England as Queen Mary and King Philip of England. The regal power did not devolve completely to the Spanish king, but the heresy laws of the Catholic Church returned. The consequent death sentence of members of the Protestant religious elite began to jeopardize Queen Mary's support in England. Many, particularly among the early Puritan leaders, fled to the Calvinist Church in Geneva where they learned and ultimately brought back elements of Calvinism. Mary's was a bloody reign that included the execution of Lady Jane, the queen of nine days, as well as three hundred high-ranking Protestants. Thankfully, Mary was sickly and died in 1558 without an heir, after only five years as queen. That same year, Emperor Charles V died in his retirement at a monastery in Spain. Almost forgotten to history and often confused with Mary, Queen of Scots, the English Queen Mary's legacy is a popular drink, the Bloody Mary.

CHAPTER 7

Coligny and the Dream of New France 1560

The idea of New France was conceived in the cauldron of a religious civil war in France that pitted the Protestant Huguenots against the French Catholic establishment.

During this same period in France, in addition to Jacques Cartier and Jean-François de Larocque de Roberval's failed attempt to colonize the St. Lawrence Valley in 1542, there were a series of attempts to establish a colony where the Huguenots, the French Protestants, could find religious freedom. In 1538, Huguenot fishermen from Dieppe established a short-lived colony in the Caribbean on St. Christophe, known today as St. Kitt's.[41]

Gaspard de Coligny, Admiral of France, one of the leaders of the Huguenots, sponsored three subsequent attempts to establish New France in Brazil, Florida, and South Carolina respectively, shortly after the French king named him admiral in 1552. He envisioned a colony that would offer freedom for religious minorities. He first attempted it by charging Vice-Admiral Nicholas Durand, Seigneur de Villegaignon,[42] with the task. A blusterer who had won his position, in part, by secretly spiriting Mary Queen of Scots to France, he rapidly abused his status. Drawing his knife against the captain of the Château de Brest over a question of the fortifications, he was in danger of losing his position of influence. He seized on the idea of making the voyage to Brazil. He was an excellent seaman.

Likely, the story of his mismanagement in Brittany had not yet reached Coligny's ears. Petitioning the king, they furnished three ships and six hundred people, setting sail on July 12, 1555. On board were sailors, soldiers, artisans, gentlemen, and men from prisons who exchanged their sentences for a chance in the New World. There were no women and no seeds for crops. They discovered an island just off the coast of present-day Rio de Janeiro. Villegaignon deemed it perfect for defence and he immediately sent a ship back to Coligny asking for more people and supplies. Next, they proceeded to build a fort, trading trinkets with the local Indigenous people for food and water.

Soon, Villegaignon over-reached himself trying to force his Indigenous hosts into building a fort. They simply disappeared, leaving the would-be colonists in a bind. Not only had they failed to bring crops or farmers, but they had also overlooked that their island had no fresh water. Miraculously, they survived. Coligny, impressed with the original report he received, sent Villegaignon's nephew along with 290 people, this time including six young women and some especially influential Huguenots.

After initial enthusiasm, a rift divided the colonists when Villegaignon discovered that he might be painted as a Huguenot, something that he had not considered before. He hadn't understood the vocation of religious freedom that guided Coligny's vision. The Huguenots were a threat to his authority and tensions were rising. He accepted to send the senior Huguenot home to consult with Jean Calvin, their spiritual leader. In this way, Villegaignon calmed the passion of the others but also eliminated their leader. As soon as the Huguenot leader was safely gone, Villegaignon denied Huguenot worship until the ruling was received. The other senior Huguenots decided to return to France, but the boat, left to Villegaignon to provision, was inadequate. Five of them abandoned the return, fearing the voyage. Villegaignon threw two in prison and the others from a cliff to their death. Those who stayed on board carried a sealed letter for the French authorities condemning them to prison as heretics, but when they arrived, the authorities declined to act on his instructions.

With the best gone or murdered, the colony was doomed and Villegaignon himself returned to France at the end of the year, abandoning the remaining colonists, one of whom was a Catholic priest named Jean Cointa. To save himself, Cointa reported the colony to the Portuguese. Soon, the Portuguese found them and served notice to the acting commander, Legendre de Boissy, to surrender. He refused, and the Portuguese under the command of the colony's governor, Mem de Sá, took the colony after a long, hard battle. After destroying the fort, and short of men to do more, the French abandoned the island, and some successfully cast their lot with the Temoyo Federation, a local Indigenous Nation. They continued to trade with France and fought for six more years under Boissy until the Jesuits convinced the Temoyo to turn them over. They were evicted in 1566.

Today, bearing the ignoble name of Ilha de Villegagnon, the island is connected to the mainland and is the location of the Brazilian Naval School.

The Brazilian New France ultimately failed, not only because of extraordinary mismanagement on the part of Villegaignon but also because of the ongoing tensions of the Wars of Religion in French society and the proximity and power of the Portuguese Catholics.

Admiral de Coligny would not stop trying.

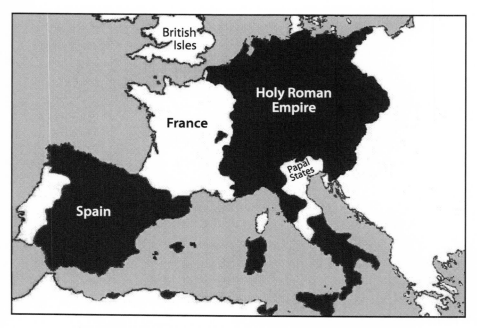

The extent of the Holy Roman Empire at the time of Emperor Charles V.

CHAPTER 8

Holy Roman Emperor Charles V

*Cuius regio eius religio (whose realm, his religion) was a doctrine that
came into force at the Peace of Augsburg in the Holy Roman Empire in
1555 to recognize Protestant princedoms. It was a worthy attempt to establish peace among the princes, but it failed the people's vision of autonomy.*

Emperor Charles V, a staunch Catholic, was the head of the empire,
including the German states, Italy, and the Burgundian Netherlands
as well as being the king of Spain and the archduke of Austria. French-
speaking, Charles's position as emperor was an elected one, and his
strongest bond in childhood was the Netherlands. His most significant
kingdom was Spain. He led military campaigns against the Ottomans and
against France, but a lot of his energies were involved in putting down
small rebellions throughout these vast holdings. The Peace of Augsburg,
delegated to his younger brother Ferdinand because he could not abide
to preside over the inevitable recognition of the Lutherans, was the last
major event of Charles' reign before his complete abdication for health
reasons in 1556.

The Peace of Augsburg was an agreement acknowledging that local
rulers could choose between Lutheranism, Calvinism, and Catholicism.[43]
The Holy Roman Empire, established in the time of Charlemagne eight
hundred years earlier, was the birth of the Catholic Western Roman Empire, and the emperor Charlemagne was crowned by the pope. Later, the
emperors were elected by the nobility and endorsed by the pope, but this
new agreement created legally recognized principalities that were not
Catholic.

Each monarch's religious choice would, henceforth, be dictated to
all his subjects and those who could not abide by the choice were free to
move to another principality. The doctrine was not based solely on relig-

ious conviction, although that played a visible role. As mentioned above, the churches took responsibility for health, education, social services, and the registry of marriages, births, and deaths. The Lutheran churches, arguably independent service providers, undermined Catholic authority, causing serious divisions, but they had the numbers to stand up for themselves. Over time, the solution proposed at Augsburg was to give local rulers the choice of established religion, at least between Catholicism and Lutheranism. This was a top-down solution proposed to address a popular reform. The reformists, the Protestants, were a movement that called for freedom of religious choice. The Peace of Augsburg made no provision for non-Christians and left no freedom to choose. Many Jews fled to Poland. At that time, Poland was the Christian country with the greatest religious freedoms in Europe. Another option for non-Christians was Constantinople, where as early as 1455 the Ottoman Sultan Mehmet II put out a call welcoming non-Christian Europeans. Bavarian Jews were among the first to respond.

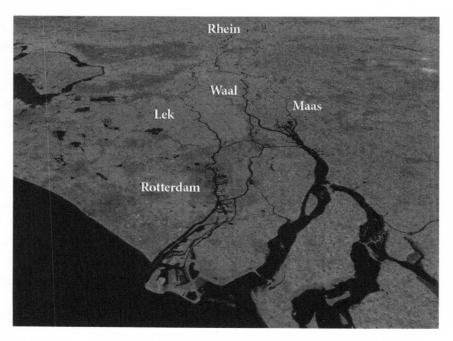

An overview of the Rhine and Meuse deltas,
where the Netherland farmers were granted title.

The new Augsburg doctrine did not sit well with independent congregations who wanted to look after their own, or who were attached to their homes and their communities and were not willing to move. The people of the Netherlands with a mixed religious heritage were a case in point. Establishing themselves on valueless swamps, they were neglected by Emperor Charles V. The ruling local hierarchy that answered to the emperor, Count Lamoral of Egmont, Philip de Montmorency, Count of Horn, and William of Orange were happy simply to see the valueless, previously uninhabited swamplands paying taxes. These events left the lowlands to develop under the radar, their aristocracy not noticing the presence of a growing number of free thinkers and entrepreneurs. The delta regions of the Netherlands grew with remarkable freedoms in this way.

These lowland farmers acquired title to rectangles of vacant swamplands, paying a modest tax for outright ownership. To dry the swamps for growing, they needed to develop specialists who would dig and maintain canals, and this gave rise to an interdependent community of skilled workers. Specialization led to markets and exchange and to the need for people to be educated. Most of the peasantry of Europe at that time lived in feudal, cashless isolation, tenants paying their way with a portion of their produce and making do with what they could keep. The Dutch swamp farmers, instead, could sell their produce and use the money creatively to explore new techniques, to acquire animals that would complement their soil's needs, and to encourage art and freedom of thought. Because they could not easily grow grains to feed their livestock, they developed cabbage and other vegetable crops to fill this gap. That resulted in more-pampered animals and better dairy production.[44] Along with these freedoms, minority religious ideas saw less resistance, and these Dutch lowlands became enriched with religious refugees from elsewhere in Europe. Things went well—at least until Charles V abdicated.

In 1556, Emperor Charles V divided the empire among his heirs and successors, the Holy Roman Empire being confirmed to his brother Ferdinand, who had been charged with Austria and with many of Charles's powers and responsibilities. The Netherlands, a Spanish colony, devolved to King Philip II, Spain's new king. Born in Spain, the wealthiest, most powerful country in Europe at the time, Philip did not share his father's laissez-faire governance but chose to rule with his own hubristic convictions. He named his sister Margaret of Parma as regent of the Netherlands, leaving her an inadequate number of troops to control the colony, and she relied on the cardinal responsible for the Netherlands to institute religious reforms – to force the Protestants back to the Catholic Church.

Counts Lamoral and Horn, and William of Orange, all Catholics, could not, or refused to, override the tradition of religious tolerance that had developed in these lowland regions of their provinces. Simultaneously, a small group of Calvinists, reacting to the cardinal's attempts to force them back into the Catholic fold, went on a rampage, destroying some Catholic churches. Margaret sent an urgent message to her brother, writing that the country had revolted against the empire and the king. Told that he must deal with such an uprising urgently, King Philip II sent the ruthless noble Fernando Álvarez de Toledo, Duke of Alba, to whip the colony back into shape.

The Duke of Alba led a veteran army of 10,000 troops, marching across Europe, picking up an additional 60,000 men, hungry and looking for booty. When this huge army arrived in the Netherlands, the Duke of Alba invited Count Lamoral of Egmont and Philip de Montmorency, the Count of Horn,[45] to dinner, ostensibly to explain the situation to the duke. When they arrived, the two counts' reception was to be thrown in prison. Despite pleas from many corners of Europe, they were tried and executed. William of Orange, upon seeing the direction things had taken, fled the country and prepared for a long war. Meanwhile, he would also watch the challenges of Protestantism in France and elsewhere in the Holy Roman Empire.

CHAPTER 9

Admiral Gaspard de Coligny Tries Again

Ever the optimist, Coligny was encouraged by Villegaignon's
colonizing attempt and decided that he would try again.

In his second attempt to create a colony based on religious freedom,
Coligny did not delegate to any one man but stayed on top of things
himself. He consulted with Protestant allies, especially his friend Renaud
de Laudonnière, and finally chose Jean Ribault, a serious man and excellent seaman, to head a new expedition. Laudonnière accepted to go with
Ribault. Their destination was to be the Spanish-claimed land of Florida.
For Coligny, the idea of baiting the Spanish or Portuguese made sense
because these countries were not at peace with France and, if challenged,
a war overseas would focus the French on an external enemy, giving the
Huguenot and Jewish minorities a respite from the Wars of Religion that
risked tearing the country apart. Also, if he could establish a colony, at
least there would be a place for the non-Catholic French to escape to.

Events like the death of Roberval would have spurred Coligny forward. Jean-François La Rocque de Roberval, who had tried to set up a
permanent colony in 1542 with Jacques Cartier, was slaughtered with his
whole congregation when they left their Protestant services in Paris in
1560.[46] The slaughter of the congregation had nothing to do with Roberval's attempted colony. It was simply Catholic violence against the Protestants, in this case the Huguenots.

The Huguenots and other reformers had been formed by the very
institution they confronted. They wanted religious and administrative
responsibilities to be shared differently, by each community, working
together as needed. They were as Christian as the Catholics with the same
passionate faith in God. They believed they could co-exist with the Cath-

olic Church. The Catholics could not tolerate a competing service provider, a challenge to their hierarchy and power. No coexistence was possible.

The Jews, present as well, just wanted to survive. Many had escaped a hell by leaving Spain and Portugal under the Inquisition, where the Catholic Church had used them to infiltrate the Muslim society and then turned on both, forcing them to become Catholic and often burning them as heretics even if they accepted. Those who had run elsewhere in Christendom felt vulnerable. Would the Inquisition follow them? France was not like Spain, but it was ruled by the majority, and the majority was Catholic. Any minority that could not stand up to it in France was in danger. Most of the Iberian Jews fled to far-away Constantinople where their community thrived under the Muslim Ottomans into the twentieth century, practising freely their culture, Jewish faith and even their Spanish language.

Coligny's new venture to establish a safe colony for the Huguenots set sail on February 12, 1562. Ribault held a course that took them straight across the Atlantic, thereby avoiding the Spanish islands. They arrived at the coast of what they called Laflorida by the end of April and they soon identified a river that would hide them from Spanish ships. They dubbed it the River Mai. Today it is called St. Johns River. As had happened often for Europeans arriving in the Americas, they were kindly received by an Indigenous Nation, most probably the Timucua, whose historic territory was northeastern Florida. There is no Oral History to find. The Timucua, reputedly large of stature and a gentle people possibly numbering 200,000 at contact, are extinct as a Nation. A small number of them had been taken to Cuba at the end of the Seven Years' War and may have been absorbed there.

With their help, the French Huguenots managed to raise a stone column that the French saw as claiming the land for the King of France. Not satisfied that the River Mai was the place to put his colony, Ribault sailed up the coast to choose instead a small place at the mouth of Archer's Creek in South Carolina. There he determined to build a colony around a fort he called Charlesfort, leaving twenty volunteers to establish it.

Jean Ribault built this monument together with the Timucua people in 1562 to mark a place of meeting. In this image, Athore is showing it to Renaud de Laudonnière in 1564.

Ribault returned to France for supplies but arrived in the middle of another outbreak of the Wars of Religion. He joined the battle for the Huguenots at Dieppe, but soon the town was lost and he was forced to flee to England, always mindful of his abandoned colony in Florida. Petitioning the queen to allow him to return to help his colony, he was initially well received but then he was inexplicably accused of being a spy and was locked up in the Tower of London.

France had three Estates, consisting of the nobility, the Church and the Third Estate, the commoners. They were called together, but rarely, for major consultation. Among the commoners, many were protesting the rigidity of the other two, and some of the commoners were opting for the Huguenot ideas of Jean Calvin with its greater freedoms of worship and management. Isolated pockets of them were being persecuted as heretics. Coligny, Admiral of France, took a public stance to protect them.

The king generally consulted with five members who made up his Grand Council. The Huguenots were being persecuted across the country, but with Admiral Coligny publicly standing up for them, three members of the Grand Council formed a triumvirate, called the Catholic League, to deal with the Huguenots, and with Coligny.

Fully aware of the huge disparity in numbers, Coligny sought only a peaceful coexistence. He acknowledged that a civil war had begun, pitting the Catholic League against Huguenot nobles, the southern Kingdom of Navarre, and members of the Third Estate. Still, Coligny managed to prolong an uneasy peace. Then he turned his energies to the rescue of the colony. This time he equipped his friend Renaud de Laudonnière to return and rescue the men at Charlesfort.

Sadly, there was little to save. The colony had been abandoned after a revolt, the fort was burned, and the rebels arrived back in France as Laudonnière was departing. Still, with the resources he had been provided, he returned to the River Mai and built Fort Caroline at the location of present-day Jacksonville. He expected reinforcements to arrive in the spring of 1565. Soon, following orders to make good relationships with the Indigenous Peoples, he managed to get stuck between two warring Nations and offended both by trying to encourage them to get along. In the meantime, unknown to him, the Wars of Religion were again delaying any chance of reinforcements.

Laudonnière was an excellent sailor but a weak administrator. Soon his men were raiding the Timucua for food and threatening to revolt. Some had even deserted with the two remaining ships, becoming pirates on the open seas. But, by good fortune, the small colony was spotted by John Hawkins, a British privateer, who was returning from a successful mission of trading slaves.[47] He offered to bring the Frenchmen back to England but Laudonnière would not abandon the colony. Instead, he traded cannon and gunpowder for food and a ship from Hawkins, reserving his plans to leave. Of the two groups who had stolen the colony's ships, one managed to alert Havana of the existence of Fort Caroline, preying as they were on Spanish shipping, and the other made it to Europe with a report of Laudonnière's misgovernment, suggesting he was living in a dissolute manner. A new peace negotiated, Coligny dispatched another company, the largest yet, to help the colony. Ribault, who had been determined harmless to the British, had been released and returned in time to lead the new expedition. He would have been better off in the Tower of London.

The denouement of the American adventures began with the departure of this new fleet of seven ships. They arrived safely on the 28th of August in time to find that Laudonnière had given up and was preparing his departure. Unknown to them, the Spanish knew not only that the colony existed but also that reinforcements were coming. A huge fleet had been dispatched under the command of Pedro Menéndez de Avilés, a capable, ruthless man who was charged with eliminating the heretics. His fleet had been hit travelling through the late summer hurricanes and had been reduced to a size similar to the French fleet. Over the following few days, while discussing their next steps, Menéndez was moving up the coast of Florida. He had been determined to arrive at Fort Caroline before the French, or at least before their reinforcements were deployed. Time was of the essence, but he still could have the element of surprise on his side. He landed south of them, sure that he was going too far, but local Indigenous inhabitants told him that the colony was further north. Returning to sea, he soon saw four French ships resting quietly at anchor. It was midday on the fourth of September and a storm was blowing in. His main ship had sustained serious damage already in the hurricane and he was obliged to spend the afternoon facing down the storm, but calm returned with the evening.

Menéndez surmised that the four ships were too large to go upriver to join the rest of the fleet. His were also too large. In the dark of night, he sidled in between the two largest French ships, intending to board at first light, but he was seen and hailed. He informed the French that he was there to execute the heretics and a round of bravado was exchanged, each goading the other. In the meantime, the French ships, undermanned for a battle, quietly cut their anchors and, while the Spanish manoeuvred to board, the French slipped out to sea. Having lost his advantage of surprise, Menéndez followed.

When Jean Ribault became aware of the event, he knew that he would have an advantage if he were to head after Menéndez right away.

Laudonnière tried to dissuade him, warning that the hurricane season was unpredictable, but Ribault did not wish to lose his advantage.

Menéndez lost no time going back south down the coast, but everything took days. Among the contents and passengers of his ships were three hundred members of the families he had intended to settle at Fort Caroline. He described them as being of no use. Remembering a river he had seen on St. Augustine's Day, August 28, he made for it and began to establish his encampment, but Jean Ribault saw his advantage and attacked. Most of the Spanish ships were in a shallows, but the tide was going out and the level was dropping. The boat Menéndez was on had not yet crossed. As the French cornered him, by some good fortune he managed to slip in over the emerging sandbank. Inside, the advantage would be his. Ribault was obliged to withdraw.

The Spanish were the masters of the south seas. They knew the force and risks of hurricanes. Menéndez understood the point Laudonnière had been trying to make. As a hurricane blew in, he surmised that Ribault would be fighting it to head back and that Fort Caroline would be weakly defended. He immediately commanded his men to prepare for a march through the shallows up the coast. Off they went, five hundred men— three hundred with arms, the rest with picks—and several days' supply of biscuits and wine. Still, they would not arrive at Fort Caroline before September 20.

He saw immediately as he approached that Ribault had not returned.

There was no resistance. Fort Caroline had about two hundred occupants, a quarter were women and children. Menéndez's army of five hundred overwhelmed the settlement and then proceeded to slit the throats of the men. He acknowledged that it was only his fear of God that kept him from killing the women and children, whom he also saw as heretics. Instead, they were returned to Havana where some managed to make it back to France, calling upon the king to avenge the killings and retake the colony. Some of the men escaped into the woods and others to the boats. Injured in battle, Laudonnière found refuge in the woods and managed to return to France.

In the meantime, the hurricane had driven the ships of Ribault's main force upon the rocks further down the coast. Over the next weeks,

Menéndez followed up on any reported sightings of survivors, found the starving crews, and cajoled them into surrendering. He separated those who said they were Protestant, tied their hands behind their backs, and marched them off to his fort, but once out of sight and hearing of the rest, their throats were slit. Ribault shared the fate of this cold-blooded massacre, all carried out in the name of His Catholic Majesty, King Philip of Spain.

The Catholic Church celebrated the elimination of the heretics. In Spain, the poet Bartolomé de Flores praised it in verse, and all Catholic Spain interpreted the fate of the Huguenots as God's will. The anger in Huguenot and Catholic France, united momentarily against a common enemy, led to the renegade action of Dominique de Gourgues, a Gascon, who returned a year later with a small elite force and captured, burned, and massacred everyone in the new Spanish fort built at Fort Caroline.

The story of Coligny's New France was not quite over. The idea of a colony where non-Catholics could find a new, safe life of religious freedom would survive in the mind of the Huguenot king of Navarre.

CHAPTER 10

The Netherlands Finds a Base in Huguenot France

*French Protestants, the Dutch and the English had reasons
to help each other in dealing with the power of Spain.*

William of Orange, who went into exile when the Duke of Alba murdered the two counts, had found a base in France. French Calvinists—Huguenots—were also fighting for toleration of their religious beliefs.

The Dutch provinces[48] were fighting a defensive war against a ruthless enforcer. Their military abilities on land were innovative, but not always effective. The first Dutch land base for William of Orange came into rebel hands serendipitously. Pirate ships flying Orange's colours raided shipping as a means of maintaining their forces. On April 1, 1572, a number of his ships were driven before a storm to take refuge in the harbour of Brielle, not far from The Hague. Finding the Spanish defenders absent, they raised the flag of Orange and declared the town their own. It was the first break they had in their long fight for independence. This victory, the Duke of Alba's inability to recapture the town, and his ruthlessness, served to drive the rebel provinces together. It led to the duke's recall in 1573.

Over the next decade, the lines became clearer as the Spanish held the southern provinces, and as William of Orange began to be accepted as the leader of the seven northern provinces. In 1581, they formally rejected Philip II as their king. By the rules of hierarchy and caste, they needed to replace him but were stymied because William of Orange was a noble, but he was not a royal. They offered the title to the king of France as well as Queen Elizabeth of England, but both declined, offering support instead. This dilemma was still unresolved when William was assassinated three years later.

With a political structure based on an equal union, where each province appointed a placeholder, called a stadholder, they looked for unanimous decisions. William's son, Maurice of Nassau, became stadholder to Holland and Zeeland in the place of his father and was also stadholder for three other provinces, giving him a leadership role. Maurice of Nassau was not the king, but simply the most important stadholder in a republic composed of seven provinces, a republic that offered an alternative for the persecuted, from Spanish Jews to French Walloons and many more. The Dutch battles with the Duke of Alba were over, but a more powerful army had left Spain and based itself in the Catholic Dutch colonies, those that form a part of Belgium today. This new army was headed by the Duke of Parma. The Spanish, though, were also counting on their duke to lead an invasion of England.

CHAPTER 11

The Dead Do Not Make War

In France, Admiral de Coligny, on whom the fate of the French Huguenots depended, was determined that he could help broker a peace with the Catholics. An opportunity presented itself with the marriage of Princess Marguerite de Valois and King Henri of Navarre.

"The shot came from that window where the smoke is!" Admiral Gaspard de Coligny declared. The bullet hit his finger, penetrated his wrist, and exited near his elbow. His men milled around in confusion as the gunman escaped.

It was midday on Friday, August 22, 1572,[49] and Coligny, the leader of the French Huguenots, had just met with King Charles. When Coligny left the Louvre, he detoured around the Hôtel Bourbon. A young man thrust a petition into his hands. Reading it distractedly, he stepped back to adjust an uncomfortable boot, an action that foiled the intentions of the assassin.

Coligny had sought valiantly for a way to resolve the Wars of Religion. Supporting the militant Huguenot Queen Jeanne III of Navarre, he had chosen to come to Paris and to trust the Court to honour its word and bless the marriage of Henri of Navarre and Marguerite de Valois, the sister of the French king, Charles IX.

Marriages between royal families were negotiated to improve alliances or forge friendships; this marriage that attempted to bring an end to the Wars of Religion had been negotiated over a long time. It was fraught with risk because the Huguenots, many of whom were property owners, formed a minority in France. They sought toleration of their religion, but coming to Paris, effectively between battles, to try to establish peace was sanctioned only nervously by many in the Huguenot community, and even then, only after Coligny had insisted that it was "better to die by a bold stroke than live a hundred years in fear."[50]

Henri, King of Navarre, located south of France but north of Spain, was a Prince of the Blood to the French Crown. His mother, Jeanne d'Albret,[51] Queen Regent of Navarre and a militant Huguenot, had him tutored as a Huguenot, rejecting the Catholicism of the early sixteenth century. His father, Antoine de Bourbon, was less committed to rejecting Catholicism. He dragged the family to Paris and tried to re-educate Henri as a Catholic, but the decision led to the breakdown of their marriage. Separated from his mother, Henri stubbornly maintained his Protestant beliefs. In 1562, when he was only nine, his father was assassinated, and Henri became the king of Navarre. Admiral Gaspard de Coligny was one of his mentors. When Henri turned eighteen, he was betrothed to Marguerite de Valois, sister of the French king, in an initiative Queen Jeanne d'Albret of Navarre had undertaken with the French Queen Mother, Catherine de' Medici, to end the Wars of Religion. Queen Jeanne died of tuberculosis in the spring before the wedding.

The wars were the French experience of the Reformation, the advent of Protestantism in Christendom. In broad strokes, it set the Catholic League, mostly in northern France, against the Huguenots in the south and west, and it was a fight for religious freedom. The de Guise family and Catherine de' Medici, the Queen Mother and regent to three kings, were the principal players on the Catholic side, and the de Guises would stop at nothing to eliminate the Protestants.

The wars stopped for the wedding and the whole Protestant leadership was in Paris to attend. New hope filled the air. The Court had assembled for the marriage despite the repeated refusal of Cardinal Bourbon to conduct it without a papal dispensation. As the summer dragged on, the cardinal rebuffed pleas from the Court. When he finally relented, the event began at the Louvre with a sumptuous meal and a ball. The ceremony was set for the following evening, August 18, at a pavilion built outside the doors of Notre Dame Cathedral. King Charles, King Henri of Navarre, and the Huguenot Prince de Condé were dressed identically in pale yellow satin as a means of publicly demonstrating their mutual trust. King Charles wryly commented, "Everybody hates me but my brother of Navarre…" The other lords were also dressed for the occasion and more than 120 ladies dazzled the crowd with silks and velvets interwoven with gold and silver. Queen Jeanne of Navarre, the one who instigated the match, had died in June.

The bride, Marguerite, wore a blue dress with a long train, and all the church bells in Paris rang, punctuated with the ceremonial firing of cannon. The Venetian ambassador was heard to say, "You would not believe there was any distress in the Kingdom." People watched from every available space, including rooftops and windows, but ominous murmurs permeated the crowds. This was not a popular wedding. The princess was being married to a heretic.[52]

Coligny's assassin ran from the building, jumped onto a waiting horse, and fled through a city gate into the open country. Coligny was carried to his room where, shortly later, the famous surgeon Dr. Ambroise Paré arrived to care for him. While his men held him steady, the doctor amputated the finger and lanced and sewed up the injured arm. Coligny bore the operation with courage and a steadfast countenance while, holding his arm for the doctor, Coligny's assistant wept.[53]

Four days after the assassination attempt, in the afternoon, as Coligny lay convalescing, cared for by the royal physician, he received a visit from King Charles himself, who swore he would find the assassin. What the king did not know until later was that his mother, Catherine de Medici, was behind the conspiracy.

That night, Catherine, who feared the rising power of the Huguenots, explained to her impressionable son Charles what had happened and why Coligny had to die.[54] The Protestants could not be trusted and sought only to take power, she told him. She also shared a rumour that they were planning to kill him in retaliation for the attempted assassination of Coligny, an idea that was ludicrous but galvanized young Charles into action. Catherine had a vengeful ally, the Duc de Guise, who held Coligny responsible for his father's death during the ongoing Wars of Religion.

King Charles ordered the assassination of the Huguenot leadership, most of whom were still in Paris. The spirit of the wedding was suddenly behind him. De Guise, assigned to fulfill the king's orders, immediately sent his henchmen to the home of the invalid Coligny, beat him senseless, and tossed him, still alive, out his second-storey window into the street.

Then, to make sure he was dead, they decapitated him and left orders to street urchins to dismember the body.

Spreading through Paris, sanctioned murders of Protestant leaders led the Catholic citizenry to rise against their Huguenot neighbours, beginning a massacre that swept beyond the capital and across France.[55] Catholic mobs chained off streets, locking their victims into certain neighbourhoods, slaughtering whole Huguenot families, leading to rumours of cannibalism.[56] Stories of such massacres have a way of feeding on horrifying rumours like this. Cannibalism has been invoked in many histories to describe our worst fears, to make the listener pay attention. Known as the St. Bartholomew's Day Massacre, it lasted much longer than a day, with the carnage running from Catholic claims of 7,000 dead to estimates as high as ten times that, while some Huguenot sources placed the numbers in the hundreds of thousands. From about ten percent, by the time the dust settled the Protestant population of France had dropped to around seven percent.

French jurists and intellectual leaders were horrified but Catholic Europe celebrated the massacre. Like at the time of the Spanish murder of Jean Ribault and the French Huguenots, the pope ordered a Te Deum, a mass in praise of God, and had coins struck depicting an angel with a sword in one hand and a cross in the other, floating through bodies, celebrating France's return to the Church.

Among the survivors was King Charles's new brother-in-law, Henri of Navarre. He was under house arrest in the care of the Court.

After the marriage and Coligny's assassination, Henri, King of Navarre, was a prisoner of the Court of the French king, Charles IX, and was forced to convert. His arranged marriage was a failure from every angle. Not only did it not end the wars, but Marguerite had also wanted to marry one of the de Guise family, the staunchest enemies of Protestantism.[57]

King Charles lost his mind over the actions of the de Guise family in the disastrous St. Bartholomew's Day Massacre. He became ill with tuberculosis and died two years after the event, declaring his sorrow to Henri until the end.

It took Henri two more years to escape the Court and rejoin the Huguenots in the south, returning to Protestantism.

CHAPTER 12

Meanwhile, in England, 1558–1610

France was in the bloodbath of the Wars of Religion, the Holy Roman Emperor was divesting himself of his responsibilities, the Netherlands were in revolt and England was an independent island kingdom.

Religious differences began at the level of the royals in England. Elizabeth, daughter of Henry VIII and Anne Boleyn, succeeded (Bloody) Mary and brought a long reign of Protestant stability. The vagrancy problem continued during her reign. Parliament passed bills in 1597 that included the building of hospitals, workhouses for the poor, penal transport, and impressment, where able-bodied men were forced into the English navy, composed largely of privateers who were raiding Spanish ships and overseas colonies, feeding the coffers of England.

It was during the reign of Queen Elizabeth that the Church of England, the Anglican Church, was established as the state religion with the monarch as its head. During this same period, the Presbyterian, the Congregationalist, and the Puritan sects insisted in their own ways that the new churches should be cleansed of all vestiges of Catholicism. There was a desire to reinvent English Christianity, reducing the power at the top. Calvinism inspired the Puritans, for whom discipline was paramount, while the Presbyterians found traction in Scotland, devolving responsibilities to the individual presbyteries. These were not the priorities of Queen Elizabeth. Once the ruler and her coterie had power, there was a strong tendency to preserve it. The role of a Protestant queen as the head of the English Church gave the ruler more power than she would have had as a Catholic monarch. There was no pope to answer to. She tolerated no competition, but on that, she had little choice. The Catholics were still present and the non-Catholics, while far from united, opposed her centralizing power. To her north, the Scottish kingdom was still ruled by a Catholic monarch. Beyond her shores, Spain, whose king was her predecessor's Catholic husband, was the most powerful nation in Europe, with a Catholic empire that stretched around the world.

Spain's King Philip II was determined that his people and his colonies would remain Roman Catholic. He took it upon himself to destroy the Protestants and return England to the Catholic realm. When Mary died leaving no heir, his kingship of England ended as well. He tried to marry Elizabeth but was rebuffed.

England still had a large population of loyal Catholics, people who might rise in support of a Catholic heir to the throne. The only Catholic candidate in the possible succession was a different Mary, the queen of Scotland.

Mary Queen of Scots was the daughter of King James V of Scotland. She was also the granddaughter of Margaret Tudor, who was the sister of Henry VIII. Her father, who died in battle against Henry VIII, was fighting to keep Scotland Catholic. Mary was his only surviving heir and became queen before she was a week old.

Mary was also a de Guise, and as the Catholic queen of Scotland, she was a perfect match for the French Dauphin. She was the same Queen Mary who Vice-Admiral Nicholas Durand, Seigneur de Villegaignon, had spirited into France in 1542 when she was a child. The two children were married and a year later, the Dauphin's father died in an accident. The young couple became King François II and Queen Mary of France, but the boy was too sickly to consummate the marriage and died himself a year later.

Mary, 18 years old, queen of Scotland and of France, was a widow. She was also superfluous to the French Court. She returned to Scotland to assume her responsibilities as queen.

To her, this included marrying her cousin Henry Stewart, Lord Darnley, and providing a male heir to the throne. She was a good queen who insisted on religious tolerance. Unfortunately, her reign was doomed by vicious infighting, exacerbated by the English queen, because Mary was also the only Catholic claimant to the English throne. To keep the peace, her advisors obliged her to abdicate in favour of her two-year-old son James VI. She fled to England, against the advice of her Court. She hoped to get help from her cousin Elizabeth. She was twenty-six years old and spent the next nineteen years safely under house arrest, prisoner of the Queen of England.

Over the next decades, English-Spanish relations deteriorated as English privateers, sailing for Queen Elizabeth, pirated Spanish shipping and encouraged the rebellion in the Dutch provinces. Following the advice of the privateer John Hawkins, England invested in its navy and improved its ship-borne guns, introducing a lower, faster ship armed with shorter, easier-to-load cast-iron cannons. Queen Elizabeth showed no fear of the Spanish Armada as it sailed up to invade her kingdom in the early summer of 1588. She could not afford to. Her shores were defenceless, and her army had to be ready to deal not just with an invasion, but also with Catholic sympathizers. The year before, her Court had finally tried and executed Mary Queen of Scots to reduce the risks of the plotting Catholics. It was this execution as much as the growing power of the English navy that had set back the Spanish invasion schedule. King Philip needed a royal, someone who was in line for the throne, for his invasion to work, and it had to be a Catholic. Catholic feudal Europe had become a society of castes, and the royals, all intermarried across Europe, were the rulers.

England's resources had been invested in its defence almost entirely through the navy. A network of guards watched the sea each day and night for signs of the Spanish, using a signalling system of torches that would be lighted upon first sight and would bring the message rapidly along the country's coast. Sir Francis Drake and John Hawkins, both pirates, undertook bold raids as Spain inexorably built up its enormous navy for the invasion. The Spanish depended upon their army, even at sea. They were dangerous if they could board the ships of their enemy. Naval war was moving away from the ramming corsairs that had served them well in the past. As long as they could grapple and board the enemy ship, or subsequently land upon the shore, England would be theirs.

England depended upon a younger navy, using tactics, speed, and distance. Their raids had set the Spanish timetable back by a year when Sir Francis Drake had attacked and destroyed a good part of the Spanish

Armada as it sat in harbour in Cadiz, preparing for battle. This, coupled with the execution of the imprisoned Scottish Queen Mary, caused King Philip to re-evaluate his plans. If his capable admiral, the Marquess of Santa Cruz, sailed against England, there was no Catholic candidate to place on the throne of England. When King Philip proposed that he, himself, would become the king, he suffered a backlash throughout the Holy Roman Empire. Even the pope, who had guaranteed his support, began to back-pedal. Now these huge sums would be withheld until his army was on the English shore and until he knew who would become its monarch.

An unforeseeable consequence of this delay was that England's nemesis, the Spanish admiral, the Marquess of Santa Cruz, died in February 1588. He had never been defeated at sea. He combined knowledge, confidence, passion, and connections to get the job done. But he could neither please, nor easily abide his impetuous king as he prepared the Armada. This could have weighed heavily on his heart.

His reluctant replacement, the Duke of Medina-Sidonia, did not want the job, nor did he feel qualified for it. Despite his protests, King Philip chose him, a general, to replace the great admiral. In doing so, he overlooked his naval corps. The historian James Anthony Froude interpreted the king's actions as expressing ambivalence about what he hoped to accomplish with his invasion force. Both Queen Elizabeth and King Philip had delegates meeting on their behalf trying to find a mediated solution, and the duke, being junior in the task, would be more likely to do the king's bidding precisely.[58] A show of force might be adequate.

After many delays, the Armada set sail under this compromised leadership. Once well underway, they discovered their stores, held too long, were putrid and their water contaminated. Winds did not co-operate, and ships were often separated. They did not see the signals of the English torches burning on the Cornish coast until July 29, two and a half months after leaving Lisbon. A part of the English fleet, waiting in Plymouth, had ample warning to put to sea.

The English navy had cut its teeth harassing Spanish shipping. The newer boats designed by Hawkins could keep their distance and still fire effectively. They were at risk, though, if the wind dropped and their gunpowder supply was not adequate. With difficulties, setbacks, and mistakes, the Spanish arrived at Calais on Saturday, August 6 with the English still harassing them at a distance. They were to meet the Duke of Parma, with his large army travelling in barges, coming from the Dutch provinces.

The Armada's main objective was to protect the 30,000 soldiers who would cross the channel to England in barges. The Duke of Parma, a general with the same kind of reputation on land as Admiral Santa Cruz had on the sea, had taken over from the Duke of Alba. The Dutch rebels would not let his barges cross, hoping to drown the whole army when it tried.

The English set burning boats in among the Spanish fleet, forcing some ships out to sea, and the harassment continued. Instead of simply landing in England and establishing a beachhead, the Spanish finally decided to withdraw downwind of the English, sailing up England's east coast. When they sailed back down the west coast, a large part of the Armada, overtaken by storms, was driven onto the shores and destroyed. The great Spanish navy had been overcome by harassment, bad weather, and bad decisions. Catholic Spain was no longer a threat to the small Protestant kingdom of England.

When the Armada sailed away, though, so did the hopes of the Dutch rebels, who would still have to face the forces of the Duke of Parma. England was their incidental ally while they fought the Spanish Armada. With the Armada retreating, the Duke of Parma set his sights on the Dutch rebels, determined to exterminate them. The seven northern provinces, Holland, Zeeland, Utrecht, Gelderland, Overijssel, Friesland, and Groningen, had been defending themselves against Spain's religious intolerance, trying to maintain the independence that had grown during the time of Charles V. It was only at this time that they began to see themselves as a republic.

With the southern provinces secured, the Duke of Parma[59] could bide his time before destroying the rebels. Unknown to both parties, the Dutch were just about to gain another incidental ally.

CHAPTER 13

Good King Henri 1610

As the first of the Bourbon kings, le Bon Roi Henri's major contribution was the creation of the Edict of Nantes, giving the French the option to end the Wars of Religion. In the short time he was king, he managed to rebuild the economy. However, his popularity really grew in the next century.

When the French King Charles died of tuberculosis, his younger brother became King Henri III, an extroverted homosexual who would not have an heir himself. He was soon fighting an attempt by the de Guises to oust him. In a strange twist of events, the new king called on Navarre for help. The king of Navarre brought his forces and joined him. While they prepared to attack Paris in 1589, bivouacked at St. Cloud, a Dominican friar arrived, claiming to have an urgent message for King Henri III. The friar attacked him, wounding him fatally. Before dying, he acknowledged Henri of Navarre as his successor. It was an almost impossible situation. The Huguenots were already vastly outnumbered, and over the next nine years, Henri of Navarre would have to reconquer all of France to be recognized as King Henri IV of France.

Henri of Navarre's first action was to divide his limited troops in three, forcing the enemy to do likewise. He took one-third to Dieppe, in the north, and found an ideal defensive position in nearby Château d'Arque, awaiting the inevitable attack of the superior Catholic League forces. With 8,000 troops, he was outnumbered four to one, but he had chosen the north because, as a Protestant, he had called upon Queen Elizabeth of England to send assistance. When the battle began in September of 1589, the year after the withdrawal and destruction of the Spanish Armada, Henri IV's strategic position protected him for the first week, but heavy losses spelled doom.

At the beginning of the second week, a small contingent of English and Scottish troops arrived and was soon supported by their main force, totalling 4,000 men. This allowed Henri IV to turn the tide and soon he was chasing the withdrawing League forces. Henri noted a particularly brave and capable soldier within his ranks, Pierre Dugua de Mons,[60] a fellow Protestant who shared the king's desire to achieve religious tolerance in France.

It would take most of a decade for them to defeat the Catholic League. Holding fast to the siege of Paris for the whole summer of 1590, he had reached a balance-point. Bombarding the city from the hills of Montmartre, burning the windmills, crippling the food supply, he was responsible for 40,000 to 50,000 deaths, mostly through starvation. By September, with the Spanish forces under the Duke of Parma successfully lifting the siege, Henri withdrew.

For the Dutch, as long as the Duke of Parma was fighting the Huguenots, the Dutch provinces had time to retrench and prepare for the attack that was sure to come.

Over the next three years, Henri and the Catholic League fought, without either side gaining the advantage. Henri realized that if he were to publicly convert to Catholicism, he would undermine the Catholic League's justification for war. Purported to have said "Paris is well worth a mass," he converted, and the Catholic League had no choice but to accept or face a rebellion. Their troops were tired of fighting. At the end of February 1594, King Henri IV was formally recognized, crowned in the Chartes Cathedral south of Paris.[61]

70

CHAPTER 14

Calm Between the Storms

The Edict of Nantes brings a period of peace to France.

One of Henri IV's[62] first actions as the undisputed monarch of France and Navarre was to declare the Edict of Nantes in 1598, a document that allowed for freedom of worship across most of the realm and became his greatest, but not his longest-lasting, legacy.

His longest-lasting legacy was to support Pierre Dugua de Mons's project to establish French colonies in Acadia and Canada. Appointed a Gentleman of the King's Chamber, Dugua de Mons visited Tadoussac, a Mi'kmaq and Innu (Montagnais) town near the Gulf of St. Lawrence. He wanted to study the potential for creating permanent French colonies in the New World where there would be a guarantee of freedom of worship. Upon his return and his report to the king, he was awarded exclusive trading rights to carry out his objectives. In 1604, he returned with colonists and experts, including Samuel de Champlain, a cartographer.

Their first settlement attempt, in what is today the state of Maine, proved disastrous, and they moved to a new location in the Annapolis Valley. They had explored down the coast of New England and were hailed from the shore from almost everywhere that had something resembling a harbour. It would generally start with the Indigenous Peoples on the shore dancing and demonstrating a warm welcome. At many places, the shore villages were surrounded by fields of maize, squash, beans, pumpkins, and tobacco. Champlain observed that any sign of disdain or lack of trust on their part could rapidly escalate into tension. They ended up having to flee most places. More than once, they watched as white smoke billowed from the Indigenous village. This was followed by more white smoke up and down the coast from other villages—a warning to the neighbourhood.

In the meantime, with Dugua de Mons working hard to create a settlement in Acadia, merchants back in France kept petitioning the king to cancel his exclusive trading rights. Finally, in 1607, those rights were withdrawn, and the colonists were forced to return to France.

Dugua de Mons knew he could convince the king to reinstate his trading exclusivity, but he also knew he would have to remain in France to protect his interests and his new colony. He had sent explorers to identify an easier site to defend and his cartographer Champlain identified Quebec as an ideal spot. Once he had secured a new exclusive trading agreement, he financed the creation of the new colony, giving Champlain all the necessary powers and money to carry it out.

Republic of the United Netherlands

In 1590 when King Philip of Spain called upon the Duke of Parma to withdraw his troops from the southern provinces and rush to the aid of the Catholic League of France, Maurice of Nassau gained two years to organize the defence of the seven provinces. By 1598, he had pushed the Spanish out. The war was far from over, but the Dutch remember that period in their history, one of victory and growth, as The Ten Years.

Shut out of Iberian ports, the ships of the United Provinces sought to bypass Spain for trade in the Far East, and in 1595, Captain Jan Huyghen van Linschoten reached Java, establishing trade relations there. Others soon followed. The impact on the economy allowed them to finance their defence. The stadholders created the Dutch East India Company. Through it, a Dutch navy was born, with the freedom to build forts overseas, create colonies, maintain an army, trade in slaves, and even to mint its own currency. Life at home was governed by the different provinces but trade and the creation of colonies were completely in the hands of the Company. It still had an appetite, as did the English, for pirating and it continued to harass Spanish shipping and colonial ports.

England and the Anglican Regime

English support of the Dutch colonies served its purpose with the Spanish, but the freedoms that the Dutch fought for went well beyond what Elizabeth was willing to abide for her people. Leiden and Amsterdam became refuges, not just for the persecuted in Europe but also for those English Protestants who objected to the singular hierarchy the queen was establishing through the Anglican Church. This led to increased confrontations and divisions in England.

One of the best-known confrontations was with John Greenwood and Henry Barrowe. Greenwood was considered the leader of the Separatists, who set up secret, separate congregations that would not be subject to the Anglican hierarchy. Arrested in 1586, he was visited by lawyer and fellow Cambridge graduate Henry Barrowe. Barrowe's reason for visiting was not to offer legal representation but simply to learn and discuss his ideas. Barrowe was also locked up without recourse. Both men wrote books on their shared beliefs on scraps of paper, hidden from the authorities and spirited out by visitors. These collections were published in Holland, one called *A Brief Description of the False Church*. When the books came to the attention of the English authorities, they did not deny their writings. They were judged intransigent and were executed.

This led to the flight of many of the other Separatists to Holland and elsewhere. During those years, the Protestant Dutch were fighting for both freedom of religion and independence from Spain and from the Holy Roman Empire. Their lands became a place for the most persecuted to find refuge. Presbyterianism found a home in Scotland. Puritanism managed to survive inside the Church of England for some time. The Separatists who stayed, sometimes known as Congregationalists, became the martyrs.

King James VI of Scotland, Mary's son, succeeded Queen Elizabeth, becoming King James I of England. His reign witnessed religious polarization with the Puritans becoming more outspoken and the Catholics trying to blow up Parliament. Guy Fawkes was convicted for that conspiracy, and he is still remembered every autumn on Guy Fawkes Day with bonfires and fireworks. King James, an educated man, surprised many by taking an authoritarian turn. His initiatives included an Authorized Version of the Bible, known today as the King James Version, and contributing to the standardization of the Anglican Church, as well as a book he authored called *The Divine Right of Kings*.

His son, Charles I, believed fervently in the divine right of kings, putting him at odds not just with the many Protestant fundamentalists who wanted to devolve the powers of the Church, but also with Parliament itself. A High Anglican married to a French Catholic, his understanding of his importance raised tensions, and by 1629, four years after his accession, Puritans began to leave for the colonies. The king's intransigence triggered his demise and execution. England became a republic under the Puritan Oliver Cromwell, slowing down the exodus, but after Cromwell's death and the return of the monarchy in 1660, tens of thousands more Puritans left England for New England.

The Leiden pilgrims on the deck of the Speedwell at their departure for the Hudson River.

CHAPTER 15

The Storm Returns, on Both Sides of the Atlantic

The United Netherland's rebellion lasted 80 years and spilled into a continental war involving every kingdom in Europe, the last thirty years of it pitting Protestants against Catholics across the German states. Estimates of up to 40% of the population died as marauding armies and starving soldiers consumed the countryside.

In 1618, the grandson of Holy Roman Emperor Ferdinand became Emperor Ferdinand II, but unlike his grandfather, he did not tolerate the rights of the Protestants. A war of religions began in the Holy Roman Empire and drew in the Dutch, Spanish, Danes, French, and Swedes. England's new king did not join partially because of infighting at home. The horrors of the war, lasting thirty years, left up to 40% of the population dead as hungry, marauding armies consumed everything in their paths. It was only at the Treaty of Westphalia in 1648 that the seven provinces of the Netherlands finally achieved their independence from Spain. The Holy Roman Empire was no longer a force as it broke into smaller nations. Spain's power also became a part of the past. France, backing the Protestant side while suppressing its own Protestant minority, became the dominant country of Europe.

Throughout this time, the seven provinces had continued to attract religious refugees. Leiden and other Dutch towns became centres of revolutionary thought and religious freedom. Among the refugees were English Pilgrims, and it was a mixture of these that made up the Leiden contingent on the Mayflower, that icon of the United States Foundational Stories. They had heard of Dutch land claimed across the Atlantic Ocean, where they dreamed of establishing themselves to live in peace by their own religious rules.

This Leiden group had acquired a ship, the Speedwell, and was to sail in company with the Mayflower, which was bringing workers to Jamestown, Virginia, but the two boats had to return to a port because the Speedwell was not seaworthy. The Mayflower accommodated many of the Leiden passengers, intending to deliver them to their destination near the mouth of the Hudson River on its way to Virginia.

Henry Hudson had claimed the river for the Dutch East India Company a decade earlier. The Mayflower never made it that far, but sailed into Cape Cod Bay in early November 1620, the crew and the passengers sick from the crossing. The iconic United States story described God's hand in the arrival of "English" Pilgrims. They found a recently vacated but fully supplied Wampanoag (Algonquian) village. God had provided this miraculous beginning of these seekers of religious freedom in America.

The Dutch influence distinguished the Pilgrims from the English Puritans who arrived later. Many of the Pilgrims had just spent key years of their lives in a highly politicized environment in Leiden and were well placed, from that experience, to conceive of and write the Mayflower Compact, another iconic element of United States Foundational Stories. Since their chosen destination was a Dutch territory, their loyalty was likely much stronger to the new spirit of independence that they experienced in the republic of the seven provinces than as a response to the lack of freedoms that existed in England at that time. The period spent in Leiden is not a highly touted part of the American story, but it is significant in that the Pilgrims' way of dealing with the Indigenous Peoples they met was more consistent with Dutch mores than with those of the Puritans.

CHAPTER 16

The Wampanoag

Wampanoag Oral History allows us to see how the English dealt with the Indigenous Algonquian Nations in New England and to contrast it with the dealings of the French and the Dutch.

Before the first European diseases reached them, the Wampanoag[63] lived in forty villages and had a population of about 12,000. The Wampanoag Confederacy comprised almost four dozen clans situated in southeastern Massachusetts, including the islands of Nantucket and Martha's Vineyard. Their neighbours to the north were the Massachusett and Nipmuck, while to the west, in present-day Rhode Island, were the Narragansett. These Nations were all Algonquian-speaking and horticultural, growing maize, squash, beans, and other crops, but they also depended on the sea and on hunting. As Algonquian peoples, their hunting territories were passed through the paternal line, but the horticulture, maintained by the women, created some matrilineal families as well. They lived communally and, as such, the children grew up in a household shared with other family groups. Their family structures do not seem to have been as consistent as the Iroquoian horticultural societies. Iroquoian influences may have been changing the horticultural areas while more classic Algonquian family structures co-existed with them.

Belief systems in both Algonquian and Iroquoian Oral Traditions described a cooperative relationship among all aspects of nature. Humans were a younger sibling, learning from their Elders, the other species, the fox, the bear, the deer, and nature itself, all animate, acknowledged as persons, and all honoured and deeply respected, with sharing as the cardinal point of focus.

Contrast this with the Judeo-Christian creation story of having been thrown out of the Garden of Eden, forced to scrape out a living while working to achieve dominion over a hostile world, and the fundamentals of the two cultures become distinct. Sailing across a stormy sea in wind-driven boats, carrying iron tools and early guns, the Europeans must have seemed like a strange sibling to honour and respect. Neither party knew that the Europeans were carrying contagions that would prove devastating. Following contact, up to 80 percent of a group could die, most often from smallpox.[64] The surviving people, with their societies weakened and destroyed, would not necessarily jump to the conclusion that the newcomers were the problem, although some, like the Wendat, concluded that the Jesuits brought the illness. The Europeans saw the illnesses as a weakness without understanding their own role either. Dancing and singing on the shores to entice the European ships to land, the original openness endured, though sometimes clouded by dispute. European egocentric concepts of possession and a personal god would have been completely opaque at first encounter as the Indigenous sense of self remains opaque to the settler mind, even today.

Before the arrival of European diseases, estimates of the overall Indigenous population of the New England region, including the Wampanoag, were over forty thousand. Political structures were based on Peace Chiefs, or Sachems, with a head Sachem. While the gender jurisdictions may have been less clearly codified than those defined by Jigonsaseh in the Great Law of Peace, there is no evidence of a gender imbalance as seen in Christian society. Women had their own agency. Different Indigenous cultures had discovered, through abstinence and in their pharmacopeia, the means to assure that pregnancy was not an accident, allowing them to have some control over the growth of the population.[65] Their respect for their elder siblings extended to respecting their space and freedom and this would lead to a balance between the human population and their sibling species.

The word *Wampanoag* means Eastern people, and there is evidence of trade with Europeans from as early as the beginning of the 1500s. In the early days, the trade was peaceful but over time European ship captains captured Wampanoag to sell as slaves. Between 1614 and 1620, three epidemics swept through the Canadian Maritimes and New England, devastating the mainland Wampanoag population, exacting a 75 percent death toll. Ten of the villages were wiped out. The colonists began to arrive in the last throes of the dying, finding perfectly habitable, stocked villages simply abandoned, and they interpreted the provision of them as signs from God—their god. The survivors, at the mercy of their historical enemies from further inland who had not yet been struck by the diseases, looked to the early colonists as potential allies with an interest in mutual defence. The Massachusett were more severely hit by the diseases and almost eliminated. As a result, a lot of their history has been permanently lost. Wampanoag numbers eventually dropped as low as four hundred, but their Oral History survived and today we can look at history through their eyes. They are the witnesses whose story can leave us to judge the civility of the Puritans who followed the original Pilgrims. In the meantime, the religious wars in Europe continued to boil over, creating a cauldron of fear, hatred, death, and refugees who would come to colonize.

CHAPTER 17

Brûlé, Savignon, and the Gift Economy, 1609

*Samuel de Champlain made a crucial decision when he promised
to go to war against the Mohawk Nation, but he sealed an alliance
that would grow to include the influential Wendat and the
Algonquian Nations of the Ottawa Valley region.*

The sixteenth-century French imagination was stirred by the existence of a country beyond Hochelaga, a country so influential that the valley of the St. Lawrence River was just a prelude to it. The French were ill equipped to travel into this country. They lacked the means of transport necessary and, in any case, Jacques Cartier's uncivilized intrusions had put the Nations he met on a war footing.

Donnacona, the headman Cartier met on the St. Lawrence at Stadacona, was probably the first to give the French an idea of a great culture to the west, but he shared many stories, as though testing European gullibility. It was not until Samuel de Champlain's time that contact was made with these central Nations. Champlain, trying to improve relations with the Montagnais and their Algonquin and Wendat allies, accepted to participate in a military sortie against their common enemies in 1609.

Champlain had accompanied some Wendat and Algonquin warriors to engage in a battle with the Five Nations of the Haudenosaunee. He met up with his partners at the Richelieu River and travelled south, a loose group of warriors looking forward to the surprise the French guns would make in a battle. Champlain hoped to prove his worth as an ally to the warriors he was with and thereby establish a trade relationship. So politically wise in other ways, it seems unfortunate that he took the course he did. Perhaps he knew of the consequences that his predecessor Laudonnière had suffered on River Mai at Fort Caroline when, in 1565, he had tried to bridge a peace between two warring Indigenous parties.

Champlain and a dozen armed Frenchmen met up with over four hundred warriors, including one hundred Wendat, at the mouth of the Richelieu River near the end of July. Military discipline among the Wendat and Algonquin was based solely on the individual's commitment to the cause and no-one was obliged to fight or was stigmatized for refusing. As a result, when they reached shallow waters before arriving at what Champlain dubbed Lake Champlain, many turned back and Champlain sent nine of his Frenchmen back with them, but he was determined to carry on. By the time they reached the lake, only sixty warriors and three Frenchmen, in twenty-four canoes, remained. When two opposing parties of canoes surprised each other late in the afternoon of July 29, they each made for shore at a good distance and exchanged messengers. They mutually agreed that they should postpone their fight until morning because daylight was failing fast. This lends an interesting perspective on what war meant to them. The formality of this agreement suggests that the encounter the next morning would have been understood as a test of strength and could have been choreographed in the minds of the opposing warriors. Champlain's allies were carrying a surprise that they anticipated with excitement.

In the morning, as the two antagonists rained down arrows on each other, Champlain hid among the ranks. At a prearranged signal, everyone else ducked and he stood up and shot his gun while his French soldiers fired from the woods.

They killed two Mohawk Chiefs. The superior Mohawk forces were surprised by Champlain's guns, having never seen or heard them before, and, with two headmen shot, pandemonium followed, and they fled. They were shocked at the break in the tradition of war. It is also evident that the Mohawk learned from this incident that their war tactics would have to change. Champlain's artistic recordings of the battle are confusing because he displays both sides as fighting nude and he gives them identical canoes. The Mohawk canoes were more probably dugouts and, while the Algonquin, considered ruthless and effective warriors, could have fought nude, the Iroquoian peoples did not, although they may not have been prepared to fight in this situation.

Champlain's allies declared victory, celebrating Champlain's actions.

He had achieved what he had hoped to and could now expect that the help would be reciprocated through increased trust and trade. Over the rest of his career, Champlain did his best to bring peace between his new allies and the Five Nations, but although he had some successes, he never achieved that goal.

After the battle, a teenager named Étienne Brûlé asked Champlain for permission to live with Iroquet's people, Algonquin allies of the Wendat. Champlain approached Iroquet, head of the Ononchateronon who lived on the South Nation River, but after much discussion, he was told that they would take Brûlé and in exchange Champlain would also take a young man to live with the French. Savignon, the brother of a Wendat Sachem, or Peace Chief, was chosen. Iroquet was Algonquin, Anishinaabe, and the Wendat were Iroquoian. The choice of the Wendat Sachem's brother suggests a cultural status that Iroquet recognized in his dealings with the Wendat, the providers of grain, maize, and hospitality in difficult times. A culture based on giving and sharing, the Wendat were being honoured with the privilege of providing Savignon.

While Champlain hoped Brûlé would learn the Algonquin language and customs, the French learned from Savignon of the central role of the Wendat, who Champlain called Huron,[66] and who farmed between Lake Simcoe and Georgian Bay. Iroquet and his people, they would learn, were allies who lived with the Wendat as winter guests.

Champlain was aware that the exchange of the two men was more than a way of learning each other's cultures. It was also an assurance of the care that would be given to the guests.

Plaque on the wall of the Old Mill Inn, Toronto, showing Étienne Brûlé.

After a winter in France where Savignon was shown at Court and interviewed and otherwise entertained, they made it to Montreal Island for the return of the young men in early June 1611. Since the other side had not yet arrived, Savignon went off hunting with a Montagnais and a Frenchman. Their canoe was upset in the rapids and the Frenchman, who could not swim, drowned while the Montagnais, a powerful swimmer, made for shore but also drowned. Only Savignon, who stayed with the upset canoe, survived. Champlain was relieved when Iroquet and Savignon's brother arrived on June 13 and he could safely return the young man to his people. He was also happy to see the young Étienne Brûlé in good health and almost unrecognizably integrated into the family of his hosts.

Savignon told his people that he had been well treated but was relieved to be home. He described the French customs that most upset him—the poverty, the beating of children, and the French tendency to argue vehemently without actually fighting. His own culture was noted for its civility of discourse and respect for children, who were seen as renewed manifestations of revered Elders. Since all property was communally held, wealth and poverty were communal experiences. Whether times were good or bad, all shared equally, something he witnessed was not the case with the French.

Brûlé, by contrast, demonstrated his comfort with his hosts, his facility with the language, and his desire to stay. He returned with Iroquet and Savignon, vanishing from French society for the next four years until Champlain met with him again in 1615 in the Wendat town of Cahiague.

Brûlé's choice is not surprising. The society he joined provided a liberating level of personal contact. Aside from the lighter hierarchical structure, the independent agency of women, and the Tradition of gratitude and sharing, there were also events that we might vulgarize as trade but that were celebrations of solidarity. These social events could happen in many places and encouraged exchange. With a deep respect for nature, these events can be seen as a flowering, and when a community flowered in this way, it had much to give, just as the berries flower in season and give in their turn. The excitement of an event of sharing good fortune would involve ceremony, Celebration, and cultural exchange, and the giving community would receive gifts that would have allowed it to exchange its surplus, further fulfilling needs. Robin Wall Kimmerer, a scientist, writer, and Citizen Potawatomi, describes these in Potawatomi as *minidewak*, a give-away inspired by the fruiting strawberries, and thereby creating a reciprocal relationship between people and also with nature.[67] We call this a gift economy. The gift is shared, being no-one's property.[68] By contrast, our market economy is based upon personal ownership.[69]

CHAPTER 18

Champlain's Choice 1610

After 1610, Champlain was forced to steer his own course in the Wars of Religion. He set the colony on an evangelical course, hoping to Christianize the Algonquian and Wendat Nations.

At the height of the French Revolution in the 1790s, when the mausoleums of the rulers were destroyed at St. Denis, the casket containing the remains of Henri IV was set aside and opened. The revolutionaries filed past his preserved corpse for two days, paying their respects. Good King Henri, who invoked the Edict of Nantes, temporarily ending the bloody Wars of Religion in France, had been assassinated 183 years earlier, on May 14, 1610. His assassin, François Ravaillac, a man the court said was mentally unbalanced and had acted alone, said he was told he would become a hero for carrying out this act. On that day, the king's carriage was caught in a small traffic blockage that may not have been accidental, and Ravaillac sprang from among the people milling around, into the king's carriage, and drove a knife into him.

The news of the king's assassination was hard on Pierre Dugua de Mons, the man who established Samuel de Champlain at Quebec. Both men knew that New France's status as a refuge from religious persecution would be threatened. The Edict of Nantes, the document that had tempered down the Wars of Religion, had lost its author and protector. Henri IV's son was only nine when he took on the mantle of King Louis XIII. His mother, Marie de' Medici, acted as regent but France went through an unstable period under her guidance. While she still respected the Edict of Nantes, her choice of advisors was Catholic, and her colony was not a priority. Champlain returned to France and had the sad fortune to watch the waters there muddy. Pierre Dugua de Mons was an unwelcome Protestant in the Court and even Henri IV's principal advisors were of no help. Dugua de Mons encouraged Champlain to contact some of the people who now had influence.

During those difficult years, Dugua de Mons managed to get Prince de Condé named as viceroy and protector of New France. Sympathetic to the French Protestants, he seemed an ideal choice, but he led a revolt against the regent and lost favour, spending three years in the Bastille.

The assassination of Henri IV

New France was the Huguenot dream, a colony where all religions would be tolerated, and there was no priesthood there. History is not clear on what religion Champlain's birth religion was, but he embraced Catholicism after the assassination of the king.[70]

He had to choose between Dugua de Mons's vision, seeking a colony free from religious persecution, and the existence of the colony itself. He had always shown more ability than his French contemporaries in dealing with the Indigenous Peoples and he could serve a function by trading with them, even Christianizing them, since that was the direction the Crown was taking. He drifted closer to the Catholic powers, obtaining the services of four Recollet Brothers who came to New France in 1614.

CHAPTER 19

The Three Sisters

Étienne Brûlé adopted his host's culture, opting for a personal freedom
that was unimaginable in any of the Christian European nations.

The missionaries and Étienne Brûlé's other French contemporaries lamented his fall from grace because he adopted the Wendat's social and sexual mores as his own. While he remained a valuable interpreter, Samuel de Champlain's notes say he "was recognized as being very vicious in character, and much addicted to women…" It is unlikely that the criticisms stung since Brûlé no longer lived in French society. He understood the mores and customs of the Wendat and other Iroquoian people, a matrilineal and matrilocal culture in which the status of women was incomprehensible to the missionaries and to Champlain. Matrilocal means that the women lived in their childhood home and raised their children there, rather than moving into their husbands' sphere, as is done in patrilocal cultures. Their role was with their mothers' families, and the vast fields were the women's responsibility.

In that society, men and women fulfilled interdependent functions. While the women farmed, the men cleared the fields of trees and built the homesteads, great communal longhouses surrounded by spiral palisades. There was no need for ministrations to the poor because hoarding wealth was shunned. Young women and men had free sexual relationships, but if a pregnancy resulted, the potential fathers would have presented themselves willingly instead of running for cover, and the new mother would have experienced neither shame nor stigma but would have chosen, or named, the father. Considering the agency that women had over their own persons, and the use of herbs that could cause abortion, this is not surprising. Each child was wanted. It suggests that pregnancy was welcomed, and the future father would be honoured by the public knowledge.

The conventional relationship that we think of as father–child would have been between another male in the mother's family—a maternal uncle—and the child. The husband would maintain the same status in his own mother's home, even if living with his wife, but as a son reached puberty, he would join his father to learn the skills appropriate for a young man. During the growing season, women lived communally in their fields, maintaining the crops, and in that environment, the maternal relationship would also have been nearly unrecognizable to us; the senior women commanded the respect and earned the affection of all the children. There was no physical disciplining because the children had total freedom, but the example of personal discipline shown by their Elders and the deep sense of belonging to Mother Earth, to the community and extended family, combined with the notion that each child was a manifestation of a revered Elder who had passed away, could be constraint enough.

Brûlé would have learned the Oral Traditions of the Wendat, based around a woman. Her name was Aataentsic, meaning the Ancient One, and she is said to have fallen through a hole in a garden in the sky clutching maize, bean, and squash seeds in her hand or pouch. She landed safely on the back of a turtle, thanks to large sea birds who cushioned her fall. The animals, birds, and the turtle worked with her to build a hospitable place for her to live on the back of the turtle, hence Turtle Island. They recognized her need for soil and one after the other, the creatures dove to procure some from the bottom of the sea. There are many different versions, but finally, it was the most humble, in one version the toad, in another the muskrat, and in still another the otter, who succeeded, and from a small amount of soil placed on the turtle's back, the forests, the fields, and the rivers were formed. This Foundational Story established some basic natural rules: that the human beginning was a woman, the grandmother; that all species worked together and were equally important and that the contribution of the humblest was valued; that soil was essential; and that the land itself rode on the back of a living creature.

The relevance of the other species, be they animal or plant, is central.

Because of their specific knowledge, they are considered as Elders, each with a special gift to offer. The humans, the most poorly equipped, learn gratefully from them and respect the gift of their knowledge. Their fundamental self-image was as a part of a gift economy, a cooperative of animate agents, not limited to human beings but comprising all life forms and including anything that had agency, including aspects of the world Europeans considered inanimate. The authority of each was respected. Their spirituality and sense of the numinous drove them to respect the jurisdiction of each member of the cooperative of being, and to hold this natural order sacred.

The Christian Foundational Story comparable to the story of Aataentsic is the story of Adam and Eve. Thrown out of the Garden for disobedience, they were condemned to struggle forever for their livelihood, and women were cursed to give birth in great pain.

Aataentsic,[71] pregnant when she fell, gave birth to a daughter who became Mother Earth, personified in the lynx. Despite her mother's admonitions, she mated with the west

Here the serpent is portrayed as female as Eve tastes the forbidden fruit of the knowledge of good and evil.

wind and gave birth to twin boys, Tawiskaron and Iouskeha, one of mischief and one of sincerity. Iouskeha had a normal birth, but Tawiskaron exploded through his mother's side, leading to her death. Some versions describe this event happening in the area we call Kentucky and describe the Kahqua people as having moved from the south long ago. The women were the farmers and the crops they grew in Ontario were not native species but thoroughly domestic ones. There are two different Origin Stories for the Three Sisters. In one, the food crops were said to have come with Sky Woman when she fell from the sky. She either grabbed them as she fell or had them already in a pouch. In a different version, her daughter was the source of them. After she died giving birth, the Three Sisters sprang from her body, and she thereby assumed her responsibilities as Mother Earth.

In Brûlé's time, the Wendat were generally larger and healthier than the Europeans. They formed a small part of the greatest horticultural civilization the world has known. One of the Three Sisters staples, maize or corn, is a food developed in antiquity. Like many of the foods bred by the original Americans, it was the product of generations of knowledge handed down by the women to their daughters. Maize today is a mystery species in that it is dependent upon human intervention to reproduce, even in the south, and the small plant considered its ancestor barely resembles it. Along with maize, they grew squash and beans in a companion-planting method. Maize stalks grow tall but need nitrogen to do it. Beans take nitrogen from the air and release it as a compound in the soil, making it available to the maize. The beans use the maize stalks to climb, keeping their seed pods clean and dry, with open flowers to present their gifts of nectar to the pollinators. Squash spreads along the ground at the base, overshadowing any weeds, and its unpleasantly rough leaves discourage foraging visitors.

The Iroquoian peoples called this triumvirate the Three Sisters and people from Mexico to the shores of Georgian Bay utilized this method of farming. They grew other crops, including sunflowers, and the women in Mexico and some points north had developed a cotton plant that was so superior to the cotton Europeans were growing that it displaced the European varieties. If the Europeans had never arrived, the Wendat would probably be growing cotton around Georgian Bay today.

Brûlé easily travelled all over the Great Lakes and even down as far as the Susquehanna in Pennsylvania and further to Chesapeake Bay. The people he met had similar Creation Stories and saw themselves as what we would call the same ethnic grouping. Today we call them Iroquoian, and they included the Five Nations of the Haudenosaunee as well as the Wendat, Tionnontaté (called Petun by the French), and the Kahqua, or Neutral. Further south were the Susquehanna, Tuscarora and Cherokee. They belonged to a large, pan-American horticultural civilization.

Brûlé did not record his experiences or if he did, they were lost. His perspective would have helped us understand the Iroquoian culture of the time and would have been a great addition to the records in the Jesuit Relations and Champlain's notes. As we learn to acknowledge the veracity of Oral History, we are beginning to have greater insights into the world that he knew firsthand.

The Three Sisters, maize, squash and beans, a gift
from Mother Earth and a symbol of the Gift Culture.

CHAPTER 20

The Route to the West

On Isle aux Allumettes, Champlain and his young protégé Nicholas de Vignau confronted the real power of the Kichesipirinis Algonquin in 1613. Did young Vignau better understand the circumstances?

The Ottawa[72] River was a busy place. It was called the Grand River by its major custodians. Its tributaries, inhabited by groups of families, clans, or small Nations, all paid their respects when passing Morrison Island, also called Isle aux Allumettes. There, the river narrowed around each side of the island; it was impossible to pass without stopping and acknowledging the Kichesipirinis, the Grand (*kiche*) River (*sipi*) people (*irinis*). That was the custom. It was customary to bring some gifts for this purpose, acknowledging their territorial protection and presence. This was also a part of the gift economy.

Paying respects involved formalities that could take several days and could even include questions about why you wanted to paddle up or down past the island and where you were going. They might insist that their guides accompany you further.

In the early 1600s, the headman of Isle aux Allumettes was named Tessouat. Samuel de Champlain had met Tessouat at Tadousac and at the Grand Sault Saint-Louys (Lachine Rapids) in 1603 and 1611. They had made a treaty that the French would fight on his side against the Five Nations of the Haudenosaunee. At their second encounter, Champlain left an adolescent named Nicolas de Vignau with him to learn Tessouat's language, following the custom Champlain had learned that indicated trust and established alliances. When Vignau came back to France in 1612, he described a trip he had taken with the headman's relative, past the island to Lake Nipissing, where they met Nipissing guides who escorted them to the shore of James Bay. There they had seen a wrecked English boat and had even taken an Englishman prisoner.

Champlain was intrigued by this news. So was the king. They both would have heard of the fate of Henry Hudson.

World trade had demonstrated its vulnerability and huge potential when the Dutch provinces, fighting a war of rebellion against Spain, were refused access to Spanish and Portuguese goods at Lisbon. The northern powers, including England, the Dutch provinces, and France, could see that the vulnerability of this trade was based on the long, arduous voyage, a full year of travelling, just to get to the wealth of trade goods in the Far East. New impetus was given to the idea of a northern hemisphere route to Asia but so far, none had been found.[73]

Just five years earlier, Henry Hudson had proposed to correct this. Approaching the Muscovy Company in London, he hoped to prove a theory that sailing over the North Pole was the solution. The idea, commonly held to be possible, was that with the long summer day at the pole, ice would have to melt each summer. Coupled with perpetual daylight, this would make it possible to sail to the Far East simply by travelling north. The company agreed to back him and that April he set off in the company's ship, the 21.5-metre-long Hopewell, with a crew of twelve, and sailed straight north. By a miracle, he and his crew survived this reckless mission, determining that the theory was wrong, and made it back to England. Even though he hadn't found a northern route to Asia, he had captured the imagination of Northern Europeans. Accepting a further commission the next year, he took the same small boat to the north of Russia, but he was convinced the Muscovy Company was wrong. He allowed himself to be blown back in a gale and determined to continue to try a route north of Newfoundland. His crew threatened to mutiny, and he found himself forced back to England. This time the company had lost its nerve or its confidence in this intrepid explorer and refused to underwrite the exploration Hudson wished to take on.[74]

Upon leaving the offices of the Muscovy Company, Hudson was accosted by a dignified elderly Dutchman, Emanuel van Meteren, who seemed to have known that the explorer would be refused a future commission.[75] Encouraged by van Meteren, he crossed to Amsterdam, where he hoped to convince the Dutch to try an American route. John Smith, a friend of Hudson's and an explorer in his own right who was involved with the governance of Jamestown for the Virginia Company, had shared a theory that the Sea of Cathay could be reached through a river further up the American coast. Hudson believed he was right but could not convince the Dutch, who were determined to have him try a route north of Norway and Russia. He accepted to try one more time to discover a northeast route. This time sailing for the Dutch in a ship called the Half Moon, he was blocked by ice off the coast of northern Norway, and once again confronted a mutiny. He turned around one more time, but on this occasion, his crew accepted to try the American route.

Hudson sailed up the river that bears his name in 1609 to what today is called Albany and thereby enabled the Dutch to found Fort Orange, and subsequently New Amsterdam, but he had once again failed to find a passage to the Sea of Cathay.

Returning to England, he found the support of three investors and set sail again in 1610, this time to explore the Northwest Passage. He made it to James Bay, where his crew mutinied and abandoned him, his son, and five sick crewmembers in a small boat. When the mutineers re-

The Half-Moon on the Hudson River in 1609.

turned to England and confirmed the mutiny, they claimed that Hudson had found a northwest passage, making themselves, the survivors, too valuable to hang. Stories about the abandoned English explorer Henry Hudson captured people's imagination, but more importantly, there was evidence that England had found a northwest passage to Asia.

Vignau reaffirmed his story before two notaries and the king encouraged Champlain to make the same trip Vignau had made. This could be the much-sought-after passage to the Orient and the English were already exploring it. Champlain and Vignau left for Quebec in the colony of New France.

The Last Voyage of Henry Hudson.
Could Vignau have seen these survivors?

Departing from the fort of Quebec on May 13, 1613, it took them almost a month to reach Isle aux Allumettes, some 140 kilometres north of the modern-day city of Ottawa. Tessouat received them with the formality of his culture and, by the end of the second day, the time had come for Champlain to state his business.

When they had made their alliance two years earlier, Tessouat knew that Champlain had made a similar alliance with the Wendat, also against the Five Nations. The Wendat had much more to trade than Tessouat's people could offer, but when it came to the delivery of goods, even the Wendat would pay their respects to the Kichesipirinis, seeking permission to travel past Isle aux Allumettes. They always had.

Tessouat and his Elders rightly saw that, thanks to the French presence, there would be a lot more people wishing to travel past their island in both directions. Tessouat's people saw themselves as intermediaries in the trade that was developing. They worried that Champlain wanted to go to the Wendat to trade; if he did, then their position would be compromised. They had to stop Champlain from going further. Tessouat explained that the trip and the Nipissing were just too dangerous. They were sorcerers and could kill at a distance. In his culture, he was saying "no" and any reason he gave was just a courtesy. It would be bad manners to question his decision.

Petulantly, Champlain complained. He would settle for two canoes instead of four. What kind of a friend was Tessouat to treat him this way? You don't understand; there are dangerous sorcerers, Tessouat explained. Champlain responded that the headman hadn't stopped Vignau with these stories when they travelled up there together the previous year.

A silence fell over the discussion. People looked shocked. Tessouat began very slowly, addressing Vignau directly in Tessouat's own language. "Nicholas, is it true that you said you went up to the Nipissing?" Nicholas de Vignau was only eighteen years old. After a long pause, he repeated what he had told Champlain of his adventures. The men around Tessouat responded with anger and aggression. Champlain and the other French withdrew, moving a distance away and hoping these men would cool down. Champlain again asked Vignau if his story was true, and Vignau confirmed it again, repeating the details and how he had been promised the English prisoner. Champlain's interpreter warned that something dangerous was happening. Men were headed off to warn the Nipissing, he said.

The Kichesipirini were shocked to think that Champlain was not accepting Tessouat's word. A bloodless battle was raging over face. Tessouat could not give in. He could not say that Vignau was right and that he, the head of the Kichesipirinis, had just lied. It was bad form for Champlain to insist. Tessouat had expressed the Kichesipirinis' decision that Champlain could not travel further at this time. The reasons he gave were simply to allow Champlain to withdraw his request without losing face.

Champlain returned to the meeting saying that he had dreamed the night before that his hosts had sent a canoe to the Nipissing to warn them. They responded saying that they were confused that Champlain would trust a liar like Vignau instead of them when they regarded him so highly.

Champlain insisted that Vignau was not abandoning his story. The tensions ran high. To believe Vignau was to suggest that Tessouat was lying, but Champlain seemed to lack the intellectual subtlety of his hosts. The Frenchmen had to withdraw again, at which point Vignau broke down in tears and told Champlain that he had made the whole thing up. He just told Champlain the story so he could come back to Canada, he explained.

When their hosts heard this, they offered to keep Vignau so they could torture him for his lies, but Champlain, terribly discouraged by having lost face and having made the trip based on a lie, said he'd deal with Vignau himself.

Champlain reiterated his alliance with Tessouat against the Five Nations, saving what friendship he could, and promising to return soon to take up a battle against them. He took his leave, returning down the river he had so recently travelled up.

Upon arriving at the Lachine Rapids on their return voyage, Champlain recorded that Vignau asked to be left there and Champlain obliged,[76] feeling that he was leaving the young man to an unhappy fate. Vignau may have had enough knowledge to join one of the Indigenous Nations and to live a happy life, but he does not reappear in any historical account and was most probably killed. Four hundred years later, many people believe that he did not lie; he just understood the gambit better than Champlain did. He realized that it was extremely bad manners to contradict Tessouat and that Champlain, insisting upon believing Vignau, had become dangerously insulting to their host. It was tantamount to standing brazenly before the King of France and telling him that what he said was a lie because he had just heard the truth from a boy, young and prone to the fantasies of youth.

Champlain salvaged his relationship by telling Tessouat that he would return as an ally in war, reminding them that they both had much more important issues to deal with together. The Ottawa River route up to Lake Nipissing and from there over to Georgian Bay was the only viable route to the Wendat, the real prize for New France, a route that Champlain needed to travel. The Five Nations controlled the southern route.

Champlain wished to learn more about the Wendat Nations, located in a dense agricultural society between Lake Simcoe and Georgian Bay on the peninsula where Penetanguishene now stands. An Iroquoian people, they had developed an agricultural and trading civilization that served as the centre of the whole Great Lakes and northern Laurentian regions. Other Nations in the neighbourhood often included people who spoke Wendat as a second language and many of those Nations depended upon the Wendat for maize, their food staple. The Wendat Nations formed part of the Iroquoian culture and spread across the northern sides of the lakes. The Wendat section to the east of the range had a population rivalling that of the Five Nations who covered a huge territory along the south side of Lake Ontario. However, any comparison of the Wendat and the Five Nations must take into account the Wendat could include in their sphere of influence the other Wendat Nations north of the Great Lakes as well as the Ojibway, Ottawa, Algonquin, Nipissing, and even some of the Cree, who were not horticultural. This cross-cultural trading led to specialization and a more cosmopolitan lifeway. There is evidence that the Wendat traded as far west as Lake Winnipeg.

The French had already established a trading relationship with the Wendat, but it was based upon the Wendat coming to Trois-Rivières and Quebec and the trade routes were controlled by Five Nations' Mohawk. For some time, the Mohawk and the other members of the Five Nations of the Haudenosaunee had found an outlet for their trade with the Dutch, but they also had a historic relationship with the St. Lawrence Valley, and the French trade was a threat to their territory.

CHAPTER 21

European-Style Warfare Introduced

*Attacking the Onondaga (or Oneida) in 1615, the French and Wendat
allies had much different objectives. The prisoner-taking skirmishes
among the Iroquoian Nations were not war as Europeans understood it.*

Champlain left France with four Recollet Brothers in 1614. By July
1615, Father Joseph Le Caron was on his way to the Wendat, to Huronia, via the same route Champlain and Vignau had travelled. History
is silent on how they passed Isle aux Allumettes and the Kichesipirinis,
but he was travelling with a significant group of Wendat traders returning
home. The Kichesipirinis knew also that Champlain was returning to
make good on his promise of war against the Onondaga of the Five Nations. Five days later, Champlain crossed over the same route and made
it easily to the Nipissing. There, he was well received and invited to return
the following spring for their annual trip to the Cree at James Bay. He recorded no regrets about Vignau.[77]

Why the Five Nations and the Wendat were at war remains confusing and seems to go beyond blood feuds. The Wendat may have had to
make treaties with their Algonquian trading partners simply to get to the
French market in Quebec, and thus may have been induced, as was
Champlain, to fight their enemies. The year before Champlain's voyage
to the Wendat, the Dutch had constructed Fort Nassau at the location of
present-day Albany, accelerating their trade, principally with the Mohawk. That explains the obvious hurry that both Le Caron and Champlain were in. The Dutch, through the Mohawk, could establish trade
with the Wendat and their allies. In the meantime, the Mohawk were
raiding the northern territories for furs being transported to Trois-Rivières and Quebec. Some historians feel that Champlain's raid against the

Mohawk in 1609 had encouraged them to stay away, look for easier pickings, and that his new initiative against their western allies, the Oneida, or Onondaga[78], would ultimately have a similar effect.[79]

From Champlain's perspective, their attack on a well-defended fort was a disaster. He demonstrated no understanding of Iroquoian methods of making war. All warriors were listened to equally and actions were based on everyone accepting a strategy. Champlain's earlier tactics against the Mohawk—simply demanding that his allies drop to the ground upon a signal to allow him to start shooting—had been understood and accepted. In this new circumstance, Champlain saw himself as the general in charge of strategic planning. Unfortunately, he had accepted Étienne Brûlé's suggestion that Brûlé leave with a separate party to seek reinforcements from the Susquehanna, thereby depriving himself of a knowledgeable interpreter. When the warriors did not understand his strategy, attacking a few Onondaga outside their fort in the hope of taking prisoners, Champlain had to open fire with his guns to save them, completely blowing the element of surprise of French guns. Of course, after that the enemy did not leave the safety of the fort to fight. Injured twice in the skirmish, Champlain aggressively reprimanded the warriors, no doubt in French, for breaking formation. He had no idea it was because they had neither understood nor accepted his strategy. His scolding rant must have mystified them. The spirit had gone out of the attackers, but they listened to him as he outlined the idea of building a European-style siege engine. With its help, they managed to inflict heavy damage beyond the walls of the fort. After that, they retreated the 120 kilometres back to where they had hidden their canoes.

The retreat impressed Champlain. Although the process was painful, he and the other injured, as well as their prisoners, were bound, confined in baskets, and carried on the backs of the strongest warriors, while the best equipped to fight surrounded the convoy, defending it against attempts of the Onondaga who gave chase hoping to capture some prisoners.[80]

This incident demonstrated the warring techniques and objectives of the Iroquoian Nations. The motivation of the Wendat in this instance was not for conquest. Champlain's encouragement of his allies to burn the fort was refused and the Onondaga exclaimed from their fort that the Wendat bringing French guns was cowardly.[81] They could not engage in proper hand-to-hand combat. The guns deprived the young men of a forum to show their courage and reduced the opportunities to properly capture prisoners for torture.

The battle against the Onondaga fort was not the only facet of the French strategy in Huronia in 1615. The other was demonstrated by the presence of the Recollets religious order represented by Le Caron. While the Dutch traded with the Mohawk without religious conditions, the objectives of the French went beyond that. They hoped to convert the Indigenous Peoples into good Catholics, allowing France to establish a Catholic colony that would not depend strictly on moving Catholic Frenchmen to New France. Before their assassinations, Henri IV and Admiral de Coligny envisaged these colonies as a place where religious minorities would be willing to relocate. Under the new regime of the time of Louis XIII, the Catholics objected to the huge number of Huguenot entrepreneurs who sailed and traded from Tadoussac to Trois-Rivières and beyond. They envisioned a Catholic colony, and the Huguenots were a threat to that vision.

The Recollets, a Franciscan order, held the objective of converting people to Catholicism and they had success in other parts of the world, where the local cultures had already been conditioned by a concept of religious hierarchy, authority, and beliefs. Their mission to Canada was supported by the Bishop of Rouen and their perspective was that the people here, particularly the Montagnais around the fort of Quebec, were too primitive to be able to understand conversion. They were wild and undisciplined and needed first to be conditioned into the French culture and language, brought into a sedentary life, and subsequently converted. The Mission began with the people around the French settlement, but the French believed that it would ultimately be easier to convert the Wendat since they were already sedentary. In the meantime, to achieve their goal, they needed to import some Catholic peasants, farmers, from France, who were sedentary and understood hierarchy and authority, to serve to some degree as examples. While their objectives were condoned by Champlain, they were at serious odds with the traders, who did not care to interfere with the local culture more than was necessary for trade. Champlain and the Recollets petitioned both the Bishop of Rouen and the king through to the mid-1620s to improve fortifications, forbid Protestant religious observance, found a residential school for Indigenous children, and institute harsher punishments for what they perceived as wrongdoing. [82]

Their project hit a financial setback when the Bishop of Rouen died. By the mid-1620s, they were in no position to oppose the arrival of Jesuits who came well financed and prepared for their mission. The first three to arrive were Jean de Brébeuf, Charles Lalemant, and Enemoud Massé. Massé had tried fifteen years earlier to set up a Mission at Port-Royal but the Jesuits were strongly rejected there because Dugua de Mons's concept of religious tolerance was still present. The Jesuits were not popular among Protestants anywhere. The Huguenot presence was still strong, and they may have been rejected again had the Recollets not housed them upon their arrival.

Despite Champlain's and the Recollets' focus on conversion and settlement, trade was the driving motivation and the main trade item on the European list was beaver pelts. Right back to the first men, such as Brûlé, described by Champlain as truchements, or interpreters, Champlain wrote that their purpose was to "learn their language, explore their country and wean them [the Indigenous Peoples] away from other traders."[83] They weren't necessarily religious themselves, but, along with the priests, they worked to bring the Indigenous communities into the Wars of Religion on the Catholic side.

CHAPTER 22

The Pilgrims and the Wampanoag, 1620

The Pilgrims of the Mayflower were a distinct group from the other English colonists. They were strongly influenced by the mores of Leiden and the Dutch Provinces.

The Wampanoag, the Nation that lived at what we call Cape Cod, were aware of the Mayflower sitting off their coast. Captain Christopher Jones, who was bound for the Hudson River in 1620, allowed his ship to become an offshore residence for his passengers in Cape Cod Bay that first winter. He was carrying people bound for the Virginia Company as well as people from Leiden in the Netherlands. The Hudson River was still claimed by the Dutch, thanks to Henry Hudson's explorations, and it would have been logical to deliver his Leiden passengers there, where they had asked to go, and then to carry on to Jamestown, Virginia. Instead, after a difficult crossing, they anchored near a deserted Wampanoag village far to the north.

At the time, Jamestown must have seemed a terrifying place. After a difficult start, colonists there had managed to find peace with the local Algonquian when their leader married Pocahontas, the daughter of Chief Powhatan. But Pocahontas died in England in 1617 and her father died a year later. Officially, the Mayflower stopped where it did because of prevailing winds and onboard illness. A diseased ship would not have been well received anywhere.

The Wampanoag carried a burden of knowledge that six years earlier, in 1614, a sea captain named Thomas Hunt, who had been given the responsibility of organizing trade, had kidnapped several Wampanoag men. Locking them in the hold of his ship, he delivered them to Spain as potential slaves. Some monks purchased one of the men to try to "civilize" him. This was Tisquantum,[84] who got away and found his way to England. Thomas Hunt was a part of Captain John Smith's mapping expedition in 1614. Working with them before he was kidnapped, Tisquantum would have had the occasion to learn English. Certainly, he and his people trusted Smith and had good reason to believe in his man Hunt until the time of the kidnapping. In reaction to the loss of their men, the Wampanoag had gone on a rampage against all Europeans and subsequently were attacked by the European diseases that tore across the New England coast, destroying Patuxet, Tisquantum's hometown.

Tisquantum got to know good people in England and made it to Newfoundland where he was recognized by Thomas Dermer, a member of Smith's 1614 mapping expedition. They returned together to England where Tisquantum accepted to act for the English in a region north of where the Pilgrim ship had landed. This would afford him the chance to go home.

On November 11, 1620, two days after their arrival on the coast, the starving passengers and crew of the Mayflower anchored in Cape Cod Bay and agreed to all sign an understanding that has come to be called the Mayflower Compact. The Compact obliged all signatories to share and work together for their survival. They spent their first months living

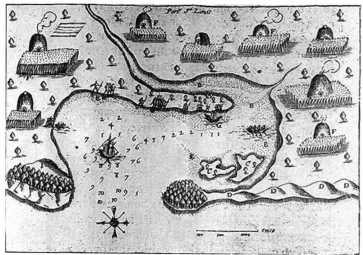

This map of Plymouth Harbour was sketched by Champlain in 1605 — fifteen years before the pilgrims arrived. Note the apparent population density.

on board the ship while slowly building storehouses ashore.

In Wampanoag accounts, they went ashore immediately. They found a Nauset Nation graveyard and began to steal the maize placed there for the departed. Attacked and chased back to the ship, they raised anchor and moved away, unwittingly anchoring near the abandoned Wampanoag village of Patuxet, not far from Plymouth Rock.

The Pilgrims'[85] descendants still celebrate the providence of finding this village as though God had prepared it for them. In the Wampanoag telling, the different Indigenous Peoples, plagued with their own serious challenges, watched the destitute passengers for some time and realized they were starving. Finally, an Abenaki named Samoset, who had learned some English at a short-lived English settlement further north in Maine, walked boldly into the village and greeted them. Samoset was representing the Wampanoag Peace Chief Massasoit (Yellow Feather), who invited the Mayflower people to become their allies. The Wampanoag were being harassed and attacked by neighbouring Nations who had not suffered through the plague and who hoped to take advantage of Wampanoag weakness. They asked Tisquantum, himself a native of Patuxet and probably the sole Wampanoag survivor of the very village where the Pilgrims found themselves, if he could become the interpreter for this new people living in his ancestral home.

To the Mayflower people, Tisquantum, whom they called Squanto, was another sign of God's providence. The Wampanoag undertook the task of nurturing them back to health and Captain Jones sailed home with the survivors of his crew.

From the point of view of the Wampanoag, the Pilgrims were good and respectful. Invited to their first Thanksgiving, the Peace Chief came with his people, bringing five freshly killed deer to the celebration with them. Peace Chief Massasoit asked the Mayflower colonists to offer him English names for his two sons, Wamsutta and Metacomet. They offered the names Alexander and Philip.

During this initial period, a second ship arrived with more colonists from Leiden. The colonists and the Wampanoag formed an alliance that served them both, with the Pilgrim presence helping the Wampanoag withstand their enemies.

Among their discussions together, the Pilgrims came to believe that the Wampanoag, who had no tradition of land ownership, had agreed that these refugees could take ownership of nearly 5,000 hectares of land. The concept of ownership of land was such a fundamental underpinning of European thought that the presumption was inevitable. European rationalization regarding individual ownership of parts of the commonwealth goes back far in European history. The misunderstanding between these two friendly groups may have grown into a disagreement later, but one that they may have been able to bridge. With the arrival of the Puritan hordes, between 1629 and 1642 when as many as 21,000 arrived in America, that which distinguished the Pilgrims from the Puritans was soon lost.

THE BREAKDOWN BEGINS
1613-1701

In the early 1600s Europe's American colonies had become a confusing reflection of the religious differences that were tearing Christendom apart.

CHAPTER 23

The Beaver Wars

The people of the sustaining cultures, living in a gift economy, accepted the Europeans as siblings but could not understand their inability to share.

U pon initial contact, the Indigenous Nations were confused and awed by what they would initially see as their siblings who came across the sea. Over time, some saw not siblings, but more a form of the Windigo.[86] A Windigo was an event of destruction centred around a character facing starvation in the forest whose voracious appetite could not be satisfied, turning him into a monster that threatened the very survival of the people. The Windigo is a powerful story. It recalls the need to share, in good times and bad, to be prepared to celebrate together but also to suffer together. In their relations with the Christians who were colonizing their homeland, Indigenous people seemed, each time, to realize too late, when nothing could save them from the greed for property, from the death of sharing.

The closest to an exception to this rule was the Five Nations of the Haudenosaunee, the Mohawk, Oneida, Onondaga, Cayuga, and Seneca. In dealing with the Dutch, the Mohawk came to understand more clearly the purely commercial style of the new European market economy, of social status vested in possession and personal property, rather than in sharing. As early as 1613, the Dutch and Mohawk established a clear agreement of jurisdictional independence and trade, called the *Kaswentha*, the ongoing respect for their relationship as separate jurisdictions,

111

and remembered in simple English as the Two Row Wampum, a Wampum Belt in white beads with two parallel purple sections running its length but not interfering with each other.

The profound insight that the Mohawk demonstrated in assuring the clear understanding of separate jurisdictions would have been a secondary, even minor, aspect of the agreement to the Dutch, whose immediate concern was safe trade. The presence of the Europeans had already disturbed the lifeways of many of the Indigenous Peoples, causing them to break their sharing bonds with nature in exchange for what were becoming essential European products. The presence of iron, guns, and gunpowder was enough to change the balance of power among neighbours, leading them into an escalation in warfare that has characterized European history.

In the early years, the Mohawk, trading with the Dutch at Fort Nassau, had a problem. Fort Nassau was in Mahican territory. The Mohawk had become dependent upon European goods. They could not trade easily with the French without respecting Algonquian/French treaty rights. If the Dutch and Mahican were to establish a similar agreement, then the Mohawk would have a similar barrier in dealing through them with the Dutch.

Since the French had long professed a desire for peace, the Mohawk took the initiative, meeting with the Algonquin and Montagnais before 1622 and finally establishing peace with the French in 1624. That same year, the Mohawk pushed the Mahican out of their historic territory, establishing themselves as the official intermediary with the Dutch. As a member of the Five Nations of the Haudenosaunee, the Mohawk were speaking for more than just themselves from the beginning of their relationship with the Dutch. They also envisaged making a treaty with the Wendat Nations that would allow the Iroquoian peoples to negotiate with one voice. But first, they needed control of the connection with the Dutch.

The peace manoeuvres of the Mohawk had the side effect of making the French nervous. While such a peace, they hoped, would allow their Algonquian trading partners to hunt and trap in the no-man's land that war had created around Lake Champlain, they were concerned about the dangers of a pan-Iroquoian Confederacy that included the Wendat and the other western Wendat Nations. Such a situation would give the Iroquoian people a strong hand in negotiations and might save their culture, pulling it out of reach of the expansionist plans of the French Catholic Church. They dispatched traders in the company of Father Joseph Le Caron to return to Huronia immediately to warn the Wendat against making peace with the Five Nations of the Haudenosaunee.[87]

The Dutch, with a practical business mentality, managed to provide the Mohawk with insights into European trade that the French did not give the Wendat. Preoccupied with religious expansion, the French objective was to replace their Indigenous culture with Catholicism. From Champlain's perspective, doing so would accomplish the creation of trade

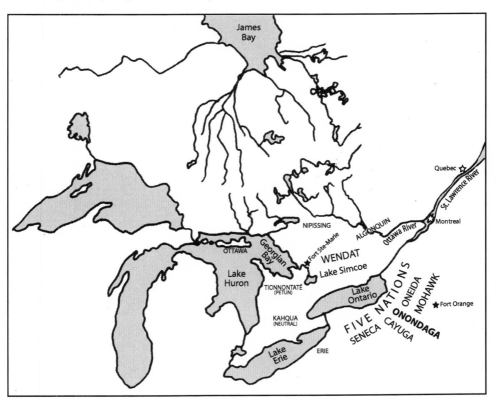

We call this period of history the Beaver Wars, but it was an Iroquoian response to the risk of the loss of their culture as well as the advent of the use of guns in inter-Indigenous warfare — the Europeans had brought military escalation to the people of Turtle Island.

loyalties that could stand up to the practical Protestant Dutch and English styles. In this way, the European Wars of Religion were being imported into America.

The Wendat Nations, long the first among the Iroquoian Nations, had little concern regarding peace as long as the French could guarantee safe passage for trade along the St. Lawrence. For the few years that it lasted, the Mohawk peace initiative did that. Huronia grew so much agricultural produce that they were the breadbasket of the Nations that surrounded them, and they received the best beaver pelts for trade. However, their central role combined with the increasing proselytizing presence of the Catholic Recollets was leading to a reduced awareness of the geopolitical manoeuvrings around them. The Mohawk were learning to play the European game and were starting to understand what the French intuitively feared: a powerful, united Iroquoian bloc could control the trade.

The timing of the Mohawk push to take over the trading territory from the Mahicans coincided with the greater Dutch investment in Fort Orange, built in 1624 to replace the earlier Fort Nassau.

CHAPTER 24
Cardinal Richelieu and the Kirke Brothers

Reaching the age of maturity, Louis XIII resorted to a coup d' état to confirm his status as king. He then named Cardinal Richelieu, the most trusted surviving advisor to his regent, as his first minister.

When Louis XIII reached the age of majority and was due to become the successor to his late father Henri IV, he had some trouble taking the French throne from his mother, the regent, and had to resort to a coup. At age sixteen, he executed his mother's most important advisor, the Italian Concino Concini, along with his wife, and sent his own mother into exile. Cardinal Richelieu, the only advisor of his mother's that he did not completely reject, managed to help mother and son patch up their differences and he even encouraged the young king to allow her to be one of his advisors. That worked until she tried to encourage him to dump Cardinal Richelieu. He exiled her permanently.

Cardinal Richelieu, whom Louis named to the Royal Council in 1624, became one of the most powerful prime ministers in the history of France, and he dealt severely with anyone whom he perceived as a threat to his king. He raised the position of the king of France to a level of almost absolute power and in the course of it executed a large number of the heads of old, noble families. He solved problems in broad strokes.

One of Richelieu's first major moves was the creation of the Company of One Hundred Associates. He gave it exclusive control of the New France market. He also informed them that they could settle only French Catholics there. Around the same time, Henri de Lévy, Duc de Ventadour and Viceroy of Canada, ruled it illegal for Huguenot sailors to sing their hymns in the colony or aboard ship on the St. Lawrence River.

There was a certain colonial logic to these decisions because the administration in New France was trying to Christianize, read Catholicize, the Indigenous Peoples to keep them trading exclusively with France, and tolerating Protestant Huguenots confused this message. Simultaneously, in France Richelieu was consolidating power in his master King Louis XIII's hands. The city of La Rochelle, the centre of Huguenot power with its special liberties accorded by King Henri IV, was in his focus. He was determined to destroy the Huguenots. During a fourteen-month siege of the city, ending in October 1628, the population of the city was reduced from 22,000 to 5,000 people.

A shrewd politician, Champlain was guiding New France toward the Catholic Church. He was placing himself on the right side of power. The Huguenot social infrastructure could not stand up to that of the Catholic Church. The social service network that the Catholic Church maintained could provide for the day-to-day needs of the young community. It was efficient to run his colony with the help of their dedicated expertise and experience. In return for his loyalty to them, he remained in command and could direct the colony's expansion.

Trade with the Wendat Nations was coloured by the inroads that the Recollets, the first religious order to arrive, and later the Jesuits, were making among them. They worked together with Champlain, restricting trade with France to those who accepted the Church. If a Wendat did not embrace the faith, he could not trade with France. Their vision was to bring them into a feudal social structure, similar to the dominant model in Catholic Europe.

The French hold on the St. Lawrence was not strong. Having forbidden the Huguenots from trading or settling in New France, Prime Minister Cardinal Richelieu had cultivated poor relations with them, and the Huguenot sailors of France figured very prominently in the French merchant marine. The colony had been conceived as a religious safe haven. The Huguenot traders had supported that idea, but they were being pushed out.

Jarvis Kirke, a London trader who had lived for over forty years in Dieppe, married a Huguenot, Elizabeth Goudon. They had five Huguenot sons, all well-informed on French naval matters. In 1627, while Richelieu was focused on beating down La Rochelle, Kirke saw an opportunity for the English Crown to establish a presence on the St. Lawrence River. He created a company for that purpose and shortly after, England and France went to war as the English fleet tried to supply the Huguenots in La Rochelle. Kirke's company-chartered ships, captained by his Huguenot sons, were commissioned by England's King Charles I to capture New France.

Cardinal Richelieu, first minister to King Louis XIII, overseeing the destruction of the Huguenot city of La Rochelle.

Led by his eldest son, David, they achieved their goal in 1629, capturing Quebec three months after England, Scotland, and France had signed the Treaty of Suza, ending their war. Blockaded and on the verge of starving, all Champlain could do was negotiate the best terms possible with them. Champlain, a prisoner, was sent to England where he learned about the treaty and the terms that obliged the English to return to France any prizes, such as Quebec, that had been obtained after the date of the treaty.

The official surrender of Quebec to the Huguenot Captain David Kirke, in the service of the King of England in 1629.

During the next three years, while King Charles of England dickered over the return of the captured colonies, the Kirkes worked the beaver trade, dealing with anyone who brought pelts, including the Five Nations. Both Champlain and the Catholic Church saw these Iroquoian as enemies to their plans. By that time, the Wendat from Georgian Bay and the Ottawa River Algonquian were dependant upon French goods. Seeing the Five Nations at Quebec could not have pleased them either. There were likely Huguenots among the French still at the fort of Quebec who may have welcomed the arrival of the Kirkes.[88] Étienne Brûlé, who seemed to move freely among the Iroquoian people, was also present, willing to trade with the Kirkes.

During those three years of English possession of the colony, even Huguenots in France must have felt a wrong had been righted and that the dreams of Admiral de Coligny and Good King Henri might yet come to fruition.

While the Kirkes, French citizens, were burned in effigy in Paris, the English King Charles worked into his negotiations a complete pardon for them with the French king, Louis XIII. When their occupation ended in 1632, David Kirke was knighted in England, not for his capture of Quebec but for the furs, wealth, and knowledge he had acquired.

Still, Cardinal Richelieu had to sort out the mess he had caused. He appealed to the Caën family, Guillaume, a Huguenot, and his cousin Eméry, a Catholic. The Caën families had controlled the trade before Richelieu created the Company of One Hundred Associates, all Catholic. Richelieu needed the Caëns to deal with the intransigent English, and their price was the possession of the colony for one year following its return to French hands, one year of furs, one year added to free trade with the Five Nations.

In 1633, Champlain returned to New France to take charge again. The friction between the Five Nations Confederacy and Champlain's Wendat and Algonquin allies had heated to the point where Champlain could no longer control it. Both that year and the next, he sent requests to Richelieu for the means to wipe out the Five Nation Confederacy. He feared for the colony's safety as much as for the wellbeing of his Catholic First Nation allies. He couldn't have known that another enemy, in the form of disease, was just about to strike with devastating consequences.

The fortunes of the Huguenots had reached a high point under Henri IV, but the hope he created and the dream of freedom from religious persecution lasted much longer than his reign. Richelieu's successor as prime minister, Cardinal Jules Raymond Mazarin, was forced into exile for a short time as the Wars of Religion began again. Maintaining the policies of Richelieu, the pressure to centralize power continued, resulting in *La Fronde*, uprisings of the lords and nobles that again involved La Rochelle. As the rebellions came to an end in the 1650s, many Huguenots converted to Catholicism so that they would be allowed to emigrate to New France.

The Huguenots continued to arrive right through the 1660s. Isaac Bédard, his wife Marie Girard, and their six children arrived in Quebec in the early 1660s,[89] where Bédard had to re-establish himself as a master carpenter, but they could not re-establish themselves as Huguenots. The dream of New France may have encouraged them and the many others who came to believe they would have greater religious freedom here, not because of the original vision of Henri IV, but because they hoped that the reach of the cardinals would be weaker.

The hope was carried in the hearts of the most oppressed religious minority, the Marranos, Spanish Jews who called themselves Protestants and Catholics, tolerated in France, incapable of returning to Spain, some of whom dreamed of going to New France. Those who went had to declare their Catholic faith and hope to find Jews or Huguenots practising when they arrived, and there may well have been secret little cohorts that survived for a while, but many, upon arriving, rejected New France and moved south. New Amsterdam had achieved what Henri IV and Dugua de Mons had dreamed of—a colony that respected religious freedom.

When Mazarin died, King Louis XIV did not replace him, taking over those responsibilities himself. He instituted measures to destroy the Huguenots, including obliging them to maintain a soldier in their houses to demonstrate they were not practising their religion. They were removed from civil appointments and other areas of recognition, but all these rules were not enough for the king, who revoked the Edict of Nantes in 1685. Those who could fled to Protestant countries, a development that would come back to haunt the French during the Seven Years' War.

CHAPTER 25
Disease Among the Nations

The Jesuits' desire to Catholicize the people of Huronia led at first to an invitation to participate in the intimate Feast of the Dead, an event they reported upon. The spread of disease led to division among the Wendat.

After the Kirkes handed the colony back to the French in 1632, the Jesuits went back to Huronia and trade returned to its old patterns, with the Mohawk of the Five Nations again shut out of French ports. When a Wendat trading party arrived at Trois-Rivières in July 1634, they discovered that disease had stricken the Algonquin and Montagnais who were there. The death toll was high. As the trading party withdrew, returning to the Ottawa River, they encountered disease at every stop and soon it was among them as well. When they arrived home, the disease rapidly spread from village to village and death followed. Fishing and harvesting were neglected. The Elders decided to try to stem the tide of death. In the village of Ossossané, they would move the Feast of the Dead[90] forward ten years.

The Jesuits, warriors for God, perceived virtually everything in terms of God and Satan, white and black. In Huronia, the Shaman was the representative of Satan and had to be carefully handled because the people were in the thrall of the devils using magic to serve Satan. The Jesuits did not believe in magic, but they did believe in divine intervention as an answer to prayer in the ongoing wars against Satan. They saw a distinction between the two, Shamanistic magic and divine intervention. This was not a special belief that pertained to Huronia but was a general truth. If a child died without Baptism, they sincerely believed the child's soul would burn in the fires of Hell forever. Of course, it served the Jesuit's mission to believe what they chose, and they believed they

121

were regularly advised by saints and confronted by Satan. The simplest trick to deal with the devil before them was to hold up their ever-present crucifix and the devil would flee.

France had sent disciples of this cult in among the people of Huronia, but both the people and the Jesuits held to beliefs that are equally foreign to us today. The priests had a goal, a focus—a mission. The Wendat saw the actions of the Jesuits in shamanistic terms. If it worked, they credited it. For the Jesuits, the objective was proselytization, but the Wendat worked simply to accommodate the French among them.

In 1636, Father Jean de Brébeuf and the other Jesuits were invited to participate in the most important feast in the Wendat community. The overwhelming intensity of this event burned so brightly that their recording of it remains one of the most extraordinary insights into the numinous intensity of Iroquoian culture.

The call was sent out to the nearby villages and friends beyond, to the neighbouring Nations, as it would be sent for any feast, but this was not just any feast. It was the Feast of the Dead. No-one refused to attend without extraordinary cause. A few thousand people might come, laden with gifts. In 1636, with the progress of disease, the people of Ossossané decided they should move their village after only five years instead of the more usual fifteen.

The move would be accompanied by the traditional Feast of the Dead, to honour and rebury those who had died, including the many lost to the epidemic. They presented to the Jesuits the honour of having two buried Frenchmen, Étienne Brûlé and Guillaume Chaudron, disinterred and included in the new ossuary, thereby confirming the kinship of the Wendat and the French.

To their surprise, the Jesuits objected, saying Christians could not be buried in the same grave as non-Christians. They reached a compromise when the Jesuits suggested that they, and any deceased Christian Wendat, could be buried in a second ossuary nearby, but the compromise itself negated a fundamental reason for the Feast of the Dead, to confirm kinship.

Disagreements began over who had killed Brûlé, an act that probably took place as a response to the departure of the Kirke brothers. The differences over this eventually scuttled the plans and the Jesuits watched as Christian Wendat were buried with their Traditional kin.

In specially decorated beaver-skin sacks they carried the bones and dried corpses of all those who had died since the previous feast. They were taken from their elevated resting places in the village cemeteries where they had dried in the air and the sun for many years. Children who had been free to run and watch during the previous feast now shared the tasks, learning that, in time, they would be among the Elders and then they too would be honoured.

The feast lasted ten days and the families stayed in their clan segment's longhouse with other members of their clan. The guests also bore gifts fulfilling their communal role, as well as other gifts to thank their hosts for their hospitality. Some of these gifts were redistributed through games and events during the feast; others were hung on the balustrade around the mortuary pit.

The men joined in the digging and preparation of the mortuary, a large pit dug three metres deep and five to eight metres in diameter. They built an enormous walkway around it where some of their gifts were displayed at their clan's totem. The whole structure spanned up to fifteen metres to accommodate the many family members. There could be a hundred corpses, especially with all the deaths from the new diseases. It was time to let them travel together through the countryside and the sky, the stream of stars that leads to the ancestors, the village of Aataentsic, and Iouskeha.

The daughters and granddaughters of the dead used flint to carefully remove the flesh from the bones of the dried, older corpses, burning it in the ceremonial fire, then separating the bones—flint is very sharp, as sharp as the sharpest knife. All the while, they commemorated these Elders. The emotional intensity must have been as powerful as anything the Jesuits had ever witnessed or imagined.

As they finished, they returned the bones to the decorated beaver-skin bags they had carried to the feast and awaited the ceremony. Emotions of loss were at a high pitch and the longhouses were filled with distracting feasting and dancing, games of skill and chance played endlessly. Everyone participated in the long feast, including relatives who had returned from great distances, some with their own departed, to participate and to honour those who would finally be left on their own to follow the footsteps of the ancestors. They exchanged stories and bets about the risks ahead for the spirits and wondered which ones might lose their courage and stay rather than risk crossing Oscotarach, who would pierce their skulls.[91] Those who had the courage would be free of the burden of life and ready to pass onto the route of the stars where they could hunt, enjoy feasts and do all they had loved to do in life.

On the ninth day, the sacks were reopened as family members mourned their dead one last time before carrying them to the mortuary pit. Toward evening, everyone assembled at their clan totems and the headmen mounted above the pit to distribute the gifts, those left by the deceased for those who they wished to honour as well as gifts brought for the deceased, and other gifts that were shared among neighbours.

There was much emotion the whole day; stories were exchanged and tears shed. Before the feast, the dead had been protected and consulted in each village cemetery, they were still with their families, they were asked for guidance and were respected, but now it was time to leave their bones in the ground while the village moved on to a place where the forest was older, and the fields could be rebuilt. No-one could forget this feast. They would experience only three or four such feasts, at different stages of their lives, before they too would be honoured and prepared for their last journey.

As evening approached, the men placed beaver robes in the pit, hundreds of beaver skins sewn into the fifty robes needed to line the whole ossuary like a giant bag folded up on the edge. Everything that the Spirits would need for their last voyage, including okis, as real as companions, carved in stone or wood, were placed to accompany them. During this last night, no-one left the ossuary. Sleep came in short fits as the fires burned, casting shadows of the posts, the raised walkway, and the decorated sacks that hung on poles over the mortuary pit. Already lowered into the pit, wrapped in more robes, were the corpses of the recently departed, whose flesh had not yet dried. All awaited the sunrise of the last day. Iouskeha would bear witness, showing the way.

After the almost sleepless night, they were greeted by sunrise and the day's events began. They raised voices in lamentation, sending shivers through the Jesuit witnesses. They climbed the balustrades and emptied their decorated sacks. Below, in the pit, men ensured that the bones were thoroughly mixed, showing that all are one people.

It was a long time ago that the practice started when the Nations agreed to live closer together. It bound the Nations together, the ancestors being all one, a single people. The Jesuits contributed no Europeans to the feast, but there were many Christian Wendat buried with the others, much to the Jesuits' consternation, worried for their souls.

The decision to hold it in 1636 was made to try to break the hold the epidemic had on the survivors, but it also showed the Jesuits the inner workings of a complex, highly spiritual society and how it dealt with great tragedy. They dutifully documented the Feast of the Dead in their Relations. After all, they financed their Mission in Huronia by reporting to their supporters in France, a macabre, voyeuristic aspect of the financial needs of their proselytization that nevertheless has allowed the light of that culture to travel through time to us.

The Feast of the Dead was celebrated among the Wendat and certain neighbouring Anishinaabe. It may have been spreading as a means of celebrating the bonds of a community through honouring their dead together. Yet, despite all the damage the Jesuits were causing them, driven by that primary ethic of sharing they worked to include the Jesuits in their lives.

CHAPTER 26

Huronia and the Jesuits

*Huronia, like the myriad other distinct societies in the Americas, was
in constant evolution, exchanging knowledge, establishing limits,
and sharing with other Nations.*

W endat self-image begs comprehension in our property and ego-driven society. They were hospitable and accepting of newcomers but expected conformity. The Shaman, a medicinal expert and magician, was often a man or a woman with a physical or other distinguishing difference or disability. He or she might disappear into the wilderness to find their way and return to offer their knowledge—of herbs, roots, or other specialties. The Shaman would be respected as long as they were not destructive to the needs of the people.

The Jesuits gave us an insight into the Wendat people that they were attempting to convert. They needed guides to find their way through the enormous maize fields, cultivated for produce for consumption and exchange, and they needed years to understand the language and to begin to understand the culture. Status among Iroquoian peoples like the Wendat was not based on what one possessed, but on what one shared.

In times of need, the Peace Chief, the Sachem, selected from childhood by the clan mothers for his values, might seem to the visitor to be the poorest person. The community might starve, but its members would do so together. Upon learning these aspects of the Iroquoian world, the Jesuits persisted in seeing them in terms of what could be incorporated into a Christian world without changing fundamental Christian values. In the Catholic model, each soul was born with sin and all the Sacraments—Baptism, Confirmation Communion, Confession, Marriage, and Last Rites—Sacraments controlled, owned, by the priestly hierarchy, were dispensed to condition each sinner to follow the narrow path to death, where they would be rewarded or punished in an afterlife. They reinforced the role of the individual. Even with the Sacrament of Holy Communion, they had no community concept comparable to the Iroquoian one. Instead, they held out the possibility of trade with the French to those who accepted the Catholic Church with its foreign concepts of person and property.

From 1636 to 1640 the rate of illness rose and fell. During each outbreak, the death rate rose higher but the Jesuits did not become ill. As the illness increased, anger with the Jesuits grew and the people held them to account. The Jesuits—dedicated men like Jean de Brébeuf, Isaac Jogues, Antoine Daniel, Charles Garnier, and Gabriel Lalemant—embraced martyrdom if necessary to establish their objective, just as surely as the early Christians did, but they were not dying, a reality that was clear to their hosts.

During this crucial four-year period, the Wendat became increasingly divided between those who accepted Catholicism and those who remained Traditional, but the French policy continued to favour trade with the Catholics, the converts. With each wave of disease, the great community of Huronia became weaker, more divided, and more inward-looking, less aware of what was happening in the greater Iroquoian world that they were a part of.

In Quebec, Champlain had died on Christmas Day, 1635. His replacement had already been named and word had been sent out recalling him to France. Cardinal Richelieu was slowly replacing everyone with loyal Catholic Knights of the Order of Malta. Charles Huault de Montmagny became the first governor of New France, guaranteeing the continuing Catholic direction. The leadership of Huronia was unaware of Richelieu's motivation but was afraid, with the increasing rate of death, that Champlain, in his dying, would take them all with him.

Focused on their internal problems, the outside world became less relevant. Through the balance of the decade after the death of Champlain, winds of change swept through the Indigenous Nations, changing the reasons for war and the balance of power. Nothing would ever be the same. Estimates of survival from the diseases run as high as 50 percent, but the most serious impact was from the loss of Elders, the peaceful guiding intelligence of the societies, and of the young.

As Wendat society was further divided between the Traditionalists and the Catholics, fears of invasion began. An eclipse was interpreted as a sign that the Five Nations would invade and destroy them. Still, the Jesuits gave guns only to those who had proven their Catholic beliefs and even then, very few. Some Traditionalists may have slipped away to join one of the other communities, bringing news of the desperate divisions.

Among those changes that Huronia was unaware of, the Five Nations of the Haudenosaunee, armed heavily because of English and Dutch rivalry for their trade, were planning to attack other Iroquoian Nations and absorb all the Iroquoian people into their federation. Their objectives were driven partially because their beaver supply was being exhausted, partially because none of the Iroquoian farming Nations had been spared the plague, leaving their critical numbers too low to maintain their society, and partially because they saw that if they succeeded, they could speak as one, and attempt to mitigate the impact of European trade. They had tried much earlier to bring the other Iroquoian people in, but the attempt to do so peacefully had failed. Forced adoption was their only option.

The Wendat should have known, may have known, as early as the summer of 1638 when a delegation of Iroquoian Wenroronon from the southeastern coast of Lake Erie reported that their villages had been invaded and they asked for refuge. Huronia was seriously suffering from population loss, and the Jesuits wanted more people to convert as well. The Wenroronon Nation was adopted, carrying their sick and wounded to Huronia.[92]

The Mohawk were acquiring muskets from the Dutch[93] while the Jesuits and Wendat converts were adapting to Father Jérôme Lalemant who replaced Father Brébeuf. Ahead of the arrival of the smallpox epidemic, Lalemant introduced a new regime that would include a new order of French laymen, the Donnés. They took vows of chastity, poverty, and obedience to their employers, the Jesuits.[94]

The first Donné was Robert Le Coq who had been with the Jesuits from 1634 and had returned to Quebec regularly to manage trade. Heading back to Huronia with a trading party of Wendat in 1639, he showed the symptoms of smallpox, with pustules breaking out on his body and face. The trading party abandoned him, fearing his state, and returned to Huronia, some with the beginnings of the disease themselves and carrying a message they claimed came from the lips of Le Coq. The Jesuits, he was purported to have said, were secretly housing an Angont,[95] a supernatural serpent that spread the illness, and that the Jesuits had found a way of firing the disease from a special gun directly at different villages. Le Coq had lived closely with the people since 1634; he was credible.

These fantastic images spread through Huronia as a new, more serious epidemic was about to divide the people from the Jesuits once again. Le Coq didn't die, but, lying in a fever, he was generally avoided and caused fear in the hearts of other travellers, although one took the time to steal his valuables. Another, a Wendat who had known him for years, brought him back to the Jesuit mission where he was nursed and where he recovered. He denied the rumours that he had been accused of spreading, but the people did not believe the new story, thinking he was simply bewitched by the Jesuits.

Lalemant's new regime changed the relationships at the same time. He had not learned the Iroquoian language, riding roughshod over the sensibilities that the priests and converts had established. He also rejected the homes the people had built for the Jesuits in the past, determining instead that a large French-style Mission would be built, in stone where possible. His ideal site was in the territory of the Ataronchronon Nation of Huronia, up a river a couple of kilometres from Georgian Bay. There he established the Mission of Ste. Marie among the Hurons, and he was determined in time to house all the Jesuits and lay French there.[96] In moving, he neglected the mission at the important town of Teanaostaiaé where they had moved only recently and where they had had some good results.

During the time of this greatest plague, the Wendat again concluded the Jesuits were malicious sorcerers and that they should be killed. At different times, friendly Elders warned the Jesuits to stay home because one or another warrior was behaving threateningly. Even the town of Teanaostaiaé turned against them. They were confronted and physically evicted, injuring one of the lay workers in the process. The people concluded that wherever the Jesuits travelled, disease followed. They and their lay helpers were the most likely vector of disease. Several village councils forbade them access.

Despite their resolve in evicting the Jesuits, the headmen realized that they could not afford a war with the French, especially in their current state. They had become dependent upon French trade goods so completely that no Nation by itself was willing to risk access to trade by being identified as the one who killed the Jesuits. Still, with deaths following baptisms, most of the people abandoned the Jesuit teachings.

One of the most significant reactions to the Jesuit occupation during the years of epidemics was due to a vision. A man out fishing reported a vision during which he was visited by the founding twin Iouskeha. This vision came at a time when many others were describing dreams of how the Jesuits were spreading the disease. The man reported that Iouskeha explained that he, the founding twin, was also the spirit that the Jesuits called Jesus. The Jesuits, according to his vision, knew little about the true story. They were also spreading disease and they would not stop until all the people were dead. Iouskeha told the man to drive the Jesuits away and gave him a ritual to perform against the disease. The man, from the village of Contarea, described his vision to the Elders, who performed the ritual, carrying water that was blessed as Iouskeha had instructed, encouraging the sick to drink it, but they did not drive the Jesuits off.

This vision was in retaliation to what they had come to see as the Jesuit's shamanism. It was the beginning of an ideological rebellion,[97] and even this did not galvanize the people enough to chase the Jesuits away.

The smallpox epidemic ran its course by the spring of 1640, but the people did not reconcile to the Jesuits as they had after the other outbreaks. Despite being frozen into inaction by their fear of the French authorities and the risk of loss of trade, they still harboured ill feelings. In the spring, Brébeuf returned, and a Shaman declared that he would die. Shortly after, Brébeuf contracted a high fever and stomach pains and was sick for a night and day. He recovered, and the Jesuits believed he had been poisoned. Subsequently, Chihwatenha, a supporter of the Jesuits who had gone to great lengths to help carry Jesuit icons from Quebec the autumn before, was found dead on August 2. He had gone with his daughters to collect squash from the fields and around noon the daughters returned to Ossossané. When he did not return, a search was made, and the headmen declared Chihwatenha had been killed and scalped by some Five Nations warriors. No-one believed them, but they were the community's authority. The headmen had determined Chihwatenha's continued support of the priests categorized him as another sorcerer. He had been warned that he and the Jesuits would be killed, but the people could not bring themselves to kill the Jesuits or their European men.[98]

Chihwatenha's murder signalled an underlying change in attitude. The religious differences between the people were breaking the Wendat into two camps, and the Traditional people were sharing concern regarding the Catholic threat to their culture and religion. Their voice was carrying through the other Wendat Nations and likely further, to the Seneca of the Five Nation Confederacy to the south.

CHAPTER 27
A Vision Called Montreal

*Jacques Cartier described a mountain above the town of Hochelaga as
Mons realis – Latin for Mount Royal. Forty years later, in 1575,
in the modestly titled Cosmographie universelle de tout le monde,
François de Belleforest recorded it as Montréal.*

During the early 1600s, the French hold on the colony was tenuous as they were faced with hostile neighbours to the south. The St. Lawrence Iroquoian people that Cartier had met were gone, extinct or absorbed into the ranks of the Five Nations Confederacy. The term *widowed country* was not used, but that description that I first heard at a conference given by Denys Delage, author of *Le Pays Renversé*,[99] is very evocative. In Champlain's time, their absence justified French settlement. According to some of the Mohawk, the Confederacy's easternmost member, the St. Lawrence Iroquoian people that the French described were simply Mohawk who had consolidated, moving to the south of their territory after Cartier left. Like the other Iroquoian people, they had farmed, fished, and hunted, following a ninety-year rotation through their territory to let the forests recover. The French presence upset their cycle and encouraged their enemies in the St. Lawrence valley. Champlain had become allied with the Algonquin and Innu Nations who hunted and fished in the same territory and had gone to war with them against the Mohawk.[100] The mystery of the St. Lawrence Iroquoian people remains. The archeological evidence shows that details like their arrowheads were different from the Mohawk, being made of bone instead of stone.[101] Whether they were all one people or in some other way connected, the Mohawk were very much present on the St. Lawrence in the early French settlement period. The settlers, refusing to recognize Mohawk territorial claims, had to always be armed and on guard against the war canoes that patrolled the river.

Jean de Lauson, the shrewd director of the Company of One Hundred Associates, staked claim to most of the territory after the colony was returned by the English in 1632. In the process, he became the first French owner of the Island of Montreal. While he was acquiring property up and down the river, the Mohawk, armed by the Dutch, were masters of the river.

Jérôme le Royer de la Dauversière, the first 'Montréaliste.'

As their power increased, threatening the very existence of the small French colony, an unlikely series of events was unfolding in France. A tax collector named Jérôme Le Royer de la Dauversière had a spiritual experience in which he heard a voice instructing him to acquire the Island of Montreal and set up a hospital there to minister to the local heathen population. Absurd as the notion sounds—and to be sure, his spiritual advisor, Father Chauveau, dismissed it as a pious chimera—he could not get it out of his head.

Le Royer had inherited responsibilities that he did not seek. He wished to become a Jesuit, but when his father died unexpectedly, he took over his father's role as a tax collector and supported his family. By 1639, when he experienced his vision, he had already experienced another spiritual command in which a voice instructed him to set up a mission of hospital workers, Sisters dedicated to helping those in need. While Father Chauveau also dismissed this more feasible undertaking, Jérôme Le Royer did manage to establish *Les Filles Hospitalières de Saint-Joseph* in La Flèche, France in 1636.

To augment his income, Le Royer rented out a room in his home to a wealthy student named Pierre Chevrier, Baron de Fancamp. Chevrier became absorbed by Le Royer's religious obsession to create a hospital on an unexplored island on the other side of the world, inhabited, to the best of their knowledge, by a hostile band of what they considered uncivilized savages. Somehow this seemed like a good idea. Together, they began to solicit support for their project, calling themselves the *Société Notre-Dame de Montréal*, or the *Société des Messieurs et Dames de Notre-Dame de Montréal pour la conversion des Sauvages de Nouvelle-France*, but soon the adherents became known simply as the Montréalistes. When they approached Jean de Lauson to buy the island, the businessman quoted the astronomical sum of 150,000 livres. With the help of the influential priest and Montréaliste Father Charles Lalemant, they managed to acquire the island in 1640. Soon a group of Montréalistes led by Paul de Chomedey de Maisonneuve, and including Jeanne Mance and other historical notables, headed off on their missionary quest.

Arriving at Quebec, the party's plans were delayed until the spring of 1642. Maisonneuve met an elderly man, Pierre de Puiseaux de Montrénault, the owner of two seigneuries, whom he convinced not only to house their party for the winter but also to join their expedition in the spring. Throughout the winter they were encouraged to stay put; in fact, they were told that they did not have permission to proceed upriver. The colony did not have the means to protect them. The governor, Montmagny, even offered them Île d'Orléans if they would abandon their irresponsible mission. Maisonneuve, speaking on their behalf, declined the offer. The intrepid and determined missionaries ignored all advice to the contrary. They paddled upriver to their destiny in the spring of 1642, landing at the place we now call Pointe à Callières, where they established the mission of Ville Marie.

That first summer was the easiest one they would have. Somehow the Mohawk did not know they were there. Among their greatest challenges, once a fort was built, was to not lose courage completely when floodwaters threatened to wash them away toward the end of their first year. As the waters rose toward their settlement, splashing against the gates of their fort, Maisonneuve exercised leadership by declaring that if the floodwaters subsided, he would carry a large cross to the summit of

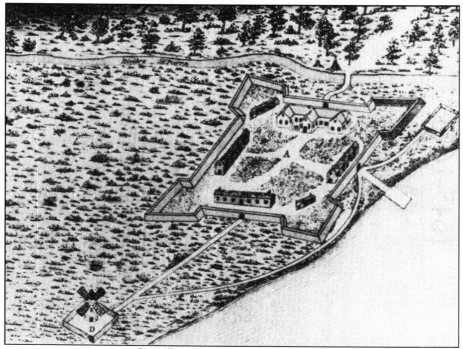

Fort Ville Marie on Montreal Island, 1645

the mountain and erect it there. His faith in this appeal gave the others courage and once the waters ebbed, he fulfilled his promise.

Eventually, the Mohawk did find them. They were only about seventy men and women, and the Mohawk warriors numbered in the hundreds. Maisonneuve wisely forbade his men from going on the offensive, limiting their strategy to defence, holing up in their fort when necessary. Jeanne Mance tended to the wounded. On one occasion, Maisonneuve authorized a foray, discovering rapidly how ill-equipped the colonists were. Maisonneuve was forced to call for a quick retreat, holding off the enemy himself to allow the others to get to safety inside the fort. Grabbed by a powerful Mohawk Chief, he managed to push his musket into the Chief's naked chest and fire it, killing the man. This was hardly the mission that Jérôme Le Royer had described in his vision. There was no ministering to hundreds of angry, taunting warriors, although between skirmishes they did receive visits from some Algonquin. Their supporters in France faithfully kept them supplied, responding to their needs and even finding other Montréalistes to join them.

Among them were Lambert Closse, who became Maisonneuve's right-hand man, Marguerite Bourgeoys, who followed in Jeanne Mance's footsteps, Mme Claude de Bullion who remained in France and discreetly backed Mance and the hospital she founded, the Jesuit Father Jean de Brébeuf, Mme Chauvigny de La Peltrie, who joined them from her mission in Quebec for a while but returned, and of course Jérôme Le Royer himself.

One person who became the key to their future survival was Jean-Jacques Olier. He was one of the founders of what became the most influential and powerful force in New France. Vincent de Paul, Jean Eudes, and Olier, all residents in France, began the *Concile de Trente*, their goal being to retrain French priests and to give meaning back to the priesthood of their time.

Only priests could benefit from their retreats and training programs. There was no congregation and there were no initiates from the lay community. Their role was pivotal in rebuilding the self-image of priests and through it they gained enormous social and economic influence. Their initiative soon came to be known as the Company of the Seminary of St. Sulpice, more commonly known as the Sulpicians. Olier was also a Montréaliste.

By the mid-1650s, the members of the Société Notre-Dame de Montréal in France were aging and not being replaced with younger benefactors. They still managed to find believers to send to the defence of the mission, but their fundraising efforts were producing less fruit. The Five Nations dominated the river and had destroyed or absorbed almost every Indigenous Nation allied to the French. Even Jean de Lauson, by then governor of New France, lived in fear of them. In one telling incident in May 1656, three hundred Five Nations warriors attacked a Wendat village under the protection of the French on Île d'Orléans, burning it and taking the survivors home. As they paddled their war canoes back past Quebec, they hurled insults at the French who stayed put, incapable of an adequate military response.

In this atmosphere, the missionaries in Montreal, even less well defended than Quebec, held on as their backers in France melted away.

French colonists further down the river at Quebec and Trois-Rivières contemplated abandoning the colony and returning en masse to France. Responding to a plea from Jeanne Mance, by this time an elderly woman, Olier, who was himself nearing the end of his life, committed the Sulpicians to support the missionaries.

It is hard to understand to what extent the Montréalistes and Sulpicians in France understood that Ville Marie was not capable of fulfilling its mission of ministering to the infidels. There were Algonquin war refugees in their care, but their major task was to fight for survival against a superior military force. The Hôtel Dieu, the hospital that Jeanne Mance founded to care for the heathens of this far-away island, was busy with sick and wounded French soldiers. The colony itself had depended upon support from Huguenot sailors out of La Rochelle and Jérôme Le Royer was also in failing health. Support for the missionaries fell almost completely to the Sulpicians. In 1657, the Société Notre-Dame de Montréal donated their seigneurial title to the Sulpicians, and the European colonization of the island picked up its pace.

CHAPTER 28

War and the Dispersal of Huronia

In the pre-contact Iroquoian and Algonquian regions, wars were fought mainly to protect alliances or to gain or maintain honour, but European expansion had destabilized the communities.

The Five Nations of the Haudenosaunee, who had tried to unite the Iroquoian people to stabilize trade since the 1620s, turned to more drastic measures. The Wendat, historically the largest Iroquoian trading culture, had rejected the Five Nations' approaches, generally following the advice of the French. From the French point of view, they saw how a union of the Iroquoian peoples would not advantage French objectives.

The records of the Jesuits documented some of the wars and torture between the Wendat and the Five Nations of the Haudenosaunee. Prisoners—men, women and children—were among the objectives of warfare and were incorporated into the social fabric of their captors. Women and children were easier to incorporate into the community and, if not killed on the spot for logistical reasons, were brought home and eventually adopted. Sexual violence against them was rare.

The Jesuit records describe the torture of male prisoners who were treated with dignity between bouts of torture, a dignity that turned to mocking when the torture resumed. Families who had lost warriors were rewarded with male prisoners, whom the women, children and men of the family proceeded to torture. This torture took place in the longhouse and was ruthless, mindful of what happened to the warrior they had lost to this enemy. Forced to run the length of the longhouse through the fires, likely with his arms bound, and goaded and tortured in more aggressive ways, the prisoner's task was to prove his courage as a way of intimidating his captors. Every young man learned his death song that he would chant to keep his strength.

At any time, the women of the family could stop the procedure. Based on their judgment, a warrior could be adopted, with him knowing that objectionable behaviour might result in a resumption of torture. His spirit would be broken so that he would accept his new family, but in time he could be fully accepted and would become a loyal member of his community of adoption and ultimately contribute to the gene pool. Conversely, if they decided to torture him to death, the death was timed for the rising sun.

Whole Nations could be adopted, absorbed through war or peaceful agreements, as the Wendat demonstrated when they peacefully absorbed the Wenroronon.

Combining this aspect of wars of honour with the need to sustain their population casts a light on what happened to the great Wendat Nations in the 1640s. Their populations, principally the Wendat, had been cut in half by disease. The Wendat, its own powerful confederacy of four Nations, was deeply involved with the French through trade and by accommodating the Jesuits. Due to the much higher presence of Europeans in its midst, it probably suffered greater losses than the other Iroquoian Nations from the plagues of the 1630s. The Jesuit presence and the French refusal to trade with those who did not accept Christianity divided them into two camps, the Catholics and the Traditionalists, but few arms were traded, even with the converts. These two factors seriously weakened the Wendat, adding to an imbalance of power between the southern and northern Iroquoian Nations.

When the diseases of the late 1630s hit, population numbers plummeted, fields could not be sustained, and social cohesion was challenged. The Jesuit Donnés carried guns and were a defence force for the Wendat Catholic towns, obliging their Wendat hosts to rely on the Jesuits for that modern aspect of their armed defence. It was probable that the French did not arm their allies properly because they feared them. To the south, the Dutch and English, competing for furs, had been trading in guns, and the Five Nations warriors were increasingly armed and familiar with the new means of warfare. Excluded from trade with the French and having practically exhausted their fur resources, they relied on raiding those Nations allied with the French to obtain furs. Their arms improved their range at the same time as their locally available beaver population was depleted.

The long-distance trading routes that the Wendat travelled to reach the French became an increasingly attractive target and way of obtaining furs. The Five Nations were also aware of the Wendat divisions in the community and of its depleted population. Traditionalists among the Wendat had come to the Onondaga of the Five Nations, concerned about the loss of their Iroquoian culture.[102]

A large Five Nations army could disperse the Wendat, eliminating the Catholics and, in the process, providing Iroquoian prisoners for adoption who could swell the ranks of the Five Nations' depleted population. The consolidation of the Iroquoian peoples would also give them more control of the European market.

Through the 1640s, the Five Nation military strength grew as they attacked Algonquin and Wendat traders, moving ever closer to the French. The small French community on the Island of Montreal, far from their original mission of carrying Christianity to an ignorant people, was only secure behind barricades. Through that same period, there was growing dissension inside the Wendat communities as the Five Nations approached.

The Five Nations' power was increasingly unopposed, and in the early spring of 1648, the attacks began against the Wendat. Cut off from the French colony and improperly armed, even their crops could not be planted or protected. To add to their desperation, some Wendat traders who had made it through to Trois-Rivières had learned that the French had started peace talks with the Mohawk. Starvation loomed as Haudenosaunee warriors raided the periphery, pushing the people together into the larger settlements and increasingly taxing their limited food resources. By the autumn, two of the four Nations of the Wendat had been destroyed. The survivors began a retreat, burning their remaining towns so they could not serve the advancing armies.

That winter, a thousand-strong Haudenosaunee army of Five Nations warriors camped out on abandoned Wendat hunting territory, preparing to attack the Wendat in the early spring. They would have to deal with Fort Taenhatentaron, which had been reinforced by the French. Reconnoitering it during the night of March 16, likely deep in snow, they assessed that it was difficult to approach on three sides because of ravines but that its watchtowers were not manned.

The occupants had not imagined an attack would happen in the winter. The reconnaissance party and its backup entered a sleeping fort. The fort was not fully occupied. Even so, in the ensuing fight, ten of the attacking warriors were killed and three of the Wendat escaped. The balance of the four hundred survivors were taken prisoner and the fort became an advance base for the Haudenosaunee army.

The escapees had time to warn the next fortified village of St. Louis. The headmen wasted no time in protecting the women and children, sending a party of five hundred along with all the assets they could carry into that same winter night towards Fort Ste. Marie. Eighty defenders stayed, including Father Brébeuf and the recently arrived young priest Father Gabriel Lalemant. Before morning, an advance Five Nations party arrived. Twice repulsed, they breached the barricades and stormed the fort, which was manned mostly by Christian warriors. Two, wounded, escaped and brought news to Fort Ste. Marie, while the ill and the aged were killed outright and the rest, including the priests, were marched back to Taenhatentaron. While the palisades were left, the houses were sacked and burned, and by 9:00 am the smoke could be seen at Ste. Marie.

The priests, stripped naked and with their fingernails torn out, were forced to walk between two rows of warriors as they were beaten. They were tied facing stakes where their torturers, including the most aggressive Wendat Traditionalists who had already been adopted by the Five Nations, continued their ministrations, baptising them with boiling water. The Traditionalists held them completely responsible for the destruction of Huronia, but Father Brébeuf's stoicism still impressed them as their torture of him increased. He died that afternoon and the warriors, admiring his courage, honoured him by eating his heart. Father Lalemant lingered until morning, the customary time when such a prisoner would be killed.

Taking advantage of their success, the Haudenosaunee army advanced immediately to take Fort Ste. Marie, the major stronghold, but in the meantime, three hundred mostly Christian Wendat from Ossossané moved to intercept them. Pushed back almost to Ste. Marie, they rallied, and the Five Nations warriors, trying to take refuge in the abandoned palisades of Fort St. Louis, were cornered.

The Wendat retook Fort St. Louis and held thirty prisoners. This battle caused the main Five Nation forces to change direction and retake Fort St. Louis instead of proceeding to Fort Ste. Marie. A vicious battle ensued, breaking tradition by continuing into the night. By the time they achieved their goal, they found only twenty wounded Wendat warriors still alive. Intimidated by the valiant defence, the Five Nations of the Haudenosaunee withdrew from Huronia.[103]

In as much as the defence of Fort St. Louis had turned back the Haudenosaunee army, the Wendat also realized that they could not withstand another advance, which would surely come. Their fields would not be safe to grow crops, their hunting grounds were insecure, and their numbers were dropping. Both the Christian and Traditional members determined that their position was untenable, and the dispersal began. They burned their villages and small groups moved west to join the remaining Wendat Nations, the Petun and the Neutral, while others moved north to islands in the north of Lake Huron and still others joined their historic Algonquian trading partners.

A large group chose to move to the Island of Gahoendoe in Georgian Bay, called Christian Island today, where they felt they could grow enough food. The remaining Jesuits went with them, burning their fort of Ste. Marie and rebuilding a smaller version on the island. It might have sustained them, but soon stragglers overwhelmed their limited resources. They had a difficult winter, but they shared and survived.

The Onondaga, the central Nation of the Five Nations, where the Tree of Peace grew, recognized the plight of the refugees and offered them succor. They could be taken back to the Onondaga villages and adopted, but the terrified refugees killed their emissaries, fearing a plot. The starving remnant tried to flee the island in the spring, but the ice didn't hold. Somehow, French traders found them and gave the Jesuits a message that they were being recalled. They left with the French traders, accompanied by a party of Catholic Wendat leaving their home forever. Carrying five thousand furs, the only wealth that they still had, they somehow succeeded in getting safely to Quebec.

These Wendat were hoping to be protected by the French and, in time, were joined by other Catholics, but as the Five Nations' raids increased over the following years, they came to learn that the French would not protect them. In fairness to the French, they were so weak themselves that they could not afford to incur the enmity of the raiding parties. Many chose instead to believe the declared peaceful intentions of the Five Nations. The Mohawk and the Onondaga were "adopting" the Wendat they captured during their raids. After one such raid, seeing the desperate state of the prisoners, some Jesuits offered to accompany them and both the Jesuits and the Wendat found themselves in the hands of Onondaga warriors, carried in canoes to Onondaga. At Montreal, the priests were turned back because their luggage was too much of a burden, and some of the refugees were tortured and killed for past wrongs they had committed against the Onondaga. Most of the others were adopted.[104]

It has been suggested that the Five Nations, aside from wanting to assimilate these cousins into their Nations, did not want them to teach the French the art of warfare. Although their Nations had been destroyed, the Wendat prowess as warriors was still feared.

Those refugees who fled west fared little better as the Five Nations determined to absorb all the Wendat and went systematically to each of the western Nations, the Petun or Tionnontaté, the Neutral or Kahqua, and the Erie. None would give up their refugees without a fight, although one of the Neutral villages refused to defend itself and accepted to become incorporated into the huge Seneca Nation, in time setting up their own town there. Ruled in linear descent from Jigonsaseh, the clan mother who had been consulted by Deganwidah at the time of the creation of the Great Law of Peace, the Clan Mother Kieunake, or Fire Woman, led her Nation peacefully into the Seneca territory.[105]

The Five Nations were challenged by the huge swelling of their populations and many accommodations had to be made. The Seneca, the largest of the Five Nations, doubled in population. By the mid-1650s, the Five Nations of the Haudenosaunee controlled the traditional Wendat territory along with trade with the Europeans, but many Wendat who re-fused to be absorbed fled further west, forming a new Nation that called itself the Wyandot. Refugees from other Nations, also trampled by the warpath of the Five Nations, moved west too. Any Nation that continued to trade with the French was chased, even the Ottawa, who lived on the scattered islands of Lake Huron.

By 1665, when a group of Frenchmen and their Indigenous allies fought their way through the territories, travelling all the way to the Win-nebago on Green Bay in Lake Michigan, they found 30,000 refugees, in-cluding Fox, Sauk, Ottawa, Mascouten, Miami, Kickapoo, Ojibwe, and Potawatomi, all attempting to co-exist with the Winnebago. The land did not lend itself to farming and hunting had exhausted the woodlands. The Wyandot, still pursued for adoption, had moved further to the south shore of Lake Superior.[106]

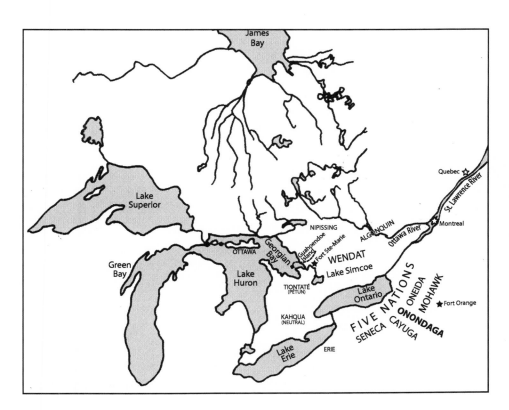

145

CHAPTER 29
"Les Canadiens"

*After the dispersal of Huronia and the expansion of the Five Nations
throughout the trading territories of New France, the Canadiens, young,
independent French traders, working with Algonquian Nations,
became a part of the new reality of life in the bush.*

Throughout the development of New France, locally born French identified as Canadiens. New France existed in Canada. The French first called the mighty St. Lawrence La Rivière du Canada. In the European French imagination, Canada was a mythical other world. It comprised that huge romantic territory that formed the drainage basin of the St. Lawrence River and the Great Lakes. It even extended into the uplands of the Ohio, the Pays d'en Haut. These Canadiens were the Europeans who integrated most closely with their surroundings. They were the French colony's face of trade, the coureurs de bois, self-reliant and independent.

Champlain encouraged exchanges of young men, such as the exchange of Brûlé and Savignon. The young French who came to the colony were not the devoted Catholics that history recalls in the first half of the twentieth century. They came from a France that was experiencing its own religious upheavals. They adapted to their environment and men like Nicholas Marsolat, a contemporary of Étienne Brûlé, refused to teach the Algonquian language to the missionaries, feeling they would bring no good.

The Jesuits deplored the fact that young men disappeared into the bush, sometimes for as long as three years, and learned to live with the Algonquian and Wendat Peoples, but these same young men understood the numinous relations with the forest, and some felt that it was better adapted to the life of their hosts than the Catholic faith was.[107] After the

147

dispersal of Huronia, New France was at risk of having to return en masse to France. Their revenues depended upon the fur trade, and not only the Wendat had been dispersed by the wars, but also many of their Algonquian partners. There was a vacuum to fill, and it was filled in part by young Canadien men who had begun to live with the Algonquin and Innu people. The mores of the whole country were strongly impacted by this interaction and a new paradigm was possible. The Catholic establishment had been set back by the capture of Quebec in 1629, and it was further knocked by the dispersal of Huronia, but it was not a spent force. These young men had grown up Christian in families that had been a part of Christendom for a millennium. They could still be reached and the man for the job was the aging Jesuit Jérôme Lalemant.

Before leaving France in 1659 to head the Catholic Church in the colony, François de Montigny de Laval asked the 66-year-old retired Superior of the Jesuits of Canada, Jérôme Lalemant, to join him in his mission. Lalemant was an experienced missionary who had served in Canada for many years, and the choice of this man, almost twice Laval's age, sheds light on Laval's priorities. The Indigenous population far outnumbered the colonials. Innu, Algonquin and Wendat Peoples were often casualties of the wars between the powerful Iroquois Nations and the French. The colony itself numbered less than 2,000 Frenchmen, most of whom were settled around the fort at Quebec, with only several hundred in Trois-Rivières, an outpost at Montreal and very little else. Even in the settled areas, few were locally born. They were often adventurous young men who had come over from France on one pretext or another. Many of those colonists were settled on seigneuries founded by the Jesuits.

Laval's attempts to institute changes, including his efforts to control the liquor trade, were rebuffed by the secular authorities. Despite a letter from the queen mother and a subsequent one from the king, which Laval had posted throughout the colony, his authority among the colonists was ignored. After all, it was ecclesiastical, not civil, and he did not yet have the authority of a bishop. He felt his only recourse was to petition the king directly, and so, leaving Father Lalemant in charge of their French and Indian missions, he returned to France in 1662.

In the meantime, life in the colony was being stoked by the arrival of young women, pulled from orphanages and poor families and sent to become wives of the colony's single men. The average age of unattached males was twenty-two and the newly-arrived females were as young as twelve, while the ratio was six bachelors for each young woman.

In early 1663, the colony filled with stories of three suns appearing in the sky on two different occasions in January, and an ominous mood hung over the colonists. With the approach of the feast of Mardi Gras, the beginning of the 40 days of Lent with its deprivations, these young people had turned the colony into a large party. There were carnivals, drinking bouts, dancing and even rumours of orgies. The Algonquin and Innu Peoples were becoming acquainted with these young French and with liquor simultaneously. Patient and experienced, Lalemant bided his time, waiting for an opportunity to establish a sober control over his congregations. It arrived on Saturday, February 5, 1663.

What would become known as the Great Earthquake, with its epicentre at the mouth of the Saguenay River, arrived at 5:30 pm, three days before the beginning of Lent. It lasted half an hour and was felt from west of Montreal all the way to Acadia, cracking chimney tops as far away as New England. The Innu thought the trees themselves had become drunk and the colonists were convinced the world was ending. In the aftermath, the shores of the river were strewn with trees, and the seismic disturbances would continue until the middle of the summer. Father Lalemant, who described the events, recorded that "Mountains were swallowed up; Forests were changed into great Lakes; Rivers disappeared; Rocks were split, and their fragments hurled to the very tops of the tallest trees; thunders rumbled beneath our feet in the womb of the earth, which belched forth flames."[108]

He also took full advantage of the event, calling upon the sinners to repent, and the effect was so strong that even the civil authorities accepted to pass a law against the trade in alcohol. By the time Laval returned with his new powers, Lalemant, the experienced old missionary, had everything under control.

The Canadiens had become intimately acquainted with the Innu, Algonquin and Ottawa and were accepted locally as a people equally capable of living in the bush and travelling with these Nations.

CHAPTER 30
Metacomet (King Philip's War);
The Covenant Chain, 1637–1675

*During the lifespan of Metacomet, named Philip by the Pilgrims,
the Indigenous Nations, from New England to Chesapeake Bay,
witnessed enormous changes as European colonies spread along the coast
and fought with each other.*

New Sweden, a small colony just south of the Hudson River on the Delaware River, was set up by Peter Minuit, the founding governor of New Amsterdam. Accused of illegal trading in the New Netherlands, he had been recalled to Holland, but felt that his dismissal and recall had been unfair. He transferred his allegiance to the Swedes in 1637. At that time, Sweden was a growing Protestant power in the Wars of Religion. Minuit offered to help the Swedes establish New Sweden, reaching up to the same rich trading grounds of the Five Nations, where the Dutch traded. He soon wooed the southern Iroquoian Nation, the Susquehannock, away from the Dutch and equipped them with firearms that were superior to those the Dutch traded. These developments left the Dutch colony vulnerable, with a competing colony literally in its back yard. England, with the large and growing Puritan settlements to the north of the Dutch colony, and the Virginia colony further south, all surrounded the Dutch. The Five Nations continued to suffer from the contagion of the plagues that had encouraged them to force the Wendat Peoples into their alliance. They were also feeling the trading presence of the English colony.

The Dutch had established their Dutch West-India Company mostly for trade, and what distinguished the Dutch from the English in the New World was that the English colonies were places of direct refuge from the

151

Wars of Religion that were dividing them at home. The Dutch settlements were operating businesses.

In England, the Puritans, objecting to King Charles I, left to set up their own colony at a location in the territory of the Naumkeag. They called it Salem. Thirteen thousand militant members arrived along the coast during the 1630s, driving all the Indigenous Nations before them. More kept coming, changing the whole dynamic of the region. The cauldron of religious righteousness that boiled throughout Europe had found purchase in England. The exodus of the Puritans became a flood, pouring across the territory we call New England without regard for the people already living there.

To the south of the Dutch, in 1632, another religious colony was awarded to Lord Baltimore to become a haven for English Catholics. In 1649, the colony instituted the first law of religious tolerance, provided of course that the religions were Christian. This tolerance law was repealed by the Protestants within six years—as soon as they represented the majority. They fought and traded with the Iroquoian Susquehannock as the colonists expanded into Susquehannock historic territory, pushing them ahead of their settlement.

Steeped in Christendom for well over a millennium, conditioned through the domestication of the Sacraments, Christians, whether Protestant or Catholic, all shone with the same light. They and their ancestors had all been moulded by the same or similar hierarchies. As thoroughly driven into submission and obeisance as was Job by his personal god, so the Christians became stamped replicas, each a believer in the righteousness of God, ultimately splitting into purer, more obsessive forms of belief.

The Puritans of New England, in dealing with the Indigenous Peoples, proselytized them, organizing them into villages of "Praying Indians" who could then be tolerated if not trusted. Ministers such as John Elliot, who oversaw many conversions, would have felt they were doing God's work. They drove these Indigenous Nations into submission while telling them that they were being blessed with the greatest gift, Christian doctrine.

Of course, some Nations did not accept to submit, such as the un-

conquered Nations of the New England region, and there were Englishmen who saw that it was wrong, such as Roger Williams, who founded
Rhode Island as a refuge for dissenting Puritans and religious minorities.
He wrote from there, contrasting the Puritan intolerance with Indigenous
virtue and became a champion of freedom of religion.[109] In his lifetime,
his efforts to maintain good relations with the Narragansett were overwhelmed in settler society by expropriation of Indigenous land and he
was dismissed for not seeing the "enemy" clearly.

As though nature was justifying the Christian belief that they were
doing God's work, disease spread ahead of them, spreading further by
warfare, to Indigenous Nations inland and up the New England coast.

The Pennacook Confederacy, residents of the Merrimack River in
New Hampshire and Massachusetts, crashed from 12,000 to 2,500 in 1620
and continued to decline through the 1600s as one wave after another of
European disease swept them away. The survivors, for a time, became a
part of the Praying Indians, trying desperately to maintain their neutrality
as wars broke in every direction around them. Throughout this time of
chaos, the Puritans pushed forward, over the rights of the original inhabitants. Even those who accepted to become Christian were forced into
submission or withdrawal. The Pennacook people were divided between
burning anger over their losses and a desire to flee north to join the Abenaki. Attempting to maintain neutrality at all costs, to stay out of the
fighting by appeasing the hungry advance of the Puritans, they gave up
land four times during the 1650s alone, until their leader, Passaconnaway,
was forced to beg for sustenance for his people.

To their north, the Five Nations of the Haudenosaunee were advancing against the Abenaki, who were allied with the French, blocking any
exit in that direction. The Wampanoag to the south, the allies of the Pilgrims, had developed a stable, cooperative relationship, even as the Puritan population exploded. Peace Chief Massasoit's son Alexander
(Wamsutta) replaced him. The Puritans, not sharing the Pilgrim-Wam-
panoag alliance, felt that the Wampanoag were acting too independently.
They invited Peace Chief Alexander to a conference, and, after a meal
with them, he fell over and died. The Wampanoag believed that he had
been poisoned and Plymouth Council records from that time list the pur-

chase of a poison acquired "to rid ourselves of a pest."[110]

Chief Wamsutta's successor, Metacomet, began what history calls King Philip's War in 1675 in response, hoping to drive the Puritans back. The situation was very unstable for the Indigenous Nations and time was running out to establish a powerful enough counterbalance to try to contain the English or push them back into the sea. Only a union of the Indigenous Nations could have accomplished this. Even then, they would have had to find a European ally to replenish their ammunition, guns, and metal. Once the English ousted the Dutch in 1664, it was probably too late. Metacomet, also called King Philip, had no choice except to try. He appealed to his traditional enemies, the Five Nations of the Haudenosaunee.

Paul Revere's caption:
A caricature of Metacomet from the book The Entertaining History of King Philip's War, written by Benjamin Church, son of the man who murdered Metacomet.

The Five Nations had long seen the need for a union of the Indigenous Nations. Their vision, based on the Two Row Wampum, the Kaswentha, was of a trading bloc represented by them that would set the terms of trade with Europeans. It had been the vision that drove their invasion of the Wendat Nations to the north. They had become hierarchical, with the Five Nations at the top, and they warred with their neighbours to force them into the trading bloc.

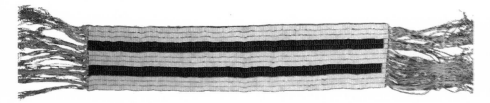

The Kaswentha, or Two-Row Wampum belt, record of the Dutch-Mohawk treaty, 1613.

With a continuous underpinning of religions tensions in Europe, the powerful Swedes developed new forts and helped the Susquehannock defend their territory against the Baltimore Catholics. In 1654, they captured a Dutch fort, but the next year they were heavily involved against the Polish-Lithuanian Commonwealth in Europe. Peter Stuyvesant, governor of New Netherlands, saw his opportunity and moved against New Sweden, taking it over.

In the next decade, the Dutch surrendered their colony to the English. The changing state of affairs was driven by European wars and must have been impossibly confusing for the different Indigenous Nations.

The Five Nations re-established the Kaswentha with their new partner, the English. Their symbol was of warriors linking arms from the English ships to the Tree of Peace on Onondaga territory, and, like any effective treaty, the English took ownership of the treaty as well. It was symbolized as a silver chain and came to be called the Covenant Chain. It was necessary to assure that the bargaining power of the Indigenous Peoples maintained a single voice in reaction to the greater consolidation that was taking place with the disappearance of the Dutch. A period of stability had allowed the two original contractors of the Two Row Wampum, and subsequently, the silver chain, to maintain their jurisdictional independence. It also assured that the Indigenous trading bloc would have European products, including arms. Five Nations' policy consolidated their bloc by conquering non-Iroquoian peoples and making treaties with them, making them second-class members of the Covenant Chain.

By the time Metacomet moved to create his alliance, the Five Nations had already established the Covenant Chain. A request for them to unite against the English would have meant accepting two impossible terms: The first was to go to war against their European trading partner, and the second was to accept their traditional enemies as a military equal in a common cause. Instead, they took the English side and moved against these traditional enemies.

Metacomet, a man of peace, was the leader of a people who had been reduced to 1,000 by recurring diseases, while the Puritans numbered 35,000 and were increasing. He had to depend on the Nations surrounding him in New England, and together they formed a total population of 15,000. Armed with English and French guns, they had also developed their own forge. Metacomet's warriors did not have the hierarchical discipline of Europeans and passions were running high. He risked not being able to start the war on his schedule.

The Puritans continued to treat Indigenous Peoples cruelly, reacting to the murder of a potential ally, a Praying Indian, by hanging three Wampanoag warriors. The Narragansett, allies of the Wampanoag, had to put their military supplies in order and needed time. The Puritans got wind of the preparations and met with the Narragansett, forcing them to sign a promise to remain neutral in any conflict. In the early spring of 1675, Weetamoo—Rock Woman—widow of Metacomet's brother and leader of the Wampanoag Pocassets, appealed to the governor of Plymouth to stop encroaching on Wampanoag territory. She received a reply making any co-operation subject to a guarantee of neutrality and of the sharing of any information that might help against Metacomet, her leader.

In the late spring of 1675, a Wampanoag was murdered near Swansea, and the warriors could contain themselves no longer, attacking an English relief column. Over that summer, the Wampanoag devastated the Puritans, forcing them into forts often undersupplied with food. The war became vicious on both sides as the Puritans systematically burned every Wampanoag village in a march towards Metacomet's headquarters at Mount Hope. In the summer of that year, the Wampanoag were trapped in a swamp near Weetamoo's Pocasset territory. As the Puritans surrounded them, the Wampanoag managed to spirit out their women and children who were transferred across the water to the care of Weetamoo. Metacomet and his warriors subsequently slipped away into the woodlands leaving a large Puritan army holding the empty swamp under siege.

Without the help of other Nations, their fate was sealed. With their villages and food stores burned by the Puritans, winter augured poorly for them. In December, the governor of their old allies at Plymouth, leading an army against the neutral Narragansett, demanded any Wampanoag in their care be released. Since the Narragansett had the care of the Wampanoag women and children, they refused, and the battle that followed, remembered as the Great Swamp Fight, almost eliminated the Narragansett, with six hundred warriors dead and huge casualties among the Puritans. Their Sachem Canonchet led the survivors away with the Puritans too weakened to follow. Canonchet and his people joined Metacomet.

In desperate need of seeds for the summer of 1676, Canonchet secretly returned to the Narragansett village to secure a cache of hidden seed stock, but on his return, he was killed. Despite their successes, this spelled the end for Metacomet. In May, thanks to Praying Indian spies, the Puritans led an army to Turner's Falls where they killed Metacomet's gunsmiths and destroyed his forges. His alliance began to fall apart, and each group tried to make the best deal it could after that. The Pocasset were destroyed and Weetamoo drowned in an attempted escape. Her head was stuck on a stake near Taunton, Massachusetts, in full view of war prisoners, setting off loud, sorrowful mourning. Thanks to information from an informer named John Alderman, rangers surrounded Metacomet on August 12. Alderman shot him. The informer and executioner was awarded Metacomet's hand as a souvenir. The great leader's head stood atop a stake in Plymouth for twenty-five years, a grotesque commemoration of the treaty between his father and the Pilgrims. His nine-year-old son was sold into slavery in the West Indies.

With the war effectively over, for two more years the Puritans continued to hunt, capture, and sell the people into slavery. Estimates of Indigenous losses range up to 11,000 people.[111]

The Great Swamp Fight almost eliminated the Narragansett in December 1675.

CHAPTER 31

La Grande Paix de Montréal

*La Grande Paix de Montréal, signed in 1701, acknowledged the
Five Nations as well as the Canadiens, and accepted the independent
Indigenous allies of the French in exchange for peace and trade.*

Even though the Wampanoag and Narragansett were not allies of the Five Nations, the latter must have been stunned by the viciousness of the Puritan destruction of their Indigenous neighbours. But they saw themselves differently. They had conquered the Wendat societies and adopted thousands of them into their Nations. They waged war with the Susquehannock, subdued many of their non-Iroquoian neighbouring Nations, and created the Covenant Chain, locking these people into a trading partnership with the English through them.

Their negotiating bloc spoke to the English with one voice and stretched from the Chesapeake to the Mississippi, and north to encompass most of the Great Lakes. They had controlled trade with the Dutch at Fort Orange. Yet, they depended upon European military technology and did not develop forges like the Wampanoag had done. They did not see the necessity of creating an infrastructure to stand up to the colonial ambitions of the European powers but, instead, became the trading middlemen with the Europeans. Accepting a hierarchical structure, they responded to their Covenant Chain partners from a power advantage and succeeded in maintaining their cultural values and territory in the face of a massive invasion.[112]

In the meantime, the French colony and trading partners were vulnerable due to the expanding influence of the Haudenosaunee-led Covenant Chain. The French Crown was of two minds about what to do. On the one hand, they wanted to consolidate their assets, maintaining a local commercial and agricultural society. On the other hand, the wealth of trade with the western Nations, such as the independent Wendat (Wyandot), the Ottawa, and other surviving Algonquian Nations that had resisted the Covenant Chain, was too tempting for the people serving in New France to resist.

During the period from 1672 to 1698, New France saw four governors. The first, Count Frontenac, was a disaster, the spoiled descendant of a well-connected family who accepted the post to avoid his creditors. He alienated all levels of local government and treated the colony as his private domain, setting up an advance trading post at present-day Kingston, called Fort Frontenac, thereby attempting to monopolize the fur trade for himself.

In his ignorance, he had located his post in territory that the Five Nations felt was theirs by conquest, but they were forced to tolerate the incursion because they were at war with the Susquehannock. When they settled with their enemies in 1675, they turned their attention upon the French and began to punish those Nations that chose to trade at Fort Frontenac. Simultaneously, the English had set up trading posts on Hudson's Bay and were drawing furs there, away from the French.

Frontenac lasted ten years before he was recalled. During that period, he undermined the structure of the colony and provided no leadership, leaving the colony weakened and vulnerable to attack. His masters back in France had no idea to what extent he had alienated the powerful Five Nations. That would be for his successor to learn. He was replaced by an over-confident soldier, LeFebvre de la Barre. While he quickly captured three English trading posts in James Bay, he moved on the Five Nations as though he were fighting a European war. He had to rapidly retreat and sue for peace. He lasted only three years before he, too, was recalled.

Next came the Marquis de Denonville, a career soldier with an excellent record. He whipped the colony into shape, insisted that the governor of Montreal should assume the military responsibility in the absence of a governor general, and explored how to deal with the Five Nations. There are many interpretations of what he did. He was asked to meet them for a peace conference at Fort Frontenac while he was quietly marshalling his troops to invade. He accepted the meeting but continued with his preparations. An advance guard captured a significant part of the Five Nations leadership on the way up the river to the conference and they were held as prisoners as an insurance policy to be able to trade for French prisoners if necessary. Some of them were sent to France to serve on the royal galleys, ships driven by enslaved rowers. Most died there. This action and others doomed the peace conference, and in June 1687 he proceeded with an invasion of the Seneca,[113] the most westerly and numerous of the Five Nations.

The Seneca disappeared into the woods. Denonville proceeded to burn villages and fields. It is argued that he had tried to undermine the leadership of the Five Nations through his kidnapping of their leaders in anticipation of his attack. Denonville was undersupplied to conduct such an attack. He needed peace but did not want his Indigenous allies, the Ottawa and others, to be forced into the Covenant Chain trading bloc. The Five Nations could not tolerate the trading practices of these French allies because it undermined the objective of the Covenant Chain trading bloc to provide only one negotiator to the Europeans.

In the meantime, the French and English in Europe were at war again, this time the English on the side of the Dutch. News of the state of war reached the Five Nations through New York before it reached Denonville. The Five Nations dropped all pretense of making peace, instead gathering an army to storm Montreal. According to one source, with the leadership having been neutralized by the kidnapping, the head clan mother, Kieunake, or Fire Woman, the same greatly respected Neutral leader who claimed descendance from Jigonsaseh, took over the plans for the attack.[114] Their advance cut through disputed territory and brought them to Lachine on August 5, 1689. There they stormed the town, burning and killing, withdrawing quickly with prisoners and leaving the French reeling. Shortly afterward, the previous governor, Count Frontenac, arrived with a notice of Denonville's recall.

Frontenac took over a changed colony, having to attend to the increased status that Denonville had accorded to the role of the governor of Montreal. The structure was more rigid, but he was also more mature and more aware of the colony's needs. That did not stop him from sending trading parties of Canadiens to trade for furs to the west in contradiction of orders for him to stabilize and centralize the colony.

Frontenac extended French influence far to the west while enriching himself and his friends, building far-flung forts, going as far as the Sioux, the traditional enemies of the French ally, the Ottawa. The Ottawa Nation, seeing their role of intermediary being bypassed by the Canadiens began talks with the Five Nations to join the Covenant Chain. Frontenac was willing to let the governor of Montreal, Louis-Hector de Callière, handle the military, but he refused to listen to him about making sure they didn't alienate the Ottawa. Callière trusted the Canadien militias, whose war techniques had been learned from their Indigenous partners, among them the Ottawa, and he trusted their relationship with these independent Nations. Frontenac saw that these Canadien militias had developed techniques that, in company with the small military force at his disposal, could stand up to the Five Nations. The fear that each instilled in the other resulted in a stalemate between the Five Nations and the French.

But time was working against the Five Nations. The French population was growing, while the Five Nations was continuously wearing down in the face of a variety of diseases to which they had little resistance. In the eleven years ending in 1698, their fighting strength was halved, dropping to less than 1,300 warriors, while the French total population during the same period rose from 10,000 to almost 13,000. Even with these disadvantages, encouraged by the Ottawa partnership, the Five Nations continued to attack the French to keep the battlegrounds centred around the settlements of Trois-Rivières and Montreal.

In 1696, Callière and Philippe de Rigaud de Vaudreuil brought the battle to the Onondaga and the Oneida of the Five Nations. Frontenac authorized a French contingent of 2,000 troops and Canadien militia to move into Onondaga and Oneida territory. He also insisted on going with them, seventy-four years old and carried in an armchair. Disappearing into the woods, the Five Nations avoided casualties, but the French army burned their villages and crops and moved on. In the aftermath, the people were reeling, struggling to feed themselves. They did not have the French advantage of a backup regular army paid by an overseas king. The Ottawa, seeing their weakness, abandoned their new allies. It was time to make peace, but Frontenac refused, against the recommendations of his advisors. He was using the pretext of war to continue to gather a huge quantity of furs for his pocket and his friends.

It may have been his extravagance in believing he was fit enough for such an adventure, but Frontenac began to weaken, succumbing to chronic asthma. With the fur trade collapsing from over supply and the cost of the colony skyrocketing, France was set to recall him. He deteriorated further and died on November 28, 1698, saving them the trouble. Frontenac had glutted the fur market and had spent a fortune with his adventuring.

The colonial leaders were faced with losing their Indigenous allies with the fur trade gone. These allies needed to trade furs to acquire arms. Without the trade, they could not use or defend the forts Frontenac had built. The French decided that they would use the forts to build an overland communication and trade route with their Louisiana colony.

Callière became the next governor of the colony and it was he who received the call for peace from the Five Nations. He saw it as an opportunity to maintain his own allies as independent traders unthreatened by the Five Nations Covenant Chain. They could establish a real, working peace that would allow the development of their upcountry trade ambitions in the Ohio and Mississippi valleys. It would be a complex negotiation involving Nations from across the region. It would involve prisoner exchange, agreements of respect of territory, trade, and the various Nations who had refused to join the Five-Nations-controlled Covenant Chain—it would also depend upon continued peace between France and England, something beyond his own mandate.

There was one man, a Wendat, who he would have to rely upon to see it through. His name was Kondiaronk, perhaps the last of the great diplomats of the Wendat Nations of the Lake Simcoe region. Kondiaronk's skills were known to, and respected by, all of the parties, even if he wasn't always trusted. His job would be to bring in the Nations that had resisted the Covenant Chain. The Five Nations could not refuse them, because without them, the governor would just be trading one set of allies for another—there would be no peace.

Over the next years, the parties progressed towards the great event of a major treaty. The fascinating diplomacy of the Five Nations was demonstrated throughout, dealing, as they were, with their most important Covenant Chain partner, the English. The four western Nations of the Haudenosaunee took the lead. The Mohawk, perhaps too close to the English, participated as observers. The Onondaga and Seneca, in their patient, rational diplomacy, repelled the English attempts to stop the whole project. Neither European party could have accommodated the other. The Five Nations speakers reminded the English on a number of occasions that they, the English, were not at war with the French, but it was clear in the European mindset that a peace made with the Indigenous Nations had nothing to do with the relationship between the two monarchies. The very existence of Indigenous Nations was not significant enough to make any real difference between the two European kingdoms. This perspective would doom any peace that was attempted.

A huge peace council to discuss the signing of La Grande Paix was organized for the summer of 1701 in Montreal. All the Nations were invited; all, that is, but the English.

It is hard to say that it was any one fact that drove the Five Nations to participate, but one factor that must have been significant was the English presumption that, through the Covenant Chain, the Five Nations and its allies were English subjects who had to obey the English king. The Five Nations went to great lengths to accommodate peace, but they were no-one's subjects.

La Grande Paix displayed the pageantry, complexity and diplomacy of the Indigenous world. William Fenton describes it in depth in his book *The Great Law of the Longhouse*.[115] Barbara Mann's *Native American Speakers of the Eastern Woodlands* addresses Kondiaronk (also Kandiaronk) in greater detail.[116]

Each side describes La Grande Paix as their initiative, as do the French, and that is how it should be for a treaty that is balanced and owned by all sides. It also represented a tacit acknowledgement among the Indigenous Nations that the French power was permanent, recognizing not just the Nations who were not in the Covenant Chain, but also the Canadiens as one among them.

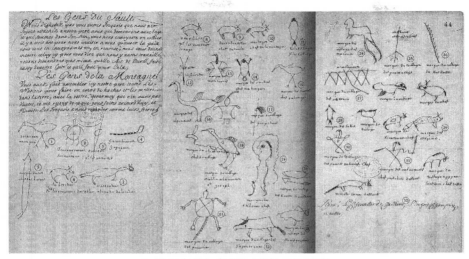

La Grande Paix de Montréal treaty, 1701

Samuel de Champlain brought the Recollets and the Jesuits, and Jeanne Mance brought the Sulpicians to New France. Their shared objectives were to minister to and convert the people who were already here. After the destruction of Huronia, French investment in converting the Wendat had left both parties weaker, one with the total loss of its historic territory. A small number who escaped and wanted to stay with the French eventually formed the Wendake settlement near Quebec City. Several Christian Mohawk, some of Wendat descent, established themselves in the territory that was whittled down to Kahnawake. Most of Ontario, including parts of the Ottawa Valley, belonged to the Five Nations by right of conquest. Other scattered Nations, allied with the French, were fighting with the Five Nations who wanted them to join the Covenant Chain. The Five Nations had conquered an immense territory, adopting the Wendat and other Iroquoian Nations into their southern regions and there were some Mohawk villages on these territories, among them the village of Kanesatake.[117]

That great conflict left refugees in its wake. By the time the dust had settled, La Grande Paix de Montréal described a new potential for stability. The Canadiens were incorporated into it, but they were still governed by France. The Sulpicians, who inherited the Island of Montreal from the

Montréalistes, could finally fulfill the original vocation of Jeanne Mance. They administered a small community of Indigenous Christians on the Island of Montreal. These people cleared and worked the land, creating wealth for the Sulpicians. Originally housed closer to the town itself, the negative influence of the French residents and a fire forced the Sulpicians to move their mission to Sault aux Récollets in 1696. The name of this new location commemorated a place where a Recollet missionary and a Frenchman had drowned in 1625, seventy-one years earlier.

In 1721, in the dead of winter, the Sulpicians relocated their charges again, to Oka on the Lake of Two Mountains, selling the four hundred arpents that these Indigenous farmers had cleared since their arrival twenty-five years earlier at Sault aux Recollets. The move was to create a homeland for the resettlement of these displaced people and by the autumn of 1722, the Sulpicians could proudly declare they had cleared more land than they had cleared over the previous twenty-five years. According to the Oral History of the Mohawk, the new arrivals were received by the residents of Kanesatake, who saved them from starving through the first winter and spring. The Sulpicians, they argue, conflated their mission land with the cleared land of Kanesatake that was already farmed, declaring that the land had been cleared in eighteen months.[118]

When the Sulpicians established the settlement, they separated the Algonquin and Iroquoian people, as though they, the Sulpicians, were necessary to make sure the two communities lived in peace. The Algonquin and Nipissing used the Sulpician Mission as a base, spending their time on their historic territories. With their hunting and trapping culture, it is hard to imagine them as having been the driving force of land clearance. The Mohawk and Algonquin cultures were different. Clearing the land and planting it was central to the Mohawk culture but rarer among the Algonquin. Of course, both groups who had come from the Sulpician missions were Catholic, but there were Traditionalists, non-Christians, who interacted with them at Oka. The Nipissing were not a part of the mission but shared territory with the Algonquin, while the Kanehsatake Mohawk discovered clan connections with the newly-arrived Christian Mohawk.[119] Whatever problems the different Catholic orders caused for their converts over time, they were attempting to incorporate them as

Sulpician property in a feudal hierarchy, where it was hoped they would eventually become Catholic peasants.

In the regions of French influence, slowly the Seven Fires or Seven Nations of Canada[120] developed. To distinguish them, I refer to them as the Seven Fires. Some of these were associated with the Jesuit missions, one with the Sulpicians, and all had some Christian influences acting on them. In spite of La Grande Paix de Montréal, the French objectives had never changed. They were creating feudal hierarchies using religious means of administration and control. Nevertheless, as mid-century approached, they experienced a period of relative stability.

The Seven Fires included different cultural origins. Jeune Lorette (Wendake, Wendat), Bécancoeur (Wôlinak, Abenaki), Odanak (Abenaki), Kahnawake (Mohawk), Kanesatake (Mohawk, Algonquin, Nipissing), Akwesasne (Mohawk), Oswegathie (Onondaga).

A MONSTER REPLICATES
1709-1760

*If the English had been invited to La Grande Paix de Montréal in 1701,
who could have represented them? Who could have guaranteed
any commitment they would have made?*

CHAPTER 32

The British Hydra

*In 1707, England and Scotland formally united, calling themselves
Great Britain, and establishing it as a dominant European power that
comprised an increasing number of almost self-governing colonies,
a Hydra, a single, multi-headed beast.*

As stable as the Five Nations wished the Covenant Chain to become, politics were getting complicated as the Hydra of British colonies grew in number and population. The separate Nations of the Covenant Chain, represented by the spokesmen of the Five Nations, succeeded in speaking to the British settlers with one voice. Instead of respecting the single voice and a single set of rules, the settlers presented themselves as a single body with many heads, each with its own authority. All separate colonies, all British, all with the same market structure that was replacing the feudal one across the Protestant world, all variations on a theme of God, a single deity, but each one capable of cheating the others and breaking promises to the Five Nations.

In 1709, Baron Christoph von Graffenreid arrived in the Carolinas, along with his settlers. He had been awarded a huge territory to settle without consultation with the people who lived there, the Tuscarora, an Iroquoian Nation. He drove off the occupants only to find that the Tuscarora retaliated, burning his new colony and killing many of the inhabitants who had driven them away. Travelling over the territory afterward, von Graffenried, John Lawson, the surveyor general of Carolina who had

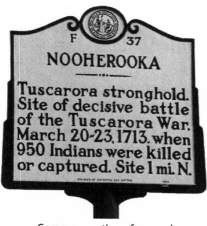

NOOHEROOKA

Tuscarora stronghold. Site of decisive battle of the Tuscarora War. March 20-23, 1713, when 950 Indians were killed or captured. Site 1 mi. N.

Commemoration of a people

encouraged him to settle, and an unidentified black slave were captured. Brought back to a Tuscarora community, they were tried by the Tuscarora in three different trials in three villages. Two of the three villages found them guilty, and the surveyor general was tortured and killed, but the baron was let go on the understanding that he could not settle on Tuscarora land without permission. The fate of the black slave was not reported, but it is not hard to imagine he joined the Tuscarora as a free man. In reaction, a settler captured a Tuscarora Peace Chief and cooked him alive without a trial at all. This led to enormous tensions that spread across the countryside, turning into heavy fighting. The British authorities sent troops to settle the differences, starting with the assumption that the problem was the Tuscarora. Taking the side of the settlers, they overwhelmed the Tuscarora villages and rounded up four hundred Tuscarora who they sold into slavery at 10 pounds sterling each to defray the costs of the war. There was no chance of having a hearing, of finding common ground. The surviving Tuscarora fled to the Five Nations, where they were welcomed as a Sixth Nation in 1722.[121]

A select group of White settlers might have understood the Covenant Chain as a means for two distinct entities to co-exist and trade as equals, but most did not even see the Indigenous Peoples as human. The population density of the English-speaking settlers had become so great that they no longer made room for anyone else, and other than slaves, they countenanced no visible minorities. It was not enough that others spoke English and traded, they also had to be English-speaking, White, and Christian.

At the same time, the British still needed to preserve the goodwill of the Six Nations in the event of any war with the French. Both the French and English could each tolerate only one jurisdiction, a hierarchy built from God down to an underclass with both men and women fitting into the social strata at their own class-defined levels. Both colonial hierarchies contrasted with the complex, multi-jurisdictional structure of the Indigenous Peoples with their jurisdictional respect extending beyond humans to the other creatures. They tried to accept both the French and English as siblings in their family of Nations, but the European social structures could only integrate them into a vertical hierarchy. While the French had been formally accepted and recognized in 1701, their driving priorities were still feudal. Nor could the British co-exist with the French in this rich, new world. These Europeans could tolerate only a single jurisdiction, and the English-Protestant one was a rapidly evolving market economy in which everything had a price while the French were still trying to maintain and expand Christendom. The European Wars of Religion were continuing.

At the Treaty of Lancaster in 1744, in which the now Six Nations of the Haudenosaunee were protesting the expansion of British colonists onto their homeland, the lieutenant governor of Pennsylvania, George Thomas, reminded them of the threat the French had always posed to them and how the British had always been their friends. The next day the governor of Maryland, Thomas Bladen, proceeded to accuse the Covenant Chain representatives of threatening war and trying to intimidate their friends, the British. The treaty process took days and involved ritual formalities. Answers needed to be contemplated. In our times, we encourage people to stop and think for a minute before responding, but for the Haudenosaunee, a night's sleep was considered a more reasonable period to reflect. On the morning of June 26, Chief Canassatego, leader of the Onondaga Nation and spokesperson for the Covenant Chain, quietly countered the many arguments of the governor, patiently explaining to him the geography that had been occupied without permission by the colonists, and then questioning the governor's reference to the great length of time the province of Maryland had existed.

Brother, Governor of Maryland

When you mentioned the affair of the land yesterday, you went back to old times, and told us you had been in possession of the Province of Maryland above one hundred years, but what is one hundred years in comparison of the length of time since our claim began, since we came out of the ground? We must tell you that long before one hundred years our ancestors came out of this very ground, and their children have remained here ever since. You came out of the ground in a country that lies beyond the seas. There, you may have a just claim, but here you must allow us to be your elder brethren, and the lands to belong to us long before you knew anything about them.[122]

Repeatedly, even through these tumultuous times, the Six Nations offered their friendship and their wisdom that was born "out of the ground" here. Their friendship was an invitation to become a part of their family, their world; to be open to learning from them. They were aware of the instabilities in the colonial world, not just because of the hierarchies that created poverty, want, and greed, but also because of the distrust the governors themselves had for each other. He gave examples in a calm, clear dissertation.

After reiterating their historic relationship with the Dutch, whom they trusted completely, and how all their partnership with the English had been built on that trust, he told how the governor of New York had advised them not to trust "Brother Onas," the governor of the Pennsylvania Colony, with any land. He encouraged them to entrust the land to him instead, so he could protect it for them against such an acquisition. Then Canassatego explained how the governor of New York, meeting Brother Onas in England, sold him the entrusted land for a great price. He made it clear that their relationships had reached a point of distrust. He calmly criticized the young Englishmen who told them that without English hatchets and guns they would have perished. He said instead that their fathers told them how much better they had lived in their land of plenty with their stone hatchets and bows and arrows."

As the British colonies expanded, built on the backs of slaves, exploited workers, and the disenfranchised, rebellions fomented in the ports. They were ruthlessly suppressed, leaving isolated underclasses. Through the first fifty years of the 1700s, this alienation contributed to the Grand Awakening, Christian Evangelism that tended to unify the religious thinking of the people in the various colonies. They all worshipped the same god, were all a part of the same market, all had similar legal systems. Evangelism found places for the disenfranchised to belong, but the real religion was the market economy based on wealth and property. Evangelism, with its focus on the individual's relationship with God, lent the underclasses a sense of belonging while incorporating them into a religious hierarchy that controlled dissension. This sense of autonomy worked well together with the market economy where individual actions and abilities could be translated into purchasing power, but where failure was personal. It was a different sense of self from the sensibilities of the French Catholic feudal system with its contained seigneurial communities all answerable to a single, bureaucratic hierarchy. Both hierarchies were foreign to the experience of communal belonging in traditional Indigenous communities.

British settlers, with their ego-centred sense of self, would not continue to respect the Two Row Wampum that underpinned the Covenant Chain. It created an obligation to respect an incomprehensible value system. By 1750, agents were claiming to have acquired land in the Ohio Valley that was under the jurisdiction of the Six Nations. As well, Albany traders claimed to have made an agreement with the Mohawk concerning 325,000 hectares of their prime New York territory. Two vastly different cultures were blind to each other's different realities. One thought as a group, seeking balance, while the other consisted of independent individuals, each one looking out for himself.

Chief Hendrick, a Mohawk of the Six Nations, met with New York governor George Clinton in 1753 and informed him,

> Brother when we came here to relate our Grievances about our Lands, we expected to have something done for us, and we have told you that the Covenant Chain of our Forefathers was like to be broken, and brother you tell us that we shall be redressed at Albany, but we know them so well, we will not trust to them, for they [the Albany merchants] are no people but Devils so... as soon as we come home we will send up a Belt of Wampum to our Brothers the other Five Nations to acquaint them the Covenant Chain is broken between you and us. So brother you are not to expect to hear of me any more, and Brother we desire to hear no more of you.[123]

The Covenant Chain broke.

CHAPTER 33

Sir William Johnson

Among English colonists and power brokers, William Johnson was a rare exception. He thought like Dutch and French traders, respecting the Nationhood of his trading partners. As a Crown liaison, he created real competition for French/Five Nation relations.

The Albany Congress was not capable of repairing the Covenant Chain; the distrust was too great. Wampum Belts sent to the other five members of the Six Nations meant that the Six Nations—and the other Nations in their Covenant Chain treaty—could be at war with the British. The British government immediately took back responsibility for diplomacy with the Indigenous Nations. In 1755, William Johnson[124] was named Superintendent of Northern Indians based in New York, dealing directly with England.

Johnson's first concern was the French. He knew already how much of the old Wendat territories were being repossessed by Algonquian allies of New France, of the success of the peace treaty in Montreal, La Grande Paix of 1701, and that the Six Nations had been signatories. He had good relations with the Mohawk but would have to act fast to reinstate the Covenant Chain.

A charismatic man, Johnson left a colourful past in Ireland, getting expelled from college. He arrived in America in 1738 thanks to his uncle, British American Admiral Peter Warren. His uncle, in his turn, had married Susan De Lancy, descendant of a Huguenot who, fleeing France, had married into a New York Dutch family in 1686. Johnson became a part of this Huguenot family, finding kindred spirits, until he felt he was ready to move to the Mohawk Valley to farm. Aside from his relations with the fun-loving De Lancys, Johnson was not a fit in Albany. He was very independent, shunning advances from Albany society. When he set up his farm, he bought an indentured servant whom he married on her deathbed to legitimize their children. Thereafter, virtually all his social contacts were with the Mohawk, a people he understood. His early years were spent wrestling with Mohawk warriors and learning their language and culture.

After his wife's death, he took a Mohawk wife, marrying her in the Mohawk Tradition, but he was away more than he was home. She could not share the house with the new, strict governess of his children who did not approve of her. There was nothing in Iroquoian culture to stigmatize her leaving—she even left him a son.

Johnson had made appeals to Mohawk families who had abandoned their traditional territory in favour of the Ohio Valley, enticing them to return. He met one of these returning families on Militia Day in 1753, a recent widow named Margaret, along with her children, who were in the company of Johnson's friend Nickus Brant, a Dutch-Mohawk trader. His regiment was involved in a horse race between British officers and Mohawk riders when one of the officers challenged Margaret's young daughter, Molly, to accompany him or to take his horse into the race. When Johnson saw her leap gracefully onto the horse, he was stricken with love. He had met his match in Molly Brant.

When he was asked to be Superintendent of Northern Indians, the Six Nations accepted him as their ambassador, a man who could speak Mohawk and understood the nuances of their diplomacy. The Covenant Chain had been repaired. Four years later, in 1759, Molly Brant took over Johnson's house with fervour. They became a power couple who shocked the Albany elite and deeply pleased the Mohawk, where she became head of the influential Society of Matrons. Molly Brant's name was Konwatsi'tsiaiénni in the Mohawk language, but history knows her also as Mary Brant.

Brant and Johnson's care of her brother Thayendanegea, or Joseph Brant, served to reinforce his status among the Mohawk. Educated in White society as well as in the Iroquoian of his birth, he would be respected among the Six Nations as a successor to Johnson.

Johnson established one the greatest fortunes in the Thirteen Colonies. A loyal Brit, a warrior who knew how to fight the French, and a

shrewd businessman, he was recognized with a knighthood. He
and his son John were also among
the most controversial characters
in early New York history. Sir William took John with him on some
of his military campaigns and
John became a respected military
leader in his own right.

Sir William maintained ethical standards in all his dealings,
honouring trade agreements as
fairly with Six Nations people as
with the English. While his principal trading partners were the
Mohawk, word of his respect and
fairness spread rapidly. He was
among the first traders to oppose
selling rum to the Indigenous
Peoples and, at the request of the
Mohawk, he acted for them as

Sir William Johnson

their liaison with White society. While he built a prestigious home and
maintained civil relations with the rich and powerful, his house would
often be filled with visiting Six Nations dignitaries sleeping willy-nilly on
the floor of the main room or camping on the grounds around the house.
His skill in listening to them and in respecting their customs, along with
his eloquence in speaking publicly at Mohawk councils, won Six Nations'
support for the British Crown. He also promoted rules of trade that would
recognize Covenant Chain trading practices. For the Six Nations, no
major agreement was valid unless the women of the clan had approved
it. Johnson attempted to have this rule enforced in any trading with the
Six Nations that involved land transactions. He, like the Six Nations, was
trying to invalidate transactions in which a Chief would be given liquor
so he would agree to an unequal deal, and, once sober, would be called
upon to respect the bargain.

Johnson was not above using Six Nations' rules to his advantage, acquiring great swaths of Mohawk land for himself and brokering the sale of parcels to his friends. During a meeting with a group of Mohawk, a Chief told Johnson he had dreamed his great friend had made a gift of a special rifle that hung above his mantelpiece. Knowing the powerful influence of dreams, Sir William promptly went and fetched the rifle, presenting it to the Chief. Some long time later, in a similar meeting, Johnson told the Chief of a dream he had had where the Chief's people had given Johnson title to a tract of land. Outsmarted, the Chief confirmed the gift but told Johnson he could no longer afford to dream with him because Johnson's dreams were too big.

Johnson understood what had to be done to protect Six Nations' territory and culture. He had an obligation to codify this knowledge but that would have obliged him to respect it himself. He never worked in a coherent fashion with the Crown to create a body that could enforce restrictions on the sale of land, as well as to establish administrative oversight and licences for traders, interpreters, and gunsmiths. He felt that kind of work could be done by raising the funds through a liquor tax to cover the costs involved.

His status was as a colonial leader whose mandate circumvented the colonies, coming directly from the Crown. His perception of the Six Nations as independent allies of the British was at odds with the perception that the governors of the British colonies held. They saw all "Indians" simply as being in the way of colonial expansion. The Six Nations came to see Johnson as their main defender.

CHAPTER 34

The Seven Years' War

The Seven Years' War for European hegemony was called the French and Indian Wars here, and it covered nine years, but it was also a war between Great Britain and France over international trade, a step towards hierarchical domination.

Running from 1756 to 1763, the Seven Years' War is considered by some historians as the first global conflict. The spark that set it off locally had happened two years earlier in the Ohio Valley.

France was working to colonize the Mississippi River Basin all the way to its colony at the Gulf of Mexico. The source area of the Ohio River, called Pays d'en Haut (highland country), describing its headwaters, was a rich area for trade beyond the influence of the Six Nations' Covenant

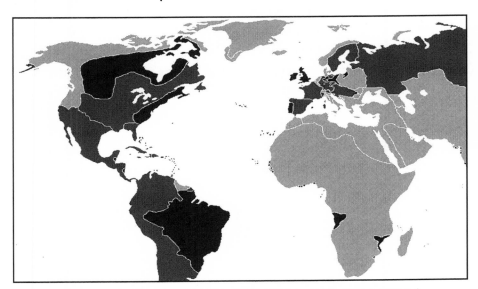

The Seven Years' War pitted British and allied kingdoms (black) against French and allied kingdoms (dark grey) in a war of hegemony over trade.

Chain. As importantly, the Ohio River, 1,500 kilometres long, joins the Mississippi River. From there, it is only a further 1,300 kilometres to the Gulf Coast. The French felt that a string of outposts along the rivers would allow them to make treaties with the different Indigenous Nations, establish trade, and secure the territory for France.

A problem arose with the European Peace Treaty of Aix-la-Chapelle, signed in 1748. France and Great Britain were signatories but not the principal antagonists, yet it obliged them to accept peace. That same war was called King George's War in the French and British colonies and involved various local players, including the Six Nations of the Haudenosaunee, who controlled the Covenant Chain alliance. War made encroachment possible, but now Britain and France were at peace.

In 1751, the French named Marquis Duquesne de Menneville as the new governor of New France with instructions to secure the trading territory on the Ohio River. He undertook to build Fort Duquesne at the junction where the Allegheny and Monongahela Rivers merged to form the Ohio River. The fort was serviced through a string of three other forts that led back through lesser tributaries and a portage to Lake Erie. Great Britain, France, and the Six Nations all claimed the Ohio country as a part of their territories. The French by the Doctrine of Discovery, the Six Nations by their presence, and the British because they interpreted their Covenant Chain treaty with the Six Nations as meaning that the Six Nation territory and its Covenant Chain members were a protectorate of the British Crown.

A part of the Ohio Valley was also the traditional territory of the Shawnee, an Algonquian people. They all cohabited with Iroquoian-speaking Wyandot and other refugee groups such as the Miami and Delaware, many of whom had been pushed out of their territories by the advance of the British settlers.

The Six Nations, when they learned of the British claim to be their protectors, ridiculed it because they did not perceive themselves as a protectorate but as a trading partner. Their comprehension was founded upon the Kaswentha, the Two Row Wampum, made with the Dutch in 1613. When the French succeeded in establishing trade with the different Nations living on the Six Nation-claimed territory, the Six Nations appointed some Wyandot Chiefs to represent themselves and the Shawnee in Six Nation council meetings, giving them the title of Half-Chief. The French proceeded to plant lead plates at strategic locations to identify the territory as theirs. The Ohio Seneca[125] objected. They appealed to the Six Nation council through their Half-Chiefs, or Half-Kings, that they did not wish to be locked into the French trading alliance.

The French knew how a show of force could change their thinking, so they appealed to their Indigenous allies in French-controlled Michili-mackinac, and a party of three hundred Ottawa and Ojibwe descended upon and destroyed a British trading post and a Miami village nearby. This caused a temporary reversal of loyalties and many came back to the French trading alliance. The Six Nations, ill equipped to start a war with the French, acknowledged some dependence upon the British and invited them to protect these lands from the French. To do so, the British began the construction of Fort Prince George at the same junction where the Allegheny and Monongahela Rivers merged to form the Ohio River.

The British Virginia Colony sent the young George Washington to peacefully protest to the French at their first fort, built on the small Le Boeuf River a short distance via portage to Lake Erie. He was politely received and accommodated, but his address was rejected. He was told that he would have to travel to Quebec, to the governor, to present it.

The French, determined to build their most important fort at the exact location where the British were building theirs, and feeling the momentum of their previous attacks, descended upon the construction of Fort Prince George, destroying it. They then built their Fort Duquesne on the same site. The French, convinced of their indisputable title to the Ohio Valley through the Doctrine of Discovery, next sent a small party to intercept George Washington who had returned to the Ohio Valley with troops, urged by Virginia to examine settlement potential.

Joseph Coulon de Villiers, Sieur de Jumonville, had been sent from the new Fort Duquesne to admonish Washington for violating the Peace Treaty of Aix-la-Chapelle, signed in Aachen, northwestern Germany, in 1748, by crossing into French territory. His role was the same as the role George Washington had filled, coming to the fort on Le Boeuf River the previous year.

One of the Wyandot Chiefs, who history remembers only as Half-King, was travelling with the French. When they had bedded down for the night, he left and went to Washington to tell him French soldiers were approaching to attack them but that with his help, they could be surprised. He led them back to Jumonville's party in the early morning.

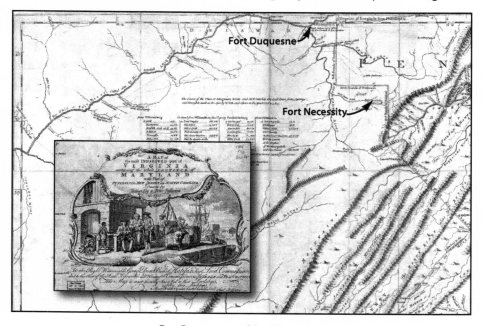

Fort Duquesne and Fort Necessity

When Washington's men saw the surprised French going for their guns, they began to fire. Jumonville managed to make his presence felt and calmed the two sides. Through his translator, he successfully communicated that he and his party were messengers representing the French authorities, and then he began to read a proclamation reminding them of the terms of the treaty. Each party was in a serious position of weakness—the French because it was just a small group of messengers and Washington's party because they were arguably in French territory with no backup. This should have been the end of the encounter, with Washington proclaiming some purpose for his being there and both parties withdrawing with messages for each other's commanders. From the French point of view, it would demonstrate the power of a small, peaceful band of Frenchmen to evict the British troops from the territory. However, as the translator repeated the proclamation in English, the chieftain recorded as Half-King shot Jumonville in the head at point-blank range. In the mêlée that ensued, nine other members of the French party were shot dead and the rest, except for one, were taken prisoner.

The sole escapee returned to Fort Duquesne. The French responded by overwhelming Washington at his hastily erected Fort Necessity. They served him with a humiliating defeat but allowed him and his men to return to British territory unarmed and on foot. The humiliation cannot be overstated. The First Nations in the Ohio Valley were crucial allies to both European powers, and, lacking any other means of evaluating these two warring European nations, they tended to back the stronger side.

Was Half-King's objective to encourage the two sides to fight so that the Wyandot, Shawnee, and others could have a clearer picture of who they should choose as an ally? He led Washington to the small French party and instigated the confrontation, but he was equally disappointed in both parties after the French overwhelmed Fort Necessity and then let their captives go.

As these things were happening, the Shawnee, Delaware, and Wyandot understood that the Six Nations had given the Ohio Valley to the British to defend it for them. Their loyalties turned against the British, but they did not join the French. When newly-arrived Major General Edward Braddock advanced again to take Fort Duquesne in July 1755, he led an advance party, leaving Virginia and heading towards the Monongahela River. His training was European; he had little or no experience in fighting in the colonies. Once he had crossed the river, he confronted a French party coming to try to block his passage. It was made up of Canadien militiamen and their Indigenous allies, most likely Ottawa and Ojibwe. Firing on them, the disciplined British troops saw them disappear into the woods on both sides of their column, firing at random from the trees. Braddock's soldiers were mowed down. The general was injured. George Washington, who had joined the advance as a volunteer, managed to control the troops, organize a retreat, and save the wounded general, who died once they were back to safety. His last words to Washington were "Who would have thought?" no doubt a reference to his incomprehension of the Indigenous and Canadien war tactics. The French side routed the attackers, but notably absent from their forces were the other Nations of the Ohio, who maintained their neutrality.

The Shawnee and Delaware had sent a delegation to protest the Six Nation's transfer of responsibility for the Ohio Valley to the English. It arrived at the same time as the unfortunate news of Braddock's defeat and death. Their delegation was hanged in revenge. The Shawnee and Delaware responded with force that summer. Over the next two years, they became the terror of Pennsylvania, Virginia, and Maryland, destroying settlements and killing 2,500 settlers.

In the confusion and violence that raged through the Ohio Valley and the fringes of the British colonies, France and England went to war again. Their differences were not limited to the Ohio Valley. England was France's major competitor for a worldwide commercial empire. In their minds, the ensuing war would be one for European—and world—hegemony. The small exchange in the Ohio Valley was just one of the sparks that ignited the flame of war that would establish an international hierarchy of power.

CHAPTER 35

British War Plans

French policy attempted to establish their feudal objectives in 'Indian' country through trade, contrasting with the English colonial explosion of religious dissidents and their territorial expansion. By 1754, the English colonists outnumbered both the French and Indigenous Peoples.

Prime Minister William Pitt the Elder, determined to win this war, looked for people of proven ability and approached General Jean-Louis Ligonier, a career soldier. Ligonier was a Huguenot who had fled Castres, France, to Holland at seventeen years old rather than convert when the French cancelled the Edict of Nantes, forcing the destruction of the French Huguenots. Throughout his adult life, he received depressing news from home of the abuses sustained by the Huguenots who stayed in France. In 1698, he arrived in Ireland as a volunteer soldier in an English regiment and began his climb up the ladder of the British army. When named the overall commander-in-chief of British forces in 1757, he was seventy-seven years old.[126] He was not the kind of enemy France needed as old grudges of the Wars of Religion continued.

Prime Minister Pitt respected Ligonier's strategy of advancing with three different forces, as well as his choice of the young, proven, Colonel Jeffrey Amherst, along with Colonel John Forbes. Both were promoted, Amherst to major general and Forbes to brigadier general. A third, the previous major general, James Abercromby, was already serving in the colonies.

Britain's North American objectives were the capture of Fort Louisbourg in present-day Nova Scotia, Fort Duquesne in present-day Pennsylvania, and Fort Carillon (Fort Ticonderoga), situated at the southern end of Lake Champlain.

Ligonier assigned Fort Louisbourg to General Amherst, who in his turn engaged General James Wolfe. Their ship reconnoitred with the British fleet under Admiral Edward Boscawen in the spring. Chosen also by Ligonier, Boscawen had learned a lot about the French in the failed siege of the French colony of Pondicherry in India in 1748.

The First Foray, Fort Carillon, July 8, 1758

General James Abercromby relied upon one of his most experienced generals, George Howe, to plan and execute the attack on Fort Carillon. Marquis Louis-Joseph de Montcalm, the defender, had 4,000 troops, while Howe had 15,000. Howe and his troops travelled up Lake George, and then along the five miles of river and portages to Lake Champlain. Along the river, they easily routed the advance parties and captured small French settlements. The first real confrontation was with troops trying to return to Fort Carillon. In the ensuing skirmish, General Howe was killed.

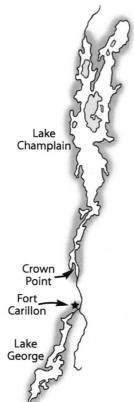

The death of this crucial leader left Abercromby at a loss for what to do. He dallied so long that his troops nicknamed him Mrs. Nambie-Crombie. By the time he had finally resumed the advance, Montcalm had received reinforcements and ordered his men to pile up barriers of brush and fallen trees around Fort Carillon. Abercromby ordered the storming of these barricades but neglected to await the arrival of his superior artillery. As the battle progressed, the British troops were bogged down and slaughtered, losing 2,000 men and being forced to retreat. The French losses were 350 killed and wounded. Abercromby, overwrought and panic-stricken, signalled a retreat and withdrew, not simply along the five miles of river and portages that they had captured, but to the far end of Lake George. When word of the catastrophe reached England, Abercromby was recalled. [127]

General Abercromby's long retreat from Fort Carillon and General Amherst's Crown Point.

Louisbourg, July 26, 1758

Amherst was a careful planner, but later strategists felt he showed too much nerve at Louisbourg, confronting the French at their point of greatest strength outside their own harbour. He commanded 27,000 troops in 157 vessels and was up against Augustin de Boschenry de Drucour, who boasted a mere 3,500 soldiers, some militia, and another 3,800 sailors in the attending French fleet of eleven vessels. The British took more than a week to land their troops for the siege.

The French did not engage or harass them. Instead, Drucour withdrew inside his fortifications and destroyed his guns mounted outside the walls above the harbour. He depended upon his navy to draw the British fire as the British forces climbed the banks in preparation for a siege, but most of the French captains wished to escape to the open sea to engage the British navy—or run for home. Only Jean Vauquelin, captain of the Aréthuse, turned his guns on the advancing British. Had other French ships fought with as much courage, some strategists feel, they may have turned the tables and repelled the invaders. Finally, on July 9, British cannon fire silenced the Aréthuse's guns. Within a few days, her courageous captain managed to slip her out to sea where she escaped to France.

Inside the fort, the outnumbered French soldiers fought with courage. Even Madame Boschenry de Drucour mounted the ramparts, shooting at the British when she was not ministering to the wounded.

British cannon fire was destroying the walls. Forced to ask for terms, Drucour and his officers learned that Amherst refused them the honours of war and insisted on a complete surrender. His soldiers refused the terms, determined to fight for their honour and property, but the risk to the civilian population was too great and Drucour accepted British terms on July 26.

The significance of this kind of surrender, aside from the loss of honour, was that the surrendering forces lost their personal property. Drucour, for instance, died in penury. The French courts judged that he had achieved the objective of delaying the British advance on the fort at Quebec by one year and had protected the civilian population from pillage, but his reward was the favourable judgment. He was not further compensated for his losses. There was a strong element of self-sacrifice in surrendering without the honours of war. The civilians, at least, would not be molested. The third option, refusing to surrender, may be considered brave but the resulting pillage was not controllable.

Leaving Wolfe to raid French ports in the Gulf of St. Lawrence, Amherst travelled to Boston to relieve General James Abercromby. Wolfe had not been the decision-maker in this battle. His skills executing the tasks Amherst set for him earned praise from his commander, and upon his return to England, Wolfe learned that he had been chosen to lead the raid on Quebec the following year.

Fort Duquesne, November 24, 1758

It fell to Brigadier General John Forbes, a Scot who came late to his military career, to take Fort Duquesne. Arriving in Philadelphia in early 1758, he had to deal with solicitations from both the Pennsylvania and Virginia colonies, each with a vested interest in the Ohio Valley. General Braddock had proceeded from Virginia, and it appeared to be the simplest route, but Forbes was concerned about the risks of flooding. He chose a route from the small town of Raystown, currently called Bedford, in Pennsylvania. Before him was about three hundred kilometres over rolling countryside, where he would have to build a road, and he determined to build supply forts not further than sixty kilometres apart. He had at his disposal 5,000 colonial militiamen plus roughly 2,000 career soldiers. His progress was slow. Forbes was aware of the raids that the Shawnee and Delaware were inflicting across the colonies, but eventually the settlers had learned that they were not allies of the French. To calm the tensions and to ensure their neutrality in the taking of Fort Duquesne, the colonial authorities had renounced their claim to the Ohio Valley.

Terminally ill as he was during this advance, Forbes, chosen by General Ligonier, was an excellent strategist and meticulous planner, but no amount of planning could have predicted what he found when his forces finally arrived at Fort Duquesne on November 25.

On September 14, without his authority, an advance party of eight hundred, led by Major James Grant, met the French and were severely beaten. The concern, aside from the defeat, was that the French knew they were approaching, but something unexpected happened. As October passed and November began, the French relaxed. They were dependent upon the Canadien militia and Indigenous Nations, allies from closer to the French home base. These non-professional fighters wanted to get back for the hunting season, to prepare stock for winter and the following spring. The French decided it was time to step down defences for the winter. A day out of the fort, Forbes sent a garrison to plant explosives around the fort and blow it up. Carried in a sling between two horses because of his advanced illness, when he arrived at the site the next day Forbes found nothing but a smouldering pile of rubble. After five months of careful preparations and slow advance, their victory was bloodless.

With his huge, well-equipped force, Forbes began immediately to build Fort Pitt on the same site. The French were gone, but the Ohio Seneca, Shawnee and Delaware watched in disillusion as the British took possession of the territory.

Vaudreuil and Montcalm 1760

Marquis Louis-Joseph de Montcalm, Seigneur of Saint-Véran, Candiac, Tournemine, Vestric, Saint-Julien and Arpaon, Baron de Gabriac and lieutenant general in the French army, was the scourge of the English in America. He is worshipped as a hero of French-Canadian history, but did he deserve the praise? Despite all of his titles, does history recognize the right man?

Born in Candiac, France, in 1712, he became an ensign at nine years of age. By seventeen, he was a captain in the Régiment d'Hainaut. He subsequently fought in, and lost, a series of European battles, was wounded in two successive ones and was taken prisoner. At the age of forty, he petitioned for a pension, but with the start of the Seven Years' War, he was forced back into service and sent to New France.

Montcalm was sternly informed he would be the subordinate of Pierre de Rigaud de Vaudreuil, governor general of New France. His responsibility would be limited to the administration of the army. This must have caused some resentment on the part of a thirty-year veteran of the French army who had at one time served in the capacity of brigadier. Vaudreuil was a lowly colonial, the first Quebec-born governor general—

a Canadien. Since Montcalm was subordinate to Vaudreuil, he was also obliged to accept the latter's battle plans. From the beginning, the two were at odds. Vaudreuil, born in the colony, had risen through the ranks to become governor of Louisiana before being assigned to New France. The colonial forces, consisting largely of Canadiens[128] who had fought the Five Nations juggernaut in the Great Lakes, knew how to fight alongside their Indigenous allies. Under Vaudreuil's guidance, they succeeded in constantly keeping the British off-balance. They used guerilla tactics that allowed their much smaller numbers to tie the enemy down in many defensive positions. Before Montcalm, Vaudreuil had had to contend with his predecessor, Jean-Armand Dieskau, another French army general without experience in the American colony. Dieskau, like Montcalm after him, insisted on a European style of fighting that involved shoring up defences and waiting for the enemy. They were also both career soldiers, men who always kept an eye on their own advancement. When Dieskau failed to obey Vaudreuil's orders in one campaign, and was taken prisoner by the British, Vaudreuil sent a plea to France asking that he not be replaced. He reasoned that the French regulars did not respect the colonials or the Indigenous allies, and the French officers were not willing to heed advice or follow orders. His request was denied, and Montcalm was sent to replace Dieskau.

In true European style, Montcalm surrounded the British Fort William Henry in August of 1757, demanding its surrender. When the commander refused, Montcalm resorted to standard siege tactics, cutting off the fort and bombarding it with cannon. Within three days, the commander offered to negotiate a surrender, and the terms were to show the British defenders the honours of war, allowing them to march out of the fort with their arms and personal property. They were even offered an escort to the next British fort. They, in turn, had to guarantee they would not take up arms against the French for eighteen months.

Their Indigenous allies, largely Potawatomi Algonquian resident at that time in the region of Detroit, did not understand the finer points of European warfare. Once they were moved to fight, they were hard to stop. The surrender of Fort William Henry confused them to such a point that the defeated British soldiers needed protection from the Indigenous allies of the French. The warriors attacked the defeated army, killing, pillaging, and taking prisoners, in some cases torturing them. The fight was in part for prisoners who could be adopted by their captors. Vaudreuil told him the Indigenous allies were indispensable, but Montcalm came away with a poor impression of them. An unanticipated result of their close fighting caused the Potawatomi to contract smallpox. Bringing it back to their villages, it spread, effectively removing many French allies from the war.

Montcalm proved much better in knowing how to vaunt his success to their French superiors than in being subordinate to Vaudreuil. In four successive battles, even one that should have been lost, Montcalm emerged victorious, reluctantly following Vaudreuil's orders. While he became a hero to the French regulars and a terror to the British, he lost the support of the Indigenous allies and the Canadien regulars. Each of his victories was earned following the strategy of Vaudreuil, but he was not gracious, seeking only his own advancement. The hero of the day was the Canadien governor general, not the general under him. At Fort Carillon, Montcalm repelled an attack by the inept General Abercromby, and his star rose. He used the victory to undermine Vaudreuil's authority.

While Vaudreuil had allies in France, coming from the French navy he did not have the necessary connections in the army hierarchy. He had, therefore, come to rely on his ability to deal with these problems in the field with finesse and patience. In one story from Louisiana, he managed to drive his Crown-appointed comptroller, a famously argumentative fellow, to the point of a fatal apoplectic fit simply through Vaudreuil's consistent civility.

Vaudreuil attempted to have Montcalm re-assigned to France, recommending him for a promotion on the understanding Montcalm would be transferred to the European theatre of war. At the last minute, the king personally cancelled the transfer, leaving Montcalm in New France, now outranking Vaudreuil thanks to the very promotion Vaudreuil had recommended.

With his new authority, Montcalm immediately changed the colony's military strategy, pulling back from Vaudreuil's guerilla tactics. Instead, he reinforced his strong position at Quebec and waited for the British to come to him. At the same time, he did not override Vaudreuil's position as governor general, because that would have made Montcalm directly responsible for failure.

His strategy was to withstand a siege in the fort at Quebec through the summer, knowing winter would force the British to withdraw. The down-river defences where the French forces could have hurt the British on their approach were being neglected and, in late May, the British arrived at Quebec in full force. Even so, it was well understood they would have until about September 20 before being obliged to withdraw for the winter, and the French could easily withstand the summer siege. The British could do no more than move threateningly back and forth along the river, avoiding or carefully towing, floating fires that the French launched upstream.

On September 13, Wolfe made a bold landing and successfully placed his army on the Plains of Abraham. No-one can explain what happened next; Montcalm was in a position of strength. He was still well defended behind the walls of Quebec. The British had only a week before they would have to withdraw. A large portion of the French troops was far upriver where they had anticipated Wolfe would land, and only a smaller force, less well trained than Wolfe's, was at Montcalm's immediate disposal. But instead of waiting coolly for his troops to return, Montcalm panicked. Leaving the security of his fortified position, he attacked the British with his inferior force. Had he simply waited, the British would have had to climb back down the cliffs to their boats within days, leaving them exposed and in retreat.

Both Wolfe and Montcalm were killed in the ensuing battle. Wolfe's forces ultimately occupied Quebec. Vaudreuil had sent urgent messages to the effect that Montcalm should remain inside the walls of Quebec and wait. Still, Vaudreuil was held responsible for the loss. The fall of Quebec, while only one of the battles that decided the war in the Americas, was symbolically the most significant. The French had held Quebec, the capital of the Royal Province of Quebec, for over a century. The morale of the defending forces plummeted.

Amherst at Lake Champlain 1760

Both General Amherst and General Montcalm learned their war methods in Europe. Neither had much use for what they perceived to be the undisciplined methods of their Indigenous allies in North America. Each general had been appointed to head his country's military operations during a series of battles that had started long before, a period remembered as the French and Indian Wars. With Montcalm dead in Quebec, the leader of the French was the Canadien Pierre de Rigaud de Vaudreuil, who understood and exploited the guerrilla tactics of the Indigenous Nations while the wily Sir William Johnson, the British Superintendent of Indian Affairs, had managed to maintain the allegiance of the powerful Six Nations Confederacy and Covenant Chain.

Amherst sent General John Prideaux west to take Fort Niagara. He intended to move up through Lake Champlain with his army and take Montreal, the same route that his predecessor, General Abercromby, had followed. When Abercromby had moved north a few years earlier, he confronted Montcalm at Fort Carillon, the French fort at the south end of Lake Champlain.

With the great distances and slow communications, as far as the French troops on Lake Champlain were concerned Montcalm was still in charge. Following Montcalm's instructions, they were waiting for the approach of the enemy behind the walls of Fort Carillon. As a result, Amherst did not meet the same kind of resistance as Abercromby and Howe had met. They were unchallenged in their march up the lakes. General François-Charles de Bourlamaque commanded 3,000 troops at Fort Carillon this time. He would face Amherst's force of 11,000 colonial and British troops. The proportions were about the same as in the previous rout, but European style did not include defending a fort against such a strong advance. Bourlamaque left only four hundred defenders whose instructions were to delay a few days and then blow up the fort as they retreated to Fort St. Frederic further up the lake.

The taking of the fort was a gift to Amherst, just like Fort Duquesne had been for Brigadier General John Forbes. Another factor was the situation of those Indigenous allies of the French along the St. Lawrence

Valley. Astute analysts of the relative strengths of the French and British opposing parties, the Seven Fires of Canada could see that their small confederacy could be crushed by the British advance.

They perceived themselves as independent allies of the French, but aware of their relatively small size, they needed to contemplate their survival in the face of the warring European nations. The Six Nations to the south, allies of the English, alerted them to their need to seek neutrality and Sir William Johnson sent a warning that if they did not, they would face obliteration. With masterful diplomatic skills, they managed to maintain their independence from both European nations from 1759. When the French called them to a strategy meeting to defend Fort Isle-aux-Noix at the south end of the Richelieu River, they were aware of Amherst's advancing army, and retiring to consider their position they returned to the French with two conditions. The first was that the French should supply 5,000 troops to aid with the siege, and second, that they reserved some time to analyse the strength of the advancing army. This was a fair test because they had to assess whether the French were fully committed before offering themselves as martyrs or cannon fodder. The French simply could not come up with the troops necessary. Acting to-

Crown Point, a monument to a careful man.

gether, they conserved their independent status, and when the war was over, they remained independent Nations with their own treaty with the British.

Once in Fort Carillon (Fort Ticonderoga), Amherst began a cautious exploration of Lake Champlain, where he discovered that Bourlamaque had abandoned and destroyed Fort St. Frederic as well, withdrawing into the Richelieu Valley. In the meantime, General Prideaux was killed in action in his attempts to take Fort Niagara. Sir William Johnson and his Six Nations allies helped to complete the job.

Military historians criticize Amherst for moving so slowly up the lake, just as they criticized him for his boldness when he took Fort Louisbourg the year before, but the news he received from the west of the death of General Prideaux was followed in the early fall with the news of the death of General Wolfe. On top of that, the strategic location of Fort St. Frederic at Pointe à la Chevelure, renamed Crown Point, was too alluring to neglect. He now anticipated confronting the full force of the French in the Richelieu Valley and at Montreal. He must have felt that the fort would be an essential defence to return to if all went wrong. He built what has been called the largest British fort in North America, a complex that covered nine hundred hectares—a monument to a careful man. Amherst also undertook to build four ships to counter the French boats his scouts had identified. With minimal losses, he proceeded up the lake, laying siege to Fort Isle-aux-Noix on the Richelieu River.

There is also much second-guessing as to what the French could have done differently. The British and French did not share the continent happily and there is little likelihood that the British would have been deterred had they lost a few more battles. Their naval superiority allowed them to blockade ports, their colonial population was vastly superior in numbers, and most importantly, they were ready to spend whatever it took to win. New France was only one small element in a global conflict for market share and control of the seas—a conflict that would not end with the Seven Years' War but would recommence in the battle against Napoleon in the next century.

Had governor Vaudreuil remained in control of the colonial forces in New France, he may have made its acquisition too expensive for the

British, in which case it may have remained a colony of France. But the outcome of the war could have been the same elsewhere—the sugar islands, access to parts of India, the Orient, and so on were still in play. It has been argued that in the battle for New France and Acadia, the French saw these possessions as expendable and failed to finance and reinforce them properly. Voltaire's famous quote that is associated with the Treaty of Paris in 1763, "*quelques arpents de neige*" (a few acres of snow), reflects indifference to these subsistence colonies. All that was being given up was the fur trade—even the Grand Banks fishing grounds would still have been part of the open seas and any small islands would give sufficient access to that. The European protagonists were so self-absorbed, so convinced of their centrality, that the several Indigenous Nations who had fought as allies for one side or the other were not informed of the treaty negotiations. In fact, the Seven Fires, having negotiated neutrality, fared better than those allied with the British.

General James Murray, who succeeded General Wolfe in Quebec, still had to contend with both the French army and the militias that came close to winning Quebec back.

Major General Jeffery Amherst is criticized for not coming faster to Montreal to draw French defences away from Quebec. Instead, he made elaborate plans to proceed cautiously to Montreal in 1760, the summer after Quebec had fallen. Leaving the Lake Champlain front to a subordinate, he took the better part of his forces up to the Great Lakes and assumed leadership of the dead General Prideaux's forces. For their part, the French, with the governor general in charge, were forced to draw their forces back to Montreal from Quebec, in anticipation of the inexorable movement of Amherst's two-pronged approach. As the French moved to protect Montreal, many of their own colonial and Indigenous allies abandoned them, leaving a hopelessly small force. Of course, Murray's forces followed them too. All would be decided there.

Amherst met serious resistance at Fort Lévis, an island east of Prescott, confronting Captain Pierre Pouchot who had surrendered Fort Niagara the year before to Sir William Johnson. Pouchot and a party of fewer than four hundred soldiers delayed the British advance by 13 days, until, on August 25, their fort was in ruins. They damaged two British ships

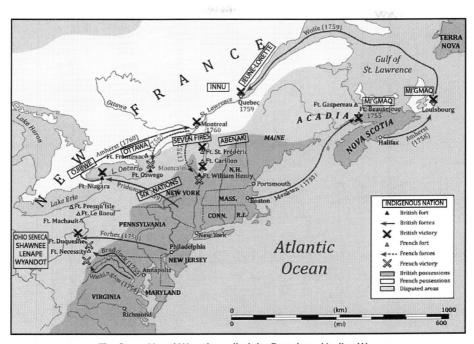

The Seven Years' War, also called the French and Indian War.
North America was no more than an abstract concept to the opposing European hierarchies.

and forced another to withdraw. When Pouchot finally surrendered, Amherst showed him deference, respecting the honours of war for such a valiant defence. The surviving soldiers could leave with their property and would not be destitute. Pouchot had been respected with honours at Fort Niagara as well, but this did not protect him from the opprobrium of the French when he returned to France. To his shock and dismay, he was accused of corruption and forced to defend himself for his contributions to the loss of the colony.

Amherst advanced on Montreal as Generals William Haviland and James Murray were already doing. The only other mishap was the drowning of eighty-four men in the rapids above Montreal on September 4. In his notes, Amherst wrote "I believe never three Armys, setting out from different & very distant Parts from each other joyned in the Center, as was intended, better than we did."[129]

On the Island of Montreal, the situation was much like it had been at Louisbourg a few years earlier. Vaudreuil led brave troops who were willing to fight for their honour and property, but Amherst was not willing to show them that respect. Despite the French soldiers' willingness to fight for their honour and possessions, and counter to the specific directions given from France, Vaudreuil negotiated a peace with Amherst that sacrificed the soldiers' property but spared the civilian population. For his decision, Vaudreuil would spend time in a French prison. The French could not hold a French officer responsible for the loss of New France because of the shame it would bring upon the army. They held Vaudreuil, a colonial and the mastermind behind Montcalm's victories, to blame. The trial was long and arduous. Vaudreuil's wife did not survive to the end, but eventually Vaudreuil was exonerated.

After Amherst's victory, he was ill suited to the peace. He never trusted his Indigenous allies, major players in the whole contest. He ignored Sir William Johnson's recommendation for how to deal with them. Likely, judging from his similar lack of respect for Indigenous warriors, Montcalm would have behaved in a similar fashion had he found himself the victor.

CHAPTER 36

Pontiac and the Proclamation of 1763

*Not shown the respect they deserved, the Indigenous Nations rebelled, led
by the Ohio Seneca and the Ottawa Chief Pontiac. Amherst, frustrated by
this new rebellion, is most strongly remembered for having suggested they
be given hospital blankets infected with smallpox.*

The Ottawa Nation distinguished itself from the earliest days, being a
trading Nation. The word *Ottawa (Odawa)* has been translated as
"traders." They were a part of the Three Fires Confederacy, the Ojibwe,
the Odawa, and the Potawatomi. When the Wendat fell, they filled the
vacuum. They refused to join the Covenant Chain because they were not
willing to surrender their trade with the French. They fought as allies of
the French against the English and the Five Nations before La Grande
Paix of 1701, carrying the French message to their client Nations and
proving to be worthy opponents, dangerous in war, dependable in trade.

After the surrender of Montreal, General Jeffrey Amherst awarded
some Ohio Seneca land to some of his officers without any regard for the
consequences. This land, territory where the French had built forts for
trade and the protection of their Indigenous trading partners, was not
French land. The Seneca, allies of the British during the war and the largest member of the Six Nations Confederacy, immediately sent Wampum
Belts out to their confederacy members, intending to create an uprising
against the British. Amherst's offer to award the land was overruled in
London. The anger died down, but the event heralded a game change.
No longer did they have an option; they were dealing with a monopoly

whose tone rang with arrogance. Dependent upon European products, the new British reality terminated the gift economy. Amherst, profoundly and wilfully ignorant of their culture, saw only the British gifts and not the exchange. He forbade the British giving of gifts, ignoring the meaning of the exchange. Both the French and Sir William Johnson understood and respected the gift economy along with its ceremony and protocol, at least for their own mercantile and political ends. Abandoning it would leave a vacuum, one the French could fill from Louisiana. Once again, Johnson had to act.

An Indigenous prophet named Neolin, known to history as the Delaware Prophet, called for a return to fundamental values and a rejection of White ways, including guns and other goods. His message resonated strongly with the Lenape, or Delaware, and soon spread across the western Nations. Pontiac, an Ottawa Chief who was encouraged by the

French, adopted the religious message of Neolin. The Ottawa and the Ohio Seneca raised an army of warriors, attacking and destroying the forts. About 2,000 British soldiers and settlers were killed in these uprisings and ten forts fell or were under siege. At Fort Pitt, Captain Simeon Ecuyer, under instructions from

The Pontiac Conspiracy, identified with one of its leaders, Chief Pontiac of the Ottawa, was a reaction to the rejection of Indigenous culture at the end of the Seven Years' War.

General Amherst, left smallpox-infected blankets to be taken by the Ohio Seneca, Shawnee and Delaware holding the fort under siege, and an epidemic slowed them down. The Ohio Valley people had little resistance, having been spared the smallpox epidemic brought back to Detroit by the Potawatomi in 1757. This deliberately started epidemic spread through the Shawnee to the Cherokee, the Creek, the Choctaw, and Chickasaw, the latter being British allies against the French in Louisiana, and from there to British settlers in the south, killing thousands.

Sir William Johnson, who had distinguished himself in the Seven Years' War with his allies in the Six Nations, succeeded in having Amherst relieved of his peace-time post. Subsequently, the British reactions included trying to find a means of pacifying the uprising. They drafted the Royal Proclamation of 1763, guaranteeing that lands west of the Proclamation Line were recognized as "Indian Territory," curbing the advance of settlers and licensing traders. The siege of Fort Detroit was the centrepiece of the uprising, continuing through the summer and into autumn.

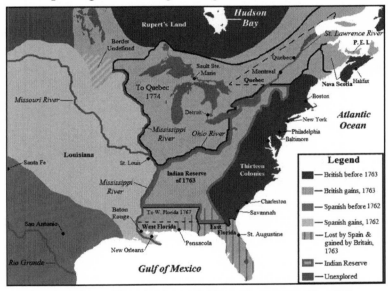

British understanding of territorial divisions after the Seven Years' War.

By mid-October, Indigenous spirits were flagging when they received a message from the French Fort de Chartres on the Mississippi, telling Pontiac about the surrender of the French. With this and the Proclamation, the uprising came to an end despite Pontiac's warnings that the British would slowly expropriate their territory. The most he could accomplish was a treaty acknowledgement that the British had captured the French forts tolerated on Indigenous territory, serving as places to trade. The treaty was signed in 1766 at Fort Ontario in present-day Oswego, NY, in the company of Sir William Johnson.

A misunderstood visionary, Pontiac was, thereafter, feared or revered among the various Indigenous Nations. Three years later, while he was living in the bush near Cahokia, west of the Mississippi, a council of the Peoria had him murdered.

James Murray became the governor of Quebec and Sir William Johnson was involved in organizing a major peace treaty, on the scale of La Grande Paix de Montréal of 1701. Called the Treaty of Niagara, it involved the presentation of eighty-four different Wampum Belts, beads, or pipes. Wampum, the method of contract agreement in many Indigenous cultures, was a sacred exchange of commitment between Nations. The British and Western Great Lakes Covenant Chain Confederacy and the Twenty-Four Nation Wampum Belt are names associated with this treaty. A third belt, the Two Row Wampum, was also presented to Johnson. It codifies the Royal Proclamation, acknowledging Indigenous jurisdiction. One of the problems that this belt presents is that, in British legal tradition, the Royal Proclamation acknowledges British title to the land with British tolerance of Indigenous jurisdiction, but in Indigenous tradition, it is an acknowledgement of separation and autonomy between two peoples. It does not acknowledge British title over the land because land title does not exist in Indigenous law. Since Indigenous law did not include ownership of the land at all, the legacy of both the Royal Proclamation and the Two Row Wampum is at an impasse. This fundamental impasse, crossing two different legal traditions, remains a major stumbling block in colonial and Indigenous reconciliation. It traces back to two different traditions; one, the Western legal system, having evolved through Christian monotheism and the English laws of enclosure, and the other, an understanding of our place in the world in which we belong to the land with the same status as other beings, our siblings.[130]

More immediately for the people everywhere, a new legal template was simply being placed over their historic homelands, and their centuries of stewardship of the forests would be ignored as many struggled with starvation and disease, watching a madness of consumption devour Mother Earth. This madness of consumption feeds on the symbiotic systems of nature. It included the beaver furs, acquired for hats in Europe. Next would come the forests themselves, followed by rules of ownership dividing the land, and subsequently everything, as though it were merchandise.

CHAPTER 37

American War of Independence

British Prime Minister Pitt fought to take over the seas, and thereby reach
world hegemony. Great Britain was within reach of that goal,
but once achieved, among the unintended consequences for the British
was that they had few friends and lots of debts.

There are a lot of reasons given for the rebellion of the American colonists against the British authority. One that captures the imagination but is not often remembered today was that the British navy retained ownership of white pine trees on land that was otherwise ceded to settlers. The navy surveyors would indicate the protected trees with the mark of the arrow, a vertical arrow carved into the tree's trunk. It was a criminal offense to touch that tree.

An early flag of the New England rebels protested the British Navy's reserve of pine trees on private property. Commemorated on a 1968 6¢ stamp, it has also been adopted in this century by the American militant Christian right.

The main mast of a British man-o'-war, or war frigate, stood to the height of a ten-storey building and had a diameter of one metre. Each ship would have two lesser masts and a dozen and a half spars, all needing straight pine timber.[131] At the height of the Seven Years' War, the British had maintained three hundred warships supporting 80,000 naval personnel. Their forestry resources long depleted, Britain was dependent upon the forests of its colonies and what could be purchased from Russia. Even during the war, the colonists were balking, not just at the threat to the pine trees on their settlements and their lack of agency over trees that were growing on their land, but also at the taxes needed to support the empire.

At the height of the Seven Years' War, the British maintained three hundred warships manned by 80,000 naval personnel.

In a book review in the *Literary Review of Canada*,[132] former Canadian diplomat and politician Chris Alexander observes that the Quebec Act of 1774, granting a protective religious status to Catholic Quebec, also exacerbated the tensions. As such, it can also be interpreted as a residual effect of the European Wars of Religion and their continuity in the Americas. Howard Zinn, in *A People's History of the United States*, expresses an even more cynical view, suggesting that it was simply a power grab by the colonial elite.

Tax revolts were increasing, epitomized in the story of the Boston Tea Party, when colonists famously rebelled and threw British tea into the Boston harbour, were increasing. In the case of the Boston Tea Party, the imperial government was administering not only the Thirteen Colonies but many others around the world. In the early 1770s, a famine devastated West Bengal, and one-sixth of its population died. Trying to balance its international network, the British imposed a tax on tea. The American rebels, led by Samuel Adams and John Hancock, had been pirating Dutch tea into the colonies, but the East India Company managed to supply the tea that came to Boston at that time at a cheaper price than the pirates' tea. Adams and Handcock whipped people up and a gang dressed to look like Indians attacked the merchant ships, throwing the tea overboard, no doubt saving the two pirates' investments. A new elite simply had the chance to take over, to push the British out. Today, Samuel Adams figures among the seven Founding Fathers of the United States, while John Hancock, heir to a valuable import-export company, eventually became governor of Massachusetts.

One of the lesser-discussed reasons why the colonists were rebelling was that their huge population was feeling bottled up, hemmed in, by the barriers established through the Proclamation of 1763. The governors of the different colonies saw the Indigenous Nations only in terms of what they could take from them. They had proven their bad faith already, at the Treaty of Lancaster in 1744 and again when Chief Hendrick told Governor George Clinton in New York that the Covenant Chain was broken. At that time, the British had to take relations with the Indigenous Nations out of the governors' hands. Sir William Johnson, answering directly to the Crown, was appointed Superintendent of Indian Affairs in 1755, at the very beginning of the breakdown of peace with the French.

The Mohawk, the easternmost of the Six Nations, had accepted Sir William Johnson as their British ambassador. They felt he was fair, but even he put British interests before those of the Covenant Chain or the interests of the other Indigenous Nations. During the Seven Years' War, he had done his job, succeeding in keeping many of these Nations neutral or on the side of the British. After the war, through the Royal Proclamation of 1763, Johnson

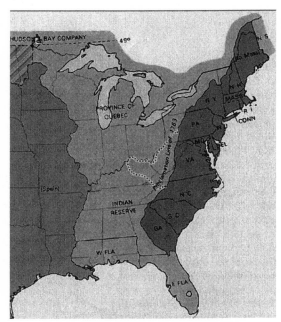

The Proclamation of 1763, defining and attempting to protect Indigenous territory from the expanding Thirteen Colonies was followed five years later with the 1768 Treaty of Fort Stanwix, indicated by the dotted line.

participated in securing them a clear border between the British Thirteen Colonies and the balance of the new British holdings as Britain saw them, assuring the containment of the Thirteen Colonies. He had trouble getting the colonial settlers to respect the Proclamation Line. He tried again with the Treaty of Fort Stanwix in 1768, pushing the southern Nations, not members of the Six Nations, further west. The Six Nations endorsed this treaty, leaving the Delaware Nation, one of the Covenant Chain allies, landless.

The colonists perceived Johnson as an impediment to settler expansion. Rebelling and becoming independent from the British Empire meant that the British Empire, through Sir William Johnson, would no longer speak for the Covenant Chain and other Indigenous Nations.

The Six Nations saw the Thirteen Colonies' aggression as a threat to their sovereignty and culture. Sir William Johnson's partner, Molly Brant, was the head of the Society of Matrons of the Six Nations, and from the Six Nations' point of view, given the power and influence of the Society of Matrons, this was a crucial liaison. From the colonists' perspective, it wasn't proper to cohabit with an "Indian." A trader and importer, Johnson was highly respected in the Mohawk Nation, but he was feared and hated in the White communities, mostly because he treated the Six Nations people as fairly as he treated the settlers, but also because his power as Superintendent of Indian Affairs came directly from London. Johnson was probably the last British American who understood the Six Nations and their trading bloc. He could attend their conferences as one of them and his home was their home. When there were problems with the colonists, he could solve them. He had called upon the Six Nations to be his allies against the French. He travelled with them and understood their society, but he was old and his health was failing. He tried to force respect of the treaties but without success. The floodgate could not be closed. Colonists murdered "Indians" as though for sport and manipulated real estate transactions that would not stand up to Indigenous or British law.

On July 7, 1774, a delegation of six hundred Six Nations leaders gathered at Johnson's home for a council, and slowly, following their customs, the talks began. Respecting protocol, it would not be until July 11 that Johnson could answer their concerns. He talked for hours in the hot sun, using all the demonstrative body language custom required. By the end, he was seized with spasms and was taken to his room. At his bedside, he told Joseph Brant, Molly's brother and Johnson's protégé, "Joseph, control thy people. I am going away." Two hours later, Molly raised her voice in the death wail of her Tradition and the knowledge of his passing was communicated to the delegation. His dramatic death marked the beginning of a period of terror and desperate attempts to organize a resistance.

Johnson Hall, the residence of William Johnson and Molly Brant.

When the war began, Sir John, the principal heir to his father's estate, and his brother-in-law, Guy Johnson (who shared the family surname), stayed loyal to the Crown. All evidence would have led them to see that negotiating with the rebels would not succeed. They were tainted with the colonial brush that stained Sir William in the rebels' eyes. The rebels, as they could see, had little use for the Indigenous Americans and were not likely to accept a state or colony of Six Nations as equal to the other states, or to respect Six Nations sovereignty over their own territory as per the original agreement with the Dutch.

All those years of resentment of the alternative lifestyle of Sir William and the opportunity to grab his estate and the Six Nations territory had left Sir John with little choice but to side with the British. The

Johnsons also had to believe the British would suppress the rebel uprising. The decision would cost Sir John dearly.

Sir John had married Mary Watts and lived peacefully in New York with a son and two daughters. When the war began, he was arrested and released on bail in an attempt to neutralize his influence in the Six Nations community. At first, as they always did, the Six Nations listened carefully to both sides, the British and American. Joseph Brant stayed loyal to the British. He was convinced that the Americans would destroy them whether they were neutral or not. Sir John's arrest confirmed his decision, and Brant became a British officer in 1775, leading warriors against the Americans in the defence of Canada.

The following spring, Sir John learned that his bail was no longer enough for the rebels. He knew he had to escape before he was imprisoned. With the help of his Six Nations allies, he managed to flee to Canada, arriving half-starved on the south shore of the St. Lawrence. He quickly recuperated and offered his services in the war.

Upon his disappearance, Mary Watts Johnson, under effective house arrest, was told if she did not stop her husband, she and her children would pay the price. She was a hostage. With the help of a dedicated enslaved black man, Tony, the brave woman organized the burying of the family valuables, including jewellery, silverware, and documents, and, taking a carriage, managed to escape the control of the rebels. They abandoned the carriage at a crossroads and made their way through the snow to eventually hire a boat and cross a river between ice floes. Tony carried her son and daughter alternately while Mary carried and nursed the baby. Upon reaching the British line, the baby succumbed to exposure and her elder sister caught a fever and died some days later.

Taking sides wasn't as open and shut for the Six Nations. They tried to remain neutral. Molly Brant and her brother Joseph dedicated themselves to uniting their people against the rising tide of the new Americans, encouraging all the Nations to ally with the British. In 1776, the Six Nations recognized the United States but also chose to remain neutral, as did the Seven Fires Confederacy. Neither would ultimately remain neutral. The Oneida and Tuscarora, holding the Presbyterian missionary Samuel Kirkland in high esteem, tended toward siding with the Americans.

The Covenant Chain was losing its influence. Members paid little heed to Six Nations' decisions in the teeming sea of change. They had not forgotten the Six Nation endorsement of the Treaty of Stanwix and its ramifications for the Delaware. The Six Nations had manipulated members to their ends too many times, perhaps following the advice of Sir William. Also, never having given full citizenship to the adopted Wendats, Neutrals, and others, they could do little as these people drifted away, joining the Ohio Seneca, along with the Wyandot, in the Ohio Valley and reducing the Six Nations' eastern core population.

Finally, when the British needed permission to travel through Six Nations territory in an attempt to split New England from the rest of their former colonies, the Six Nations itself extinguished the Council Fire.

An epidemic had taken the lives of several respected Sachems making it difficult to find a consensus. The Oneida Sachem Skenandoah refused to take any action that would alienate the Americans. Kirkland had succeeded in negotiating some real estate understandings with the American authorities. The Oneida did not want to jeopardize what they saw as a potential peaceful coexistence. Brant represented the Mohawk whose territory was to their east and more exposed to Albany and its uncontrollable advances. They had tried in the past to negotiate with the governor, George Clinton, and had no illusions about the outcome. Brant could not convince the Oneida of the bad faith the Americans would show them.

The Seneca and Cayuga, the western members, and over half of their total population, backed Brant. The Onondaga, Keepers of the Fire whose home was the location of the Tree of Peace, were the central Nation. They were obliged to extinguish the Six Nations' Fire and they sided with the majority. After uncounted centuries of peace, the confederacy Nations would be at war with each other, with four of the Nations and well over half the population seeing themselves as allies of the British. As they would learn, the British saw them as allies when it suited them, but often didn't see them at all.

During one of his many incursions into the rebel-held territories, Johnson, a terror to the rebels, reached his abandoned estate and recovered the buried valuables. They were loaded up and carried back to

Canada in the knapsacks of forty soldiers. From there, they were loaded on a ship bound for England for safekeeping, but it was not to be. The ship foundered in a storm in the Gulf of St. Lawrence and was lost.

Joseph Brant and the Johnsons fought using Indigenous guerilla warfare techniques and they were very effective, but Brant could not defend the Onondaga and Seneca territory when George Washington sent three armies with 4,000 troops into their villages in 1779, guided by Oneida scouts. The central Onondaga village of Kanadaseagea, the historic capital of the Six Nations' Confederacy, was burned to the ground, along with forty other villages and all their crops and food. Thereafter, Washington was called *Caunotaucarius*, meaning destroyer of towns. The rebel troops, largely an underclass that the war managed to keep busy, saw the rich, cultivated fields of the Seneca and would not forget them.

When the British finally sat and negotiated with the new United States of America, they did so in Europe, neglecting to invite their Indigenous allies to the table once again, not even bothering to consult with them first. The negotiations took place in Paris where France and Spain, protagonists in the war, could also deal with their issues. The French had the least to gain or lose, but a strong desire to see the war end. Their foreign minister looked for a peace that would bring the Spanish onside as well and found it with a recommendation that would protect Spanish territory bordering the new independent nation on the south and also included a clause that would see the Ohio Valley, south of the river, become Indigenous buffer states while the British would possess the territory north of the Ohio, to the Mississippi. There was no Indigenous representation present at these discussions.[133]

The American negotiator, John Jay, felt that he could get a better deal negotiating directly with the British, cutting the Spanish and French out. His hunch proved correct. When he met with William Petty, Earl of Shelburne, in England, Shelburne saw the opportunity to establish a lucrative trade relationship with its old colony. He gave the new country the territory all the way to the Mississippi in exchange for the Loyalists having an opportunity to recover their property.

Joseph Brant and the other leaders heard of the end of the war and its terms as though they themselves were irrelevant. Their villages were

Spanish proposal to end American War of Independence. The concept of a buffer state would have committed the negotiators to recognizing an autonomous Indigenous political reality.

destroyed, their leaders were dead, and their food supply was gone, all in the service of a war against a common enemy. The British forces on the ground in America could see that a much better outcome should have been negotiated. Instead, the British government had conceded Indigenous land as though they owned it. Refugees of the Six Nations in their war-ravaged land faced the advancing hordes of the new Americans, mostly discharged soldiers and militiamen looking for ownership of land whose title was no longer protected by treaty. The new treaty had recognized neither Indigenous jurisdiction nor Indigenous territory, and American soldiers became homesteaders on Six Nations' land. Forced off their productive farms during the war and having lost many of their young men, the Indigenous Nations were faced with subsistence survival as their ancient civilization crumbled before their eyes.

The British had been very generous to the new United States in the treaty, hoping to turn their lost colony into a trading partner. The British were forsaking their Six Nations allies just as the French had forgotten the Wendat at their moment of greatest need in the previous century, trying to turn the victorious Five Nations of that time into a trading partner to replace the Wendat.

Major British forts set up on Indigenous territory to facilitate trade—acknowledged by earlier treaty as being on Indigenous land—were promised to the Thirteen Colonies along with the land the forts sat upon, as though these lands had been British territory. This was the very same land that Pontiac had fought for only a few decades before, that he predicted the British would steal.

The local British leadership was so astonished by the terms of surrender that they tried to hide it. General Frederick Haldimand declared, "My soul is completely bowed down with grief." The British prime minister, Lord Shelburne, said, "[T]he Indian Nations were not abandoned to their enemies; they were remitted to the care of neighbours… who were certainly the best qualified for softening and humanizing their hearts." His statement reflected racism that assumed "the Indians" to be a part of the local wildlife with no society or order, sort of wild human-animals of no consequence, not military allies, nor even a British colonial people.

The people, the Six Nations and the residents of the Ohio Valley, entertained no further illusions. One of the most respected of them, Seneca Chief Kaienkwaahton, an erstwhile ally of the British, described the Americans at the time: "If we had the means of publishing to the World the many Acts of Treachery & Cruelty committed by them on our Women and Children, it would appear that the title of Savages would with much greater justice be applied to them than to us."

Chief Kaienkwaahton, known as Old Smoke for his role in peace discussions, was seventy-eight years old when he said that in 1783. He died at eighty-one. He was the undisputed Warrior Chief of the Seneca, the most powerful of the Six Nations, and he had led men in battles from his mid-forties, at the beginning of the Seven Years' War. His Nations were independent allies of the British in the American War of Independence. They judged that the Americans were uncontrolled, uncivilized interlopers who would destroy all that they found. He distrusted the much younger Joseph Brant, who was only forty when the Chief made his statement in 1783. Brant had been educated in White society, but the Whites dismissed him as an "Indian." He lived in both worlds but was not fully accepted in either.

Both the British and the Americans feared the Six Nations and their allies. Resorting to their lack of natural resistance to the effects of alcohol, the British gave them gifts and plied them with rum to try to pacify them for their loss of … everything. The British in the outposts refused to turn the forts over to the Americans, arguing that the Americans were not respecting the Treaty of Paris in other areas, such as Lord Shelburne's condition that the treaty agreement was contingent on the honouring of Loyalist land claims. Their argument was true. The Americans were on the verge of bankruptcy and could not afford a war, so Congress encouraged a stalemate, a cold war, while it sought to neutralize the Indigenous Nations.

The Oneida and the Tuscarora who stayed with Kirkland fared no better than the other members of the original confederacy as everything that Brant had predicted came to pass.

Our history has always underestimated the wealth that was stolen bald-facedly from the Six Nations. Advisors to Congress felt that as long as the "Indians remained free," they were a threat. They were better warriors and were adept at guerrilla warfare. General Philip Schuyler argued in Congress that the Six Nations could be lured back into their historic homeland and onto reservations where they would be surrounded by White settlers and become incapable of mounting an organized resistance while their fertile historic lands were appropriated. He said they "would dwindle comparatively to nothing as all Savages have done who … live in the vicinity of civilized people, and thus leave us the country without the expense of a purchase." The greatest fear that the Americans had was that the Six Nations would find a base of operation on British territory, allowing them a secure homeland from which to launch a guerrilla war. The British wanted a buffer-zone of Indigenous Nations to cushion their remaining colonies from any American attack.

In 1784, British Governor Frederick Haldimand made a sincere offer to the Six Nations, through Joseph Brant, of a large holding that the British first had to purchase from the Mississauga, a branch of the Ojibwe. It was a business concept that sounds strange for several reasons, not the least of which was that much of the land was Six Nation territory through their Wendat adoptees and by right of conquest. They shared parts with their Mississauga neighbours. The land in question was the Grand River watershed, described as being ten kilometres deep on either side of the river from Lake Erie to the headwaters. Governor Haldimand's offer might have made it possible for the Confederacy to re-establish its culture and thrive as a sister state to the west of Canada, but he did not record the legal ratification before the end of his term as governor. His proposal was made in compensation for the British having negotiated peace with the new United States without inviting their Indigenous allies to the table, effectively ceding the Six Nation land to the new country. As soon as the agreement to cede the Grand River watershed to the Six Nations was made, the British began to qualify the terms and never properly ratified it.

Six Nation members returned to New York, and eventually relit the Confederacy Fire. Joseph Brant, in large part thanks to his elder sister Molly Brant's enormous influence, established representatives of all Six Nations at the Grand River settlement. There, they also relit the Confederacy Fire. Two Fires burned, as the Six Nations' people struggled to see themselves as a part of their own Confederacy, separate from and separated by the modern new nation states whose borders cut arbitrarily through their ancestral ground. Meanwhile, struggling Nations of the Ohio Valley appealed to their old Covenant Chain masters for help dealing with the Americans. The New York-based Confederacy tried to help but had no traction, ignored by the United States government as they fought to maintain their shrinking land share. Their real risks were the total loss of their culture and history. They found a spiritual solution through a modern prophet called Handsome Lake.

Describing a vision, Handsome Lake began a new religion called the Longhouse Religion, based on Iroquoian Tradition with elements of Christianity mixed in. It worked to their advantage in several ways, giving hope and identity while maintaining some of their Tradition, and keeping out Christian missionaries with their hierarchical hidden agendas, but it risked losing other important elements of Tradition.[134]

In the meantime, Shawnee, Delaware, and Wyandot leaders in the Ohio Valley knew better than to trust the Americans. They worked to organize an alliance. Joseph Brant led this initiative but soon lost control because many of his people moved to the promised lands of the Grand River and others returned east to their New York homeland, enticed by General Schuyler's promises. During the decades following the war, the Nations of the Ohio region and the Six Nations worked to establish an alliance to negotiate with the Americans, but a single Indigenous voice did not suit the Americans, who sabotaged their efforts. Even so, the U.S. frontier justice system held any "Indian" they captured as responsible for the actions of all Indigenous Nations. The great Shawnee Chief Cornstalk, recognized as the leader of a large Shawnee group that refused to take sides with either the Americans or the British during the American War of Independence, was present at treaty discussions in 1775 and 1776, each time demonstrating that a settlement could be found peacefully. In 1777, when he arrived for discussions at Fort Randolph on the Virginia frontier, the American captain in charge of the fort threw him in prison in an attempt to hold him hostage. The captain's militia broke into the prison and killed the Shawnee party, including Cornstalk and his son. The murderers went unpunished because no Americans would testify against them.

As the Ohio Seneca, Shawnee and others tried to form a federation to stand against the Americans, the British delayed the transfer of the Grand River land title to the Six Nations. Molly Brant, responsible for a dozen children, some hers, some orphans, settled at Cataraqui (Kingston). She died there in 1796.

While local names such as Brantford commemorate these historic figures, Joseph Brant spent the balance of his life fighting a losing battle with the British-Canadian authorities and passed away in 1807 at sixty-four years of age. The Six Nation fight for the land title continues today, over 230 years later; it has surfaced in the news in this new century, associated with the name Caledonia.

CHAPTER 38

The War of 1812

The War of 1812 was mostly about the Nations in the Ohio Valley, but it is hard to understand what was happening in North America without reviewing the ongoing European power struggle.

In 1791, the British had divided their Province of Quebec into the two provinces of Lower and Upper Canada, providing the citizens with a constitution and the right to elect members to an assembly. While each assembly was an advisory body only, Britain had created two separate colonial identities. The predominantly French-speaking Lower Canada was more populous. The English governor-in-chief resided in Quebec City and surrounded himself with a coterie of British businessmen. The biggest losers in this new arrangement were the Indigenous Nations, especially those whose traditional territories now spanned two different colonial administrations.

The Canadiens, who had learned the art of war over the centuries from the Indigenous Nations, recognized in the creation of Lower Canada a sincere attempt by the British to protect their rights, religion, and culture. After the creation of the new governments, the Quebec City lawyer Pierre-Stanislas Bédard recognized the efforts by declaring in 1792 that, under the *Ancien Régime* (the governance of New France), "the people counted for nothing, or less than nothing. A

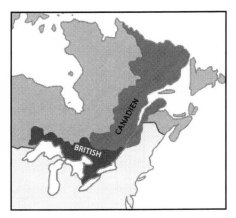

The British divided Quebec in two, giving both Canadien and British colonists their own distinct local administrations.

217

[French] governor would have considered he was demeaning himself if he had let anyone contradict him in the slightest," while under the British administration "we now enjoy a constitution under which everyone has his place, and in which a man is something. The people have their rights; the powers of a governor are laid down and he knows them."[135] These newly recognized Canadiens were not willing to jeopardize their rights and were willing to defend them.

In Upper Canada, many of the new citizens were people who had fled the Thirteen Colonies because of their deeper loyalty to the British Crown. They crowded into locations beyond the line of the Proclamation of 1763, "welcomed" through treaties by the Mississauga and a few Chiefs of other Nations. The intention in these treaties, from an Indigenous perspective, was driven by an obligation to share, something that was a fundamental humanitarian concept among most Indigenous Nations. The "payment" made for this openness involved trifling articles such as "clothes for their families, some guns and ammunition, 12 lace hats and enough red cloth to make 12 coats,"[136] items accepted, no doubt, with grace. Most of the Proclamation territory was shared through numerous treaties. The colonists filled the space as though it had been unpeopled before, as if the treaty was an acknowledgement made by the Indigenous Peoples that the territory was no longer theirs, as if they had simply ceased to exist. Confronted with a new legal code, Indigenous codes and national status lost effect as the Indigenous Peoples became overwhelmed by newcomers and their diseases.

The Constitutional Act, separating the Province of Quebec into Lower and Upper Canada, and giving assemblies to both, came into force three months after France's newly formed National Assembly wrote a constitution for France. The spirit of change triggered by the creation of the republic of the United States had fired the imaginations of peoples across Europe. The timing of the two constitutional acts was entirely coincidental, but the new constitution in France was very disturbing to the European hierarchies, while the division of the Province of Quebec was nothing more than a small, local administrative change. It did, however, help to keep the Canadiens focused on what they had and not on a popular rebellion in their mother country.

Two years earlier, in 1789, King Louis XVI of France had called an Estates General because the treasury was empty. It was the first time the French Estates General had been summoned since 1614, when it dealt with the aftermath of the assassination of King Henri IV.

The Third Estate, the commoners, refused to cooperate with the other two in the traditional choreography and re-invented itself as the National Assembly. They were reacting to the influence of cardinals Richelieu, Mazarin, and de Fleury who served three successive kings in their roles as chief ministers. These cardinals had done much to suppress any kind of religious independence, even into the reign of Louis XV, when they identified the Dutch Catholic thinker Cornelius Jansen as expressing Calvinist (Huguenot) ideas in his thinking. The Wars of Religion also extended to the purification of the faith.

By 1793, the guillotine was invented, the king was dead, and the nobility that could leave had fled the country. Church property was confiscated, and priests were forced to declare their first allegiance to the state. Next, the French army had repulsed the Prussian army, part of a coalition that was supposed to bring France back to its senses.

Then, the tables turned. The French army marched into Germany. Two years later, twenty-four-year-old Napoleon Bonaparte was promoted to the rank of Brigadier General in recognition of his tactical skills in battle. He went on to prove himself, leading the French army to victory in Italy and subsequently in Egypt on July 21, 1798. Napoleon's objective was British India, where he hoped to cut British trade with India, to isolate Great Britain, the only remaining kingdom of the coalition that had attacked France several years earlier that was still able to fight.

Napoleon's string of victories was short-lived. Aware of the risks and dangers of Napoleon's advance, Vice-Admiral Horatio Nelson led the British Mediterranean Fleet, following the French navy across the Mediterranean, slowly catching up. On August 1, he boldly attacked it at anchor in Abu Qir Bay, east of Alexandria. He destroyed French naval capacity, leaving Great Britain's as the dominant world navy.

After the naval defeat in Egypt, with a large army effectively stranded there, Napoleon returned to a France that was in turmoil, not from any of his actions, but from divisions among the revolutionary leaders. With the help of his brother and a few trusted confidants, he organized a coup. By December 1799, he was elected First Consul of the newly governing Consulate. In his new position, Napoleon recognized that the wholesale rejection of the Catholic Church was feeding a counter-revolutionary movement. He tried to bring the Catholic Church back, under his control, declaring freedom of religion, but his terms controlled the Church and did not return their confiscated properties. In May of 1804, Napoleon was declared Emperor of the Republic and obliged Pope Pius VII to be present at his coronation.

France's First Republic expanded over Europe, appealing to the common people. Many of the historic Catholic hierarchies came crashing down, only to be subsumed into a new one where Napoleon controlled the Church. But his war was expensive. In 1803, having negotiated the acquisition of Spanish North American territory and its annexation to the French colony of Louisiane, he promptly sold the whole colony to the United States, all under European law, with no consultation of its residents.

This sale may have tied the United States to a neutrality in the wars with Great Britain, but it also sandwiched the whole Ohio Valley between the expanding American colonies and their newly acquired territory.

The British hegemony, established at the end of the Seven Years' War, had been challenged by the breakup of its empire and the secession of the Thirteen Colonies to form the United States. The French Revolution, inspired by that bold break, had grown under Napoleon to challenge the entire royal structure of Europe. One after the other, the kingdoms toppled, but France could not topple Great Britain. Napoleon had to invade it and to do so he needed a stronger navy.

That possibility collapsed when the French and Spanish navies were defeated in 1805 at the Battle of Trafalgar by a smaller fleet under the same Admiral Nelson of Great Britain. Next, frictions on the Iberian Peninsula began to be evident. There, the common people were not enamoured with the French. When France and Spain together took Portugal in 1807, France turned against Spain as well, unsure of its loyalty. What ensued was the Peninsular War, fought on two fronts, with guerrilla[137] forces fighting sabotage actions.

During this same period, Napoleon confiscated the Papal States. Pope Pius VII, pushed back into his palace, became only the spiritual head of the Church. In retaliation, the pope refused to recognize Napoleon's appointments of bishops and finally excommunicated the emperor. That was the last straw. In 1809, Napoleon's General Radet, ostensibly on his own initiative, invaded the papal palace and kidnapped the pope who spent the next five years under house arrest.

The greater war reached a standoff when the British blockaded all European ports controlled by France, and the French seized any ship that had traded with Great Britain and was subsequently trading in any of the European ports. The blockade was so effective that the French navy could not train its sailors, contributing to the victory of Admiral Nelson at the Battle of Trafalgar. It was also seriously crippling the British economy, including access to materials for shipbuilding. Maintenance of warships took precedence over the maintenance of the merchant marine.

This standoff was felt in New Brunswick, the Canadas, and the United States. The British navy could not access Baltic ports for timbers for shipbuilding and they had lost access to the New England pine forests. They turned to the colonies of New Brunswick and the Canadas, stimulating the growth and development of settler communities in the centuries-old Algonquian and Iroquoian cultivated forests.

The British struggled to maintain a huge navy, effectively trying to control world trade. Among their challenges was manpower. From the beginning of the English navy in the time of Queen Elizabeth, impressment served as a method for rounding up crews, drawn from commoners who had been driven off their lands. The navy would treat any able-bodied man as fair capture, and he would become virtually a slave on a war vessel.

Desperate for crew, the British did not hesitate to continue to snatch and impress able-bodied men who were unlucky enough to be found in a maritime environment, forcing them to work as crew. Some of these men were Americans, but escaped British sailors also tried to pass as Americans, hoping to avoid recapture. In 1807, sailors from a British warship, the HMS Leopold, forcibly boarded the American frigate USS Chesapeake to retrieve four deserters, three of whom were Americans who had been impressed into service. The fourth was a British citizen who had deserted the British navy and signed up with the American navy under a pseudonym. The action became a *cause célèbre* in the United States, and together with the difficulty the Americans were having because of the closed ports during the war in Europe, various governors and senators began sabre-rattling.

The reasons for the desire for war were many. In 1803, the United States had purchased Louisiana, the territory west of the Mississippi, from France. During the early 1800s, the American population was also exploding into the Ohio Valley, rising in the territory of the future state from 42,000 to 230,000 between 1800 and 1810.[138] This expansion was being made against the will of the Indigenous Nations, the Shawnee, Delaware, Miami, Wyandot, and others. Their numbers throughout the Ohio Valley were miniscule in comparison but they were a terrifying reality along the frontier. Also, the British had not fully respected British Prime Minister Shelburne's promise to abandon these lands, seeing the

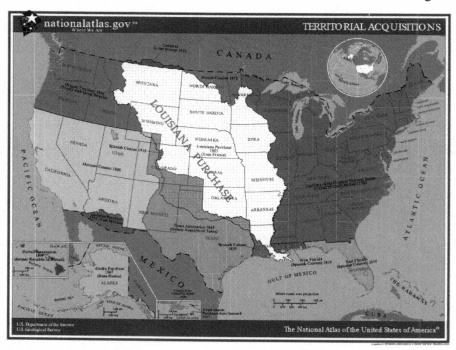

France acquired Spanish territory, selling it to the Americans almost immediately in 1803.

importance of maintaining these Nations as a buffer against the expanding United States. In 1802, Shawnee Chief Black Hoof had travelled to Washington and met with Secretary of War General Henry Dearborn. He proposed that a deed be created in American law, recognizing a specific territory where the Shawnee could live in peace under the American system. Taken by surprise, Dearborn left him to wait for an answer. After consulting frantically, the general came back to him, rejecting the proposal. It became clear that the Americans would not co-exist with the Nations of the Ohio Valley.

Tenskwatawa, remembered as the Shawnee Prophet, shared a vision with his people. He said they must eschew the White man's ways and go back to living the way they had in the past. The Shawnee, by far the largest of the Nations, led the others. Tenskwatawa's elder brother, Tecumseh, worked during this period to create a confederacy to defend their remaining territories. He knew that the Americans could not be trusted. There was no sincere interest in the wellbeing or even the continued existence of the Indigenous Nations.

Chief Michikiniqua of the Miamis had tried to organize a confederacy in the 1780s. In 1791, he led the defence against the advancing army of Major General Arthur St. Clair, inflicting the worst loss the Americans ever experienced in a single offensive against an Indigenous force. Aware that the victory would not remain unanswered, Michikiniqua concluded that a confederacy was not the solution, and communicated that to Tecumseh and the other chiefs. The power differential was just too great, and the British had shown their hand as unreliable allies even as late as the Battle of Fallen Timbers in 1794 when the British gates of Fort Miamis were closed to defeated, retreating warriors. That same year, the war against France was intensifying. The British signed the Jay Treaty, accepting to abandon their forts in favour of improved relations with the U.S., proving Michikiniqua's assessment.

Rejecting Chief Michikiniqua's cautionary advice, the Shawnee Chief Bluejacket had led the Indigenous forces in the Battle of Fallen Timbers. General Anthony Wayne and the United States Army carried the day. After his victory, he described what he found. "The very extensive and highly cultivated fields and gardens show the work of many hands.

The margin of those beautiful rivers [the Maumee and the Auglaize] appear like one continued village for a number of miles both above and below this place; nor have I ever beheld such immense fields of corn in any part of America from Canada to Florida." Then he proceeded to destroy them.

Acknowledging the presence of the Prophet Tenskwatawa, historian Julius Pratt, writing in 1925, showed how the United States citizens saw the people who lived in the Ohio Valley as little more than itinerant bands, fed and armed by the British, who had to be removed from United States property.[139]

The British were little better. The British colonial elite was shocked by the blunt assessment of their prime minister, Lord Shelburne, and he was sacked for his accord with the Americans after the Treaty of Paris, but Shelburne was on the mark of how the settlers felt. The Indigenous Nations could be directed, like trained dogs, in war, but were a pesky burden in peace. In the words of Sir James Henry Craig, Governor-in-Chief of British North America, "if we do not employ ["the Indians"] there cannot exist a moment's doubt that they will be employed against us."

The "Indians" were neither romantic nor autonomous at that time. They were the refugees of great Nations that had been destroyed by successive plagues of European disease, wars, and market rapacity. Craig instructed his people to court Chief Tecumseh as the United States boiled towards war. Even so, in November 1810, when Tecumseh confided to the British that the Shawnee Confederacy had little choice but war, the message was transferred to Craig who, fearing American retribution, had his chargé d'affaires in Washington warn the Americans that Tecumseh might attack. That same year, seeing his coterie of British acolytes lose seats in the new assembly of Lower Canada to the Parti Canadien, Craig threw the leaders of the Parti Canadien, the lawyer Pierre-Stanislas Bédard and his partners, into prison, closing their newspaper, Le Canadien. Fearing that any victory by a French-speaking party in Lower Canada was the beginning of an insurrection mastered by Napoleon, Craig was running scared and lacked the sophistication necessary to govern the complex colonies that fell to his responsibility.

Governor William Henry Harrison of the Indiana Territory was not running scared. He had become skillful at playing Indigenous Nations against each other, looking for the best opportunity to grab land through sympathetic treaties and insincere promises of support. He did not underestimate Tecumseh's abilities. In his words, "if some decisive measures are not speedily adopted, we shall have a general combination of all tribes against us."[140] He did not want peace.

After reiterating his refusal of any accord with Tecumseh in a meeting in late July 1811, Harrison confided to his war secretary, "if it were not for the vicinity of the United States, (Tecumseh) would perhaps be the founder of an empire that would rival in glory that of Mexico or Peru. No difficulties deter him."[141]

Learning that Tecumseh had left for the south of the territory to meet other Nations, he marched 1,000 soldiers up the Wabash River to Tippecanoe, and Prophetstown, Tecumseh's and Tenskwatawa's home village. He hoped to goad the prophet into defending their home and to precipitate a battle. Tecumseh had warned his brother to avoid confrontation with Harrison.

On November 7, in the early hours of the morning, the inevitable fight began when a small band of defenders stormed Harrison's bivouac. The warriors had no chance of winning. They believed the prophet, who had told them that their defence of Prophetstown would render them invincible. They may have completely routed Harrison's troops, too, if their ammunition had not run out. Harrison's men, regaining the advantage, built defences in fear of Tecumseh's return. Next, they proceeded to Prophetstown, looting and destroying the quickly abandoned village. The death toll from the skirmishes was around 120, with each side losing about the same number of men.

Harrison was right about the reaction he would create. The Tippecanoe story became the flashpoint for war. Newspapers carried the story as a defeat of the United States Army while others called it a British-incited attack against the United States. Andrew Jackson, at that time a Tennessee Supreme Court judge, called for vengeance for "the blood of our murdered countrymen." He went on to call for the destruction of "this hostile band which must be excited to war by the secret agents of Great

Britain." War talk ran rampant. The British were held responsible for inciting the "Indians" to "disturb and harass our frontiers, and to murder and scalp helpless women and children."[142] The needs and sufferings of the Indigenous Nations were invisible to them, as if they did not exist.

Peace had failed. Tecumseh and his loose, nascent confederacy were driven into an alliance with the British. From Tecumseh's point of view, the War of 1812 was only a continuation of the American War of Independence. That lost war had followed quickly after the British victory over the French. Each time, the Indigenous Nations were the forgotten allies. The Elders living in 1812 well remembered how much easier it was to deal with the Europeans when the French and English were both vying for their cooperation and products. The French had been accepted by, and forced to acknowledge the existence of, the Indigenous Nations at La Grande Paix de Montréal in 1701. Neither the British nor the Americans had acknowledged the humanity—the right to exist—of the people from here.

In early 1812, the United States newspapers and congressmen were talking war. When Isaac Brock, the British general and acting lieutenant governor of Upper Canada, met with the legislature at York (Toronto) in February of 1812, he left discouraged, unable to convince the representatives of the imminence of war. A big man, six-foot-three, forty-two years old, he was in the prime of his career. Key areas of vulnerability that he identified included the British Fort Amherstburg below Detroit on the Detroit River and the Island of Michilimackinac, called Mackinac today, that controlled access between lakes Huron and Michigan. Brock is recorded to have said, "Unless Detroit and Michilimackinac be both in our possession at the commencement of hostilities, not only Amherstburg but most probably the whole country, must be evacuated as far as Kingston."[143] Sending a coded message off to a reliable contact, Robert Dickson, who had all but joined the Dakota Sioux, he did as many British and Frenchmen had done before him. He called upon the Indigenous Nations to be his allies.

The Americans declared war on June 18, 1812. Still riding upon their successes in their war of independence, they relied initially on some very senior generals, including General Henry Dearborn. A portly man with the distinction of having chronicled Benedict Arnold's failed attempt to take the fort at Quebec in 1775, his first preoccupation was to bring the northeastern States onside. They failed to give him support, leaving the New England coast undefended. When he arrived to lead the army, he had trouble motivating his troops.

Brock heard from Robert Dickson only after the American declaration of war. He was on the move. By June 30, he and three hundred Sioux warriors arrived at Fort St. Joseph, north of Michilimackinac. With the commanding officer, Captain Charles Roberts, and the help of two hundred Canadiens, fur traders, and 250 Ottawa and Chippewa, they planned a night-time invasion of Michilimackinac. They climbed up a steep unguarded hill behind the fort. They took Michilimackinac without a battle.

MACKINACK, FROM ROUND ISLAND

Fort Michilimackinac (now Mackinac)

The news stunned the Americans.

Chief Tecumseh and General Brock were both anticipating meeting. Tecumseh had already captured U.S. mail in raids on the supply lines of General William Hull, another veteran of the American War of Independence. The young Canadien, Lieutenant Frédéric Roulette, had boldly captured one of Hull's boats on the Detroit River, finding among its contents Hull's strategic plans. Brock had information showing not just the size of Hull's army, but also information on seriously flagging morale. They also discovered that Hull was almost catatonically afraid of "Indians."

After their meeting on August 13, Brock and Tecumseh both expressed deep respect for each other, with Brock commenting that, "A more sagacious or a more gallant warrior does not, I believe, exist," while Tecumseh said of Brock, "This is a man."[144] Within two days, they marched on Detroit, where Hull was securely installed with a much larger, better-equipped army. Warriors, half-naked, painted, and chanting, along with many militia soldiers dressed in discarded British uniforms, were marched in a continuous loop within view of Detroit, giving the appearance of a huge force. Brock demanded General Hull surrender immediately. Inside Fort Detroit, in a town that was 90 percent Canadien, Hull refused, so Brock began a cannon attack on the fort. A single ball crashed into the officer's mess. Shaking in terror, Hull accepted to surrender Fort Detroit. After being paraded to Montreal, Hull and his men were traded back to the United States where Hull faced a court martial for cowardice and would have faced the firing squad if President James Madison had not intervened.

The War of 1812 tested both American and Canadian identities. The Americans needed to run through a series of inferior generals before beginning to take their own war seriously. During this run of poor leadership, the United States was faced with the risks of breaking apart just from the stress of the war. Canada, hopelessly outnumbered, was a tiny outpost of the British operations against Napoleon. The United States was more of an aggravation than a serious problem. In their opening salvo, the battle of Queenston Heights, General Stephen Van Rensselaer's own militia refused to obey him. They feared the war-cries of the Six Nations warriors fighting on the British side. The militiamen argued their constitutional right to not be obliged to fight on foreign soil.

General Isaac Brock, aware of the importance of keeping Queenston Heights, allowed hubris to guide him as he led his men on a difficult uphill attack in an attempt to regain the heights lost to the United States early on the morning of October 13. Hit twice by gunshot, he was killed, but the British, under his second-in-command, Major General Roger Sheaffe, took the heights as resistance collapsed. Fear of being scalped overrode discipline and defeated the Americans as much as actions taken by the British.

What changed the direction of the war was American naval actions on the Great Lakes. American naval officers, like Oliver Perry, made special efforts to study the famous British admiral Horatio Nelson. They used his strategies to wrest control of the Great Lakes from the British. On September 10, 1813, while General Harrison was moving toward Detroit with 8,000 troops, Perry engaged the British fleet on Lake Erie. While the battle went badly for him initially, his own ship, the USS Lawrence virtually destroyed, he rejected British commander Robert Barclay's request to surrender. He rowed to the USS Niagara and resumed command. Boldly charging the British fleet in a classic Nelson manoeuvre, he managed to separate the fleet and pounded it from an off angle until Barclay had to surrender.

His success allowed him to cut the supply lines for the British army under General Henry Proctor. Soon, Proctor determined the only safe route was withdrawal. On October 5, 1813, the British army formed lines to defend itself from the American advance. Tecumseh and his warriors were holding the right flank, but Proctor was nervous and broke. He left Tecumseh to hold the massive American forces at bay while his men withdrew.

Tecumseh was killed. Along with him died the hopes of the Indigenous Nations in the Ohio Valley. The confederacy created by Tecumseh melted away upon his death. The Americans had accomplished what they set out to do. They had destroyed the Indigenous resistance in the Ohio Valley.

Much ink has been spilled declaring who won the War of 1812, but the correct question was who lost. The combined forces of the Americans and the British finished their battles without succeeding in changing any pre-existing borders, except for those of the Ohio Valley. At the Treaty of Ghent, signed on Christmas Eve in 1814, the Americans dropped their claims regarding impressment and the British dropped their defence of the Indigenous Nations in the Ohio Valley on the condition that the Americans return Indigenous lands that had been taken as a result of the war. This promise was meaningless. The Americans had defeated Indigenous resistance. They resumed their tactics of displacing the people of the Ohio Valley, finally passing the Indian Removal Law in 1830.

The War of 1812, a small sideshow in the great war against Napoleon, succeeded in establishing American dominance over North America. It was a major loss to the British Empire. The Nations of the Ohio Valley were the real victims of the war. The great Shawnee Chief Tecumseh had risen to lead a new confederacy that allied itself with the British. A remarkable and able leader, he was the only hope left that the Shawnee and their allies might salvage some territory they could call their home. The British knew this but even so, in October 1813, General Henry Procter and his troops broke ranks, fleeing in the face of an American advance through Moraviantown. They left Tecumseh and his vastly outnumbered warriors to face annihilation.

After the war, the Americans practised genocide and ethnic cleansing over the next decades, culminating in their policy of Manifest Destiny. They forced the survivors to follow the Trail of Tears, to take refuge on reservations, pushed eventually to Oklahoma. Canada followed their example during the 1800s.

The policy of Manifest Destiny carried forward the Puritan vision of their God-given mandate to create a perfect Christian society. For the Indigenous people, it was the route to expulsion from their homes, following the Trail of Tears.

CONCLUSION

"In minobimaatisiiwin, [the good life] we honor one another, we honor women as the givers of lives, we honor our Chi-Anishinabeg, our old people and ancestors who hold the knowledge. We honor our children as the continuity from generations, and we honor ourselves as a part of creation." -Winona LaDuke.[145]

As I learned about the Wars of Religion, contact and the differences between the two cultural systems, one contrast that has stayed with me is the market economy and the gift culture. On the one hand, the market economy is based on personal ownership that is an endowment of a personal God giving agency to the possessor, and on the other, the gift culture expresses the agency of the whole, of Mother Earth.

In a market economy, the owners speak for what they perceive they own. It is an entitlement that mirrors the concept of terra nullius, the doctrine that allows a European power to claim ownership of land that no other European power has claimed. The law, a human artifact, presumes ownership for those defined by the law.

In a gift culture, the people belong to Mother Earth, and act as stewards. Personhood is not limited to people. All forms of life and many inanimate things have, and can declare, their personhood. In that sense, COVID-19 has declared its personhood.

I grew up in the market economy with its entitlement through ownership, and the gift economy is something I had to learn to understand. Generations of hierarchical subjugation have conditioned me to the notions of property. When a group that does not obviously include me speaks up and declares that there is a problem, my first reaction is to feel that I am being asked to give something up.

It is just as difficult, if your experience is of the gift culture, to make the presumption of ownership. Someone living in a gift culture doesn't need sharing to be explained. The market economy is incapable of operating without the concept of property, of ownership. The gift culture does not presume personal property or ownership.

The market economy is fast moving and progressive. It has grown rapidly since its inheritance from the personal god. The personal god is based on concentration of community power in a hierarchy, itself perhaps having grown out of the hierarchy of herding, in which property and ownership are concentrated and bestowed or withheld from above.

The gift culture is about the reception of the gift of life, its mysteries and its bounties, life being intimately bound into, and an expression of, the totality of being, of the universe. We are all a part of it, and our role is to maintain it through maintaining each other, the whole community of Mother Earth.

Our modern culture is driven by ideological imperialism, hierarchies that must destroy all others in their self-justification and must ultimately feed on themselves. The speed of its growth took thousands of years to reach maturity. It now spans the planet and continues to grow at a harrowing rate, growing exponentially since the beginning of the nuclear age only a single lifetime ago. It is not limited to the Laurentian hills, to the greater drainage basin of the Great Lakes and the mighty St. Lawrence, or even to North America. It manifests itself through religion, money, and property. The current frontier can be found in such seemingly obscure places as the Bijags archipelago off the coast of Guinea-Bissau in Africa, where Brazilian Christian evangelicals expand their ideology in an attempt to absorb and destroy the protective influence of the priestesses, or in the story of John Allen Chau, the American missionary who violated protective laws to try to convert the inhabitants of North Sentinel Island of the Andaman and Nicobar Islands in the Indian Ocean in 2018.[146] It is also expressed through the accelerating rate of its growth. Vaclav Smil, in his recent book *Growth: From Microorganisms to Megacities*, observes that "China consumed more cement between 2008 and 2011 than did the United States throughout the entire twentieth century." Growth is not limited to consumption. There is a corresponding growth of the concept of what is legally considered property and, therefore, is subject to ownership. Our system creates new definitions of property for acquisition. Concepts are patented as are biological modifications. This leads to the patenting—ownership—of living things, empowering the owner even if those living things move onto the property of someone else, such as Monsanto's Roundup Ready seeds. Large companies, catering to profit-driven shareholder investment schemes, are striving to own us, to market that ownership, through cultivating our dependence upon their products. Seeds are becoming their property. Even elements of our bodies can be patented, meaning that individuals risk losing ownership of parts of themselves. Even information about you and your property becomes a product that can be sold through data harvesting. All of this is an outgrowth of our ancient hierarchical system centred on power and property ownership. It is the same force that drew Britain to seek world hegemony. This is not an inevitable function of the human condition, but one adopted through acceptance of a concentration of power in the hands of a few people who we accept as being at the top of a hierarchy. It results from the concept of a single God who has given us dominion, ownership, of all we can take. It leads from the Creation Stories of the herding-based civilization.

We can change our course and some people are experiencing mixed success in their attempts to do so, but the system itself is the problem. A simple comparison to the Great Law of Peace and the gift economy shows us that it could be different. For us to achieve change, we must be ready to dismantle the legal and religious hierarchies that we are a part of. It was not the churches, the kings or later even the fascists or communists, but the hierarchies themselves that acted all in the name of singular, centralized power.

The first step is to acknowledge what hierarchies have done and continue to do. With the United Nations Declaration of the Rights of Indigenous Peoples, we have taken that first step in acknowledging the wrongs our system has inflicted. In an ideal world, we might have the time to nurture and learn to respect different ways of thinking and governing, to remodel our societies on these old, non-hierarchical sustaining communities, but ours is not an ideal world and too many among us are driven by the absolutes that the hierarchies demand, convinced that there is only one solution: that growth and power must dominate and control, that a strong leader will solve the problem.

Even in Canada, which has shown moments of openness, the hierarchical system continues to consolidate control. Its reach can be clearly seen in the examination of attempts by individual autonomous Nations inside our presumed frontiers seeking recognition. The list is long.

Shiri Pasternak spent five years living with the Barrière Lake Algonquin in Quebec, north of Ottawa. Studying a period spanning the 1990s and the first decade of the current century, she learned how they, working within the framework of their Customary Governance, managed to negotiate a trilateral agreement with Quebec and Ottawa in which they would be the stewards of their unceded territory. These Algonquin community members, the residents of these forests for thousands of years, understood themselves to be responsible for their elder siblings' habitat. They were willing to have the extraction industries do their work, but with their community's input and oversight. The arrangement was full of promise. Moose reproduction areas as well as bear dens, sensitive maple groves, and fish spawning waterways could be protected, the whole comprising no more than twelve percent of the territory. Some of the forestry and mining interests expressed satisfaction as well, but there was a serious dilemma for their two partners, the Quebec and Canadian governments. The Trilateral Agreement acknowledged a jurisdiction not governed by Quebec or by Ottawa but by Customary Governance, not an elected government. Its revenues would come from the extraction industries and, while everything might work, it was a jurisdiction apart with no elected officials or elections and with access to independent revenue streams.

Customary Indigenous Governance is a threat to Canadian and American governments. Its implications are too threatening because to acknowledge them is to acknowledge a separate jurisdiction outside the existing hierarchy. The essential role of the sustaining community is dismissed in favour of central control. Throughout our shared colonial history, the Crown and Indigenous parties had agreed to the concepts of Customary Indigenous Governance through foundational treaties represented by Wampum Belts and other means. The nation states that succeeded the Crown elected governments that unilaterally reneged on these treaties, concluding that the Nations involved had simply been subjects of the Crown, existing on territory that belonged to the Crown, based on the doctrine of terra nullius.[147] There was no regard for the ancient presence and sustaining nature of these communities, and the opportunity that they provided for us to learn about sustainability. The old agreements had become inconvenient and risked setting a precedent to the Crown's successors, the nation state governments. It is inconsistent with their centralizing control. According to the Barrière Lake Algonquin people, the governments chose to renege.

Our governance system is built around patriarchy and steep hierarchies. We can change it, but change has to come from within. Change through changing ourselves, one at a time. Rebellion or a "successful" revolution is a solution from a simplistic past when we believed that one group could replace another and really change anything. In any case, it is too late. The system today has led to such a severe hierarchical imbalance and human redundancy that rebellion would precipitate a bloodbath and demonstrate that our current hierarchies are more powerful than those of the days of absolute rulers.

How can we step away from this seemingly insatiable hunger without losing those good aspects that our technically developed society has given us? How can we incorporate the aspects of the modern into a Good Life that honours all of our siblings in the family of Mother Earth? How can we learn to live as sustaining communities?

We must understand the voices of the sustaining communities, teaching us how we belong to the world, to Mother Earth, not the other way around. They can help us comb the snakes out of our hair, help us find fulfillment in our place on Mother Earth, and work together to improve her bounty. They can help us learn to satiate our hunger and to cherish our role as siblings among the children of Mother Earth, to live a Good Life, to allow rivers to flow teeming with fish, and the sky to carry clouds of birds.

Each of us must embrace a Good Life and do our best to live it, take the steps one at a time and trust each other's judgment. There is no magic solution. We must each think and act holistically with every action, investment, and purchase, with every breath.

A detailed path back to a non-hierarchical society has to be conceived and I believe we have started down the right road. We are no longer a herding culture and patriarchy is being challenged. This trend will continue if we nurture it, support it, and do our best to live it.

Womankind will find an equilibrium. In the story of Deganwidah and the Great Law of Peace, it was Jigonsaseh, the woman Deganwidah consulted, who encouraged the men to stop supporting the hierarchy centred around Adodaroh. Each person, one at a time, had to understand the peace that was being proposed, to learn to live a Good Life. As a reader of history, I see that there is a growing body of historical research led by women, revealing a much different past than our predominantly male historians have laid out for us.

COVID-19 has addressed every person in the world, all individually. It is a powerful address from life itself, making us slow down. It underlines that the responsibility for dealing with COVID is shared equally. Learning from it, we can see that we are all equal and we all need each other. How can we live our lives in our communities in a way that can help us flatten the hierarchy of inequality in a similar way to the efforts we made to flatten the curve of new infections? In the story of the people who confronted Adodaroh, everyone came onside, one by one, to find balance in nature. Can we, one at the time, change our fundamental ethic from our social Darwinian owner-driven economy to a gift economy in which our role is stewardship?

Acknowledgements

This work has been done with the steady, unmeasurable support of Sheila Eskenazi, my life-partner and closest friend. In spite of her profound clarity of understanding of the world we cohabit, she has never lost her conviction that I am trying to make sense. To understand her efforts in this mission, examine the index in this book, a conceptual key to the various ideas that came together in the long study of the subject.

When I was entangled in three different historical strands, it was Sheila who suggested I contact Ruth Bradley St. Cyr, a structural editor. Ruth, who acted as a sounding board, helped me see that there was a braid of influences that, while they did tangle, constituted the flow of the story I needed to tell. She also gave me the important advice to go to my friends and ask them to be readers.

Sheila agreed. She had read it for me many times and told me I needed some fresh eyes. The first friend I went to, John McLaughlin, has known me since adolescence. When I asked if he could read the manuscript, he told me to summarize it so he could decide. What I said somehow enticed him and he was in, giving me the confidence to reach further.

There are a huge number of friends whose intellects provided feedback. Carmel Chiacchiarello was deeply helpful as were Tom Eades, Denis Gaspé, Nadia Korths, the late and missed Luc Matter, Brian Parsons, Beryl Puddifer, Bonnie Shemie, Fabio Sousa, Eric Pouliot Thisdale, Patricia Young and the many readers of my columns in the Quebec Heritage News and in Main Street, our local English newspaper, where I began to explore some of the ideas in this book.

The next step in the process was to find a publisher, and that search led me to new friends at Black Rose Books. Clara Swan Kennedy immediately understood and responded, along with Jason Toney, and I have been well looked after and helped in the rounding out of this story. Kaitlin Littlechild ensured that I dealt with Indigenous Peoples with respect and helped further with the editing.

Once the manuscript was 'finished,' I shared it again, with retired history professor Michel Allard, who gave me an in-depth analysis and encouraged my perspective. I was hugely helped with the straight-for-ward advice from my cousin, Anthony Paré, who showed me how to hear my own voice. I also approached a number of authors whose work had helped me. Such people do not always respond, and I can understand that, through the old Scottish attitude of not talking to someone to whom you have not been introduced. A few did respond, however, and Barbara Alice Mann immediately became a life-guide. She and Lee Maracle, both very busy in their own fields, found the time to give me the confidence to believe that what I was doing was important and they seemed to under-stand independently what Sheila worked so hard to help me believe. My only regret is that I waited so long before approaching both of these ex-ceptional people.

Rita Bauer took over from there. She designed the book and cover, making the whole process real, giving it endless days of detailed work and consideration. Her patience leant a happiness to the project

Claude Bédard, a lawyer, and a descendant of the Huguenot Bé-dards, including that fine early Canadien lawyer, Pierre-Stanislas Bédard, also contributed to my knowledge, as did Jean-Pierre Miljours, a local expert on history who grew up learning Anishinaabemowin among his neighbours. Thanks also to Stuart Graham and Michelle Sullivan for their perseverance and help.

Years ago, when receiving recognition for the progress of a heri-tage/historical association that we had built and guided, I thanked every-one, sure I had covered all the people whose help I had deeply appreciated. Beside me stood Erik Wang, a member of our committee and retired diplomat. As I wound up, I heard my life-partner's clear voice ring across the room: "What am I, chopped liver?"

Without missing a beat, the diplomat observed: "Amazing selfless-ness. He remembered everyone except his own family." I understood the success he had in his career. No doubt I have forgotten someone's valued help. It may be small comfort to you that you are in good company, as close to me as family.

As helpful as so many were, I must accept the responsibility for the inevitable errors that managed to survive through to the final text.

Influences and further reading

Long before this book began to take form, Thorkild Jacobsen, the author of *The Treasures of Darkness, A History of Mesopotamian Religion*, showed where hierarchies were before the beginnings of monotheism and confirmed how I must look beyond monotheism to understand the world and my place in it. Bruce Trigger, the author of *The Children of Aataentsic, A History of the Huron People to 1660*, brought that view into focus, close to home. Barbara Alice Mann, the author of *Spirits of Blood, Spirits of Breath, the Twinned Cosmos of Indigenous America*, gives a deep explanation of a world that we should have learned about in school, or better still, with our mother's milk. Towards making up for that absence, Lee Maracle's *My Conversations with Canadians* is essential reading.

Claudio Saunt's book *Unworthy Republic, The Dispossession of Native Americans and the Road to Indian Territory*, starts where this book ends, after the shameful British abandonment of Tecumseh and the people of the Ohio Valley.

If you find this all too heavy, read Robin Wall Kimmerer's *Braiding Sweetgrass, Indigenous Wisdom, Scientific Knowledge, and the Teachings of Plants*. I read this book years ago, when a dear friend left it without comment in our mailbox. Kimmerer taught me how to overcome my anger and the importance of joy and hope.

Notes

INTRODUCTION and CONTACT 1534-1541

1   Martin Prechtel, *The Unlikely Peace at Cuchumaquic: The Parallel Lives of People as Plants, Keeping the Seeds Alive* (Berkeley: North Atlantic Books, 2012), 35–67 in which he describes the people at Cuchumaquic in Guatemala that he set out to "rescue" after an earthquake and that the army had isolated. He found them in a calm state of acceptance of their last days and hours.

2   Timothy J. Motley, ed. *Darwin's Harvest: New Approaches to the Origins, Evolution, and Conservation of Crops* (New York: Columbia Univ. Press, 2006), 67.

3   Céline Carayon, *Eloquence Embodied: Nonverbal Communication among French and Indigenous Peoples in the Americas* (Williamsburg, Virginia: Chapel Hill: Omohundro Institute of Early American History and Culture; University of North Carolina Press, 2019), 62n.

4   Jean-Pierre Miljours, historian, Mont Laurier, personal communications; Michel Allard, historian; Val David, personal communications; Canada East census 1851.

5   Denis Gaspé, Kanehsatake, personal communications.[1]

6   Truth and Reconciliation Commission of Canada: *Calls to Action, National Centre for Truth and Reconciliation*, University of Manitoba; Jonathan Sisson, A Conceptual Framework for Dealing with the Past, https://www.kairoscanada.org/wp-content/uploads/2015/06/UN-Joinet-Orentlicher-Principles.pdf. Accessed 2020/08/25.

7   Rev. A. E. Burke, *Jacques Cartier's First Voyage and the Landing at Cascumpec*, The Prince Edward Island Magazine, October 1899 Vol 1 No. 8, 294 to 299. https://www.islandimagined.ca/articles. Accessed February 15, 2017.

8   Hiram B. Stephens, *Jacques Cartier and His Four Voyages to Canada* (Montreal, Canada: W. Drysdale & Co., 1890), 23.

9   Stephens, *Jacques Cartier,* 24. The Three Sisters, maize, beans, and squash were the mainstay and varieties suitable to their locations were grown from Mexico to the Great Lakes. Potatoes had already arrived in Mexico from South America.

10 Bruce G. Trigger, *The Children of Aataentsic: A History of the Huron People to 1660.* Reprint. with a new preface, 1st paperback ed. (Kingston: McGill-Queen's Univ. Press, 1987) The Individuals and Society p 75-91.

11 The use of the figure 8 is used in some writings to indicate the sound "oo" or "ou."

12 Julien d'Huy, "The Evolution of Myths," *Scientific American* 315, no. 6 (December 2016): 64.

13 Lee Sultzman, N*eutral History*, http://www.dickshovel.com/neutral.html. Accessed 2011-12–20.

14 Stephen Arthur *"Where License Reigns with All Impunity" An Anarchist Study of the Rotinonshón:ni Polity*, http://nefac.net/anarchiststudyofiroquois. Accessed 2011/09/25; see also http://libcom.org/library/where-license-reigns-all-impunity. Accessed 2019/05/01. This story is told in many forms with many interpretations. The serious reader should find the more complex and nuanced studies expressed here: Barbara A. Mann, and Jerry L. Fields, "A Sign in the Sky: Dating the League of the Haudenosaunee," *American Indian Culture and Research Journal* 21 no.2 (1997): 105–163, https://meridian.allenpress.com/aicrj/article-abstract/21/2/105/211735/A-Sign-in-the-Sky-Dating-the-League-of-the?redirectedFrom=full. Accessed 2021/01/09; William N. Fenton, *The Great Law and the Longhouse: A Political History of the Iroquois Confederacy*. The Civilization of the American Indian Series, v. 223, (Norman: University of Oklahoma Press, 1998), chapters 2 and 3.

15 Adodaroh can be read as a title, rather than as a name.

16 Also spelled Tekanawita.

17 Jigonsaseh can also be read as a title.

18 Laura DeVries, *Conflict in Caledonia: Aboriginal Land Rights and the Rule of Law*. Law and Society Series (Vancouver: UBC Press, 2011), p.83; Victor P. Lytwyn, *A Dish with One Spoon: The Shared Hunting Grounds Agreement in the Great Lakes and St. Lawrence Valley Region*, https://ojs3.library.carleton.ca/index.php/ALGQP/article/viewFile/262/249. Accessed 2017/01/29.

19 Barbara Alice Mann, *Iroquoian Women: The Gantowisas* (New York: P. Lang, 2000), 36-38.

20 Cassandra Clifford, "Rape as a Weapon of War and It's Long-Term Effects on Victims and Society," peacewomen.org. 7th Global Conference Violence and the Contexts of Hostility, 05 2008. https://www.peacewomen.org/sites/default/files/vaw_rapeasaweaponofwar_stopmodernslavery_may2008_0.pdf. Accessed 2021-01-22.

21 Anke Becker, *Herding and Male Dominance*, Harvard University Department of Human Evolutionary Biology, November 11, 2017 published November 14, 2017, revised August 29, 2018 https://papers.ssrn.com/sol3/papers.cfm?abstract_id=3069684. Accessed November 20, 2017.

22 *The Torah, The Five Books of Moses: A New Translation of the Holy Scriptures According to the Masoretic Text*. (Philadelphia: The Jewish Publication Society of America, 1962) Genesis 4,5. Translations may vary depending on their source.

23 Sean Illing. *Why a leading political theorist thinks civilization is overrated*, interview with Vox https://www.vox.com/conversations/2017/11/22/16649038/civilization-progress-humanity-history-technology?wpisrc=nl_todayworld&wpmm=1. Accessed November 28, 2017.

24 Charles Q. Choi, *Hunters and Herders: Ancient Civilization Made Rapid Switch*, *Live Science*, https://www.livescience.com/45188-neolithic-transition-hunting-herding.html. Accessed December 4, 2017.

25   Käthe Roth and Denis Vaugeois, *America's Gift: What the World Owes to the Americas and Their First Inhabitants* (Montreal: Baraka Books – Les Éditions du Septentrion,1992), ISBN 978-0-9812405-2-7.

26   Charles C. Mann, 1491: *New Revelations of the Americas before Columbus*. 1st ed (New York: Knopf, 2005), 71.

27   Stephens, Jacques Cartier, 30–31.

28   Stephens, *Jacques Cartier*, 31–33. Note that I cross-referenced these various quotes with the archaic French of Cartier's records called *Relation Originale de Voyage de Jacques Cartier au Canada en 1534*.

29   Stephens, *Jacques Cartier*, 49.

30   To estimate the size of the whole palisaded area would be challenging because Cartier's estimates of the width seem improbably wide if we assume a step is roughly a yard or a metre (even if the length is correct) and because there is a question of whether the longhouses would have been placed in parallel southeast/northwest orientation for thermal gain (as one study has shown, see below). Presuming the efficient parallel orientation and accepting Cartier's sizes but making no allowance for the space between the buildings, the construction would have covered six to eight acres of land.

31   Stephens, *Jacques Cartier*, 87.

32   Stephens, *Jacques Cartier*, 41-94.

33   Eric Pouliot-Thisdale, lecture, Laval Historical Society, Laval, Quebec. 2018-03-16.

34   John P. Rafferty, Stephen T. Jackson, *Little Ice Age Geochronology*, https://www.britannica.com/science/Little-Ice-Age. Accessed 2019-03-12.

35   Mann, 1491, 97–99.

36   Alexander Koch, Chris Brierley, Mark M. Maslin, Simon L. Lewis. *Earth system impacts of the European arrival and Great Dying in the Americas after 1492*, Quaternary Science Reviews 207 (2019) 13. https://www.sciencedirect.com/science/article/pii/S0277379118307261/pdfft ?md5=7640a392ed3d133a81e194f56b244627&pid=1-s2.0-S0277379118307261-main.pdf. Accessed 2019-03-19.

37   Denys Delâge, *Le Pays Renversé: Amérindiens et Européens En Amérique Du Nord-Est, 1600-1664*. (Montréal: Boréal, 1991), 97.

WARS OF RELIGION 1530-1630

38   Joseph Patrick Henrich, *The Weirdest People in the World: How the West Became Psychologically Peculiar and Particularly Prosperous* (New York: Farrar, Straus and Giroux, 2020), 185.

39   C.N. Trueman, *Henry VII and the Economy*, https://www.historylearningsite.co.uk/tudor-england/henry-vii-and-the-economy/. Accessed 2020-10-16.

40   John Simkin, *Was Henry VIII as bad as Adolf Hitler and Joseph Stalin?*
      https://spartacus-educational.com/spartacus-blogURL48.htm. Accessed 2020-
      10-26.

41   *Basseterre* https://potbs.fandom.com/wiki/Basseterre. Accessed 2020-10–15.

42   Whitehead, Gaspard de Coligny, 312–319.

43   Britannica. *Peace of Augsburg,* https://www.britannica.com/event/Peace-of-
      Augsburg. Accessed 2017-12-07.

44   Delâge, *Le Pays Renversé*, 22–27.

45   Encyclopedia Britanica 1911. *Lamoral, count of Egmont*,
      https://theodora.com/encyclopedia/e/lamoral_count_of_egmont.html. Ac-
      cessed 2021-01-23;

      World Heritage Encyclopedia. *Philip de Montmorency, Count of Horn*,
      http://self.gutenberg.org/articles/eng/Philip_de_Montmorency,_Count_of_H
      orn. Accessed 2021-01-23.

46   R. La Roque de Roquebrune, *Jean-François de La Rocque de Roberval*, Diction-
      ary of Canadian Biography, http://www.biographi.ca. Was his New France in-
      terest also an attempt to create a safe haven for Huguenots?

47   Whitehead, *Gaspard de Coligny*, 323–324. This same Hawkins, years later, re-
      ceived a knighthood for his role in defeating the Spanish Armada. He also
      brought the first potatoes to Ireland in 1565.

48   Bamber Gascoigne, *History of the Netherlands* HistoryWorld. http://www.his-
      toryworld.net/wrldhis/PlainTextHistories.asp?groupid=3102&HistoryID=ac90
      &gtrack=pthc. Accessed 2017-02-23; Geoffrey Parker. The Spanish Road to the
      Netherlands, http://www.historynet.com/the-spanish-road-to-the-nether-
      lands.htm. Accessed 2017-02-23.

49   Julian calendar

50   Whitehead, *Gaspard de Coligny*, 237.

51   Renaissance and Reformation 1500-1620: A Biographical Dictionary. *Albret,
      Jeanne D'*, https://renaissance_and_reformation.enacademic.com/8/AL-
      BRET%2C_Jeanne_D%27. Accessed 2020-11-12.

52   Whitehead, *Gaspard de Coligny*, 256.

53   Whitehead, *Gaspard de Coligny*, 260.

54   Whitehead, *Gaspard de Coligny*, 255: The Dead do not Make War. Anonymous
      Spaniard's comment upon the execution of the Flemish nobles Lamoral,
      Count of Egmont, cousin of King Philip II of Spain and Philip de Montmorency,
      the Count of Horn, in1568. Their death sparked the rebellion that led to the in-
      dependence of the Netherlands 80 years later, but the comment was also re-
      ported in Whitehead's book.

55   François Dubois, *The Saint Bartholomew's Day Massacre* http://www.reforma-
      tion.org/bart.html. Accessed 2011-12-17.

56   Cătălin Avramescu, *An Intellectual History of Cannibalism*. Translated by Alistair

Ian Blyth. (Princeton University Press, 2011), 255. The St. Bartholomew's Day Massacre is described as a cannibalistic nightmare in which human hearts, livers, and so on were sold in the streets. They point out that this was a much more disgraceful cannibalistic event than any in New World history because this was an orgy of feeding upon its own.

57   Whitehead, *Gaspard de Coligny*, 253.

58   James Anthony Froude, *The Spanish Story of the Armada and Other Essays* (London: Longmans, Green and Co., 1892), 21.

59   Jean-Léon Charles, *Alessandro Farnese, Duke of Parma and Piacenza* https://www.britannica.com/biography/Alessandro-Farnese-duke-of-Parma-and-Piacenza. Accessed 2019-02-04.

60   Jaenen, *Les Huguenots de la Nouvelle France*, Pierre Dugua de Mons (1558-1628), http://www.erq.qc.ca/stmarc/huguenots.html. Accessed 2014-03-12.

61   Monteil, Pierre. *La huitième guerre de religion sous le règne d'Henri IV*, http://www.histoire-fr.com/bourbons_henri4_2.htm. Accessed 2014-11-02;

62   James W. Casavant, *Henri IV et l'Edit de Nantes*, https://sites.google.com/site/casavaniajwm/trivial-importance/henri-quatre-et-l-edit-de-nantes. Accessed 2010-10-21:

PROTESTANT BEACHHEAD 1600-1620

63   Sultzman, *Wampanoag History*, http://www.tolatsga.org/wampa.html. Accessed 2016-02-07.

64   James Daschuk, CBC Secret Life of Canada podcast, *Why some folks feel weird about Hudson's Bay blankets*, https://www.cbc.ca/radio/secretlifeofcanada/why-some-folks-feel-weird-about-hudson-s-bay-blankets-1.4846059. Posted: 2018-10-02.

65   What-When-How. *Birth Control, Native Americans of California*. http://what-when-how.com/birth-control/native-americans-of-california-birth-control. Accessed 2018-11-14.

William Engelbrecht. *Factors Maintaining Low Population Density among the Prehistoric New York Iroquois*, https://www.academia.edu/12753626/Factors_Maintaining_Low_Population_Density_among_the_Prehistoric_New_York_Iroquois?email_work_card=view-paper. Accessed 2020-10-23.

66   Huron came from an old French term that referred to the people's hairstyle rather than anything more substantial. A hure is the hair that stands up on a boar's head. It was not an endearing term, but it stuck in settler vocabulary.

67   Robin Wall Kimmerer, *Braiding Sweetgrass: Indigenous Wisdom, Scientific Knowledge and the Teachings of Plants*. 1. edition. (Minneapolis, Minn: Milkweed Editions, 2013), 380.

68   Robin Wall Kimmerer, *The Serviceberry – An Economy of Abundance*. https://emergencemagazine.org/story/the-

serviceberry/?utm_source=pocket-newtab. Accessed 2020-12-25. This is an excellent podcast and more accessible to those who prefer to listen.

69   Heide Goettner-Abendroth. *Matriarchal Society and the Gift Paradigm* http://www.gift-economy.com/womenand/womenand_matriarchal.html. Accessed 2018-12-06.

70   Biography Newsletter. *Henry IV Biography* (1553–1610) https://www.biography.com/royalty/henry-iv. Accessed 2014-11-08; Delors, Catherine. 14th of May 1610: assassination of King Henri IV, http://blog.catherinedelors.com/*14th-of-May-1610-assassination-of-King-Henri-IV/*. Accessed 2014-11-08.

71   Like the element of the story that describes the different humble creatures who returned with a mouthful of soil, there are different names for different characters in the various retellings of the Foundational Stories.

72   Graham, Joseph. *Naming the Laurentians: A History of Place Names "up North."* Lachute, Québec: Main Street, 2005. 37

73   Russell Shorto, *The Island at the Center of the World: The Untold Story of Dutch Manhattan and the Founding of New York* (London; New York: Doubleday, 2004), 30.

74   Shorto, *Island at the Center*, 24.

75   Shorto, *Island at the Center*, 27.

76   Bruce G. Trigger, *The Children of Aataentsic: A History of the Huron People to 1660*. Reprint. with a new preface, 1st paperback ed. (Kingston: McGill-Queen's Univ. Press, 1987), 279–285 and David Hackett Fischer, *Champlain's Dream: The Visionary Adventurer Who Made a New World in Canada*, (Toronto: Vintage Canada, 2009), 308–310 differ on this story.

77   Trigger, *Children of Aataentsic*, 299.

78   The real identity of this fort has never been confirmed. It could have been Onondaga.

79   Trigger, *Children of Aataentsic*, 309.

80   Trigger, *Children of Aataentsic*, 327–335.

81   Trigger, *Children of Aataentsic*, 308–315.

82   Trigger, *Children of Aataentsic*, 381.

83   Charles Garrad, *Petun to Wyandot: The Ontario Petun from the Sixteenth Century*. Edited by William Fox and J.-L. Pilon. Mercury Series 174 (Quebec: Canadian Museum of History and Ottawa: University of Ottawa Press, 2014), 165.

84   Johnson *Tisquantum ("Squanto")*, http://mayflowerhistory.com/tisquantum/. Accessed 2016-02-03.

85   Jeremy Dupertuis Bangs, *Who Were the Pilgrims* http://www.leidenamerican-pilgrimmuseum.org/Page31K.htm. Accessed 2016-01-15;

Bangs, *The Pilgrims and Other English in Leiden Records*, https://jhowell.com/tng/histories/PilgrimsAndOtherEnglishinLeidenRecords-

ByJeremyBangs.pdf. Accessed 2016-01-16;

Caleb Johnson, *The Mayflower*, http://mayflowerhistory.com/pilgrim-history. Accessed 2016-02-03.

THE BREAKDOWN BEGINS 1613-1701

86 Lynn Gehl. *The Truth That Wampum Tells: My Debwewin on the Algonquin Land Claims Process* (Halifax: Fernwood Publishing, 2014), 110.

87 Trigger, *Children of Aataentsic*, 382–85.

88 Fischer, *Champlain's Dream*, (Toronto: Vintage Canada, 2009), 423–424;

Marcel Trudel, *Samuel de Champlain; Guillaume de Caën; Émery de Caën*. Dictionary of Canadian Biography, http://www.biographi.ca;

George MacBeath, *Pierre Dugua de Mons*. Dictionary of Canadian Biography, http://www.biographi.ca;

Jaenen, *Les Huguenots de la Nouvelle France*, http://www.erq.qc.ca/stmarc/huguenots.html.

89 Study led by Quebec Professor Yves Tremblay at Centre de Recherche d'Histoire Quantitative Université de Caen, Programme de Recherche sur l'Émigration des Français en Nouvelle-France, in collaboration with Maison de l'émigration française en Canada consacrée au peuplement de la Nouvelle-France, Tourouvre (Orne), France 2001-2006 entitled Huguenots leaving France 1650s-60s, http://www.apointinhistory.net/larochelle.php and http://www.unicaen.fr/mrsh/prefen/index.php. Aaccessed March 3, 2018;

Personal discussions with Claude Bédard, a descendant of the family with knowledge of his family's history.

90 Trigger, *Children of Aataentsic*, 85–90.

91 Mann, Barbara Alice. *Spirits of Blood, Spirits of Breath: The Twinned Cosmos of Indigenous America*, 210. The piercing of the skull helps to release the spirit of breath; Trigger, *Children of Aataentsic*, 85-90.

92 Trigger, *Children of Aataentsic*, 562.

93 Peter Lowensteyn, *The Role of the Dutch in the Iroquois Wars*, http://www.lowensteyn.com/iroquois/. Accessed 2011-11-10.

94 Trigger, *Children of Aataentsic*, 575.

95 Trigger, *Children of Aataentsic*, 589.

96 Trigger, *Children of Aataentsic*, 587.

97 Trigger, *Children of Aataentsic*, 594.

98 Trigger, *Children of Aataentsic*, 598–600.

99 Delâge, *Le Pays Renversé*, 97. 'une sorte de «no man's land»' called Pays Veuf at a conference, Montreal, 2017. Francis Jennings first used the expression in 1975 in *The Invasion of America: The Cant of Conquest*.

100 Eric Pouliot-Thisdale, lecture, Laval Historical Society, Laval, Quebec. 2018-03-16, describing the St. Lawrence Iroquois as a part of the Mohawk people.

101 William Engelbrecht, and Bruce Jamieson, *"Stone-Tipped versus Bone- and Antler-tipped Arrows and the Movement of the St. Lawrence Iroquoians from Their Homeland,"* Ontario Archaeology, no. 96 (2016): 76.

102 Trigger, *Children of Aataentsic*, 744–745.

103 Trigger, *Children of Aataentsic*, 762–766. The description of the battle is a précis of Trigger's description.

104 Trigger, *Children of Aataentsic*, 759 -840.

105 Mann, *Iroquoian Women*, 146–152.

106 Sultzman, *Iroquois History*, http://www.tolatsga.org/iro.html. Accessed January 7, 2018.

107 Jean-François Beaudet, *Dans les filets du Diable*, (Paris: Médiaspaul, 2009), 62

108 Jesuit Relations and Allied Documents. *Volume XLVIII, Lower Canada, Ottawas 1662-1664.*

http://moses.creighton.edu/kripke/jesuitrelations/relations_48.html

109 Ted Widmer, *Carter Roger Williams Initiative*, http://www.findingrogerwilliams.com/essays/native-americans. Accessed 2019-03-13.

110 Sultzman, *Wampanoag History*, http://www.tolatsga.org/wampa.html. Accessed 2017-11-27.

111 Sultzman, *Wampanoag History.*

112 Francis Jennings, *The Ambiguous Iroquois Empire: The Covenant Chain Confederation of Indian Tribes with English Colonies from Its Beginnings to the Lancaster Treaty of 1744* (New York, NY: Norton, 1984), 145–171.

113 W.J. Eccles, *Jacques-René De Brisay, Marquis de Denonville*. Dictionary of Canadian Biography http://www.biographi.ca/.

114 Mann, *Iroquoian Women*, 150–51.

115 William N. Fenton. *The Great Law of the Longhouse, A Political History of the Iroquois Confederacy*. The Civilization of the American Indian Series, v. 223. (Norman: University of Oklahoma Press, 1998), Chapter 22: The Grand Settlement at Montreal, 1701.

116 Mann, Barbara Alice, Ed. *North American Speakers of the Eastern Woodlands, Selected Speeches and Critical Analysis*, Greenwood Press, 2001, Chapter 2, "Are You Delusional?": Kandiaronk on Christianity..

117 Brenda Katlatont Gabriel-Doxtater, Arlette Kawanatatie Van den Hende, and Kanesatake Education Center. *At the Woods' Edge: An Anthology of the History of the People of Kanehsatà:Ke*. Kanesatake (Quebec: Kanesatake Education Center, 1995), 14–16.

118 Gabriel-Doxtater, Van den Hende, and Kanesatake Education Center. *At the Woods' Edge*, 31–32. Current spelling of Kanehsatake includes the 'h'. I have left both spellings in because of different source material.

119 Gabriel-Doxtater, Van den Hende, and Kanesatake Education Center. At the Woods' Edge, 20.

120 Darren Bonaparte, *The Seven Nations of Canada, The Other Iroquois Confederacy* http://www.wampumchronicles.com/sevennations.html. Accessed 2020-11-15. Also called Seven Tribes and Seven Lands.

A MONSTER REPLICATES 1709-1760

121 Carl Waldman, *Atlas of the North American Indian*. (New York, NY: Facts on File, 1985), 104; Lee Sultzman, *Iroquois History*, http://www.tolatsga.org/iro.html. Accessed 2018-01-07.

122 C. Van Doren, and J.R. Boyd, eds. (1938), *A Treaty with the Indian Six Nations, 1744*, http://treatiesportal.unl.edu/earlytreaties/treaty.00003.html. Accessed 2018-03-28.

123 Howard Zinn, *A People's History of the United States*. 1st ed. (New York, NY: Harper Perennial, 1990), 85–86.

124 Graham, *Naming the Laurentians*, 45

125 Private consultation with Barbara Alice Mann, 2021-07-21. The term Ohio Seneca refers to that part of the Seneca Nation residing in the Ohio Valley.

126 Anacharsis Combes, *Jean-Louis Ligonier, Feld-Marèchal d'Irlande,* 1680-1770, (Castres, 1866). The story of Ligonier is another chapter in the Wars of Religion.

127 Graham, *Naming the Laurentians*, 77. The small Township of Abercrombie running southeast from Ste. Adele commemorates General James Abercromby, and being in Canada, it is not surprising that his name was misspelled. Exactly why he should have been so honoured is a bit of a mystery. It could be someone's sense of humour—an encrypted message to the future assuring that his incompetence not be forgotten.

128 The Canadiens were already an ethnic group by this time and their name cannot be translated to "Canadians" without confusing their ethnicity and identity.

129 C. P. Stacey, *Amherst, Jefferey, 1st Baron of Amherst*. Dictionary of Canadian Biography, http://www.biographi.ca.

BRITISH HEGEMONY 1763-1814

130 Lynn Gehl, *Claiming Anishinaabe: Decolonizing the Human Spirit*. (Saskatchewan: University of Regina Press, 2017), 105–106.

131 Robert Hughes, *The Fatal Shore*. 1st American ed. (New York: Knopf, 1987), 60.

132 Chris Alexander, *A Wretched and Motley Crew, The Struggle that Defined Two Nations*. Literary Review of Canada, November 2020, also at https://reviewcanada.ca/magazine/2020/11/a-wretched-motley-crew/.

133 Hunter Miller, Ed. *Declaration Signed by the American Commissioners plus Preliminary Articles of Peace; November 30, 1782*. http://avalon.law.yale.edu/18th_century/dec783.asp and

http://avalon.law.yale.edu/18th_century/prel1782.asp. Accessed 2019-03-14.

134 Mann, *Iroquoian Women*, 291-354

135 Fernand Ouellet, *Pierre-Stanislas Bédard*. Dictionary of Canadian Biography

136 David Shanahan, *Land for Goods: the Crawford Purchases* http://anishinabe-knews.ca/2018/11/08/land-for-goods-the-crawford-purchases/. Accessed 2018-12-31.

137 The now commonly used term guerrilla, meaning "little war" came from this time. It was similar to the war methods used by the Indigenous Peoples in the French and Indian War.

138 *Population of Ohio State, Historical Population*. https://population.us/oh/. Accessed 2019-01-03.

139 Bradford Perkins, ed., *The Causes of the War of 1812: National Honor or National Interest?* (New York: Holt, Rinehart and Winston, 1965), 56.

140 Kenneth Kidd, and Jim Coyle, *Crucible of Flames, Canada's War of 1812*. http://stardispatches.com/2012/12/crucible.pdf, 8. Accessed 2013-09-24.

141 Kidd and Coyle, *Crucible of Flames*, 9

142 Perkins, ed. *Causes of the War of 1812*, 54.

143 Kidd and Coyle, *Crucible of Flames*, 12.

144 Kidd and Coyle, *Crucible of Flames*, 23–27

CONCLUSION

145 Winona LaDuke, *'Minobimaatisiiwin: The Good Life'*. Accessed 21 January 2021. http://www.culturalsurvival.org/publications/cultural-survival-quarterly/minobimaatisiiwin-good-life.

146 Al Jazeera News Agency, November 22, 2018, *US missionary killed by endangered Andaman island tribesmen*. https://www.aljazeera.com/news/south-asia/2018/11/tourist-killed-arrow-shooting-andaman-island-tribesmen-181121074347304.html. Accessed 2020-07-01.

147 Gustavus Adolphus College. *Terra Nullius*, http://homepages.gac.edu/~lwren/AmericanIdentititesArt%20folder/AmericanIdentititesArt/Terra%20Nullius.html. Accessed 2020-09-08.

Bibliography
Printed Sources and Inspirations

Asch, Michael, John Borrows, and James Tully, eds. *Resurgence and Reconciliation: Indigenous-Settler Relations and Earth Teachings*. Toronto; Buffalo: University of Toronto Press, 2018.

Asturias, Miguel Angel, and Gerald Martin. *Men of Maize*. Critical ed., The Pittsburgh Editions of Latin American Literature. Pittsburgh: University of Pittsburgh Press, 1993.

Avramescu, Cătălin. *An Intellectual History of Cannibalism*. Translated by Alistair Ian Blyth. Princeton University Press, 2011.

Axtell, James. *After Columbus: Essays in the Ethnohistory of Colonial North America*. New York: Oxford University Press, 1988.

Barbeau, C.M. *Huron and Wyandot Mythology*. 1915. Reprint, Ottawa: Canada, Department of Mines, Geological Survey, Anthropological survey, 2017.

Beahen, William, and Stan Horrall. *Red Coats on the Prairies: The North-West Mounted Police, 1886-1900*. Regina, Sask.: Centax Books, PrintWest Pub. Services, 1998.

Beaudet, Jean-François. *Dans Les Filets Du Diable: Les Coureurs des Bois et l'univers Religieux Amérindien*. Montréal: Médiaspaul, 2009.

Biggar, H.P. *The Early Trading Companies of New France*. University of Toronto, 1901.

Brizinski, Peggy. *Knots in a String: An Introduction to Native Studies in Canada*. 2nd ed. Saskatoon: Univ. Extension Press, 1993.

Brody, Hugh. *The Other Side of Eden: Hunters, Farmers and the Shaping of the World*. Vancouver: Douglas & McIntyre, 2000.

Cahill, Susan Neunzig, ed. *Wise Women: Over Two Thousand Years of Spiritual Writing by Women*. New York: W.W. Norton, 1996.

Campeau, Lucien. *"Bédard, Marc-André, Les Protestants en Nouvelle-France. Cahiers d'Histoire, nº 31. La Société Historique de Québec, 1978."* Revue d'histoire de l'Amérique française 32, nº 4 (1979): 630.

Carayon, Céline. *Nonverbal Communication among French and Indigenous Peoples in the Americas*. Williamsburg, Virginia: Chapel Hill: Omohundro Institute of Early American History and Culture; University of North Carolina Press, 2019.

Cartier, Jacques. *Relation Originale du Voyage de Jacques Cartier au Canada en 1534*. Edited by Henri-Victor (1811-1890) & Alfred (1826-1886) Michelant & Ramé. 1867. Reprint, Paris: Librairie Tross, 2007

———. *Voyage de J. Cartier au Canada*. 1545. Reprint, Paris: Librairie Tross 1863, 2004.

Chatwin, Bruce. *The Songlines*. London: Picador, 1988.

Clément, Daniel, and Musée Canadien des Civilisations, eds. *The Algonquins*. Mercury Series, Canadian Ethnology Service Paper, 130.1996. Hull, QC: Canadian Museum of Civilization, 1996.

Combes, Anacharsis. *Jean-Louis Ligonier, Feld-Maréchal d'Irlande; 1688-1770*. Castres,

France: Imprimerie de veuve Grillon, 1866.

Cornplanter, Jesse J., and Sah-nee-weh. *Legends of the Longhouse*. Ohsweken, ON: Iroqrafts, 2007.

Culin, Stewart. *Games of the North American Indians*. New York: Dover Publications, 1975.

Cutler, Ebbitt, and Bruce Johnson. *I Once Knew an Indian Woman*. Montreal: Tundra Books, 1975.

De Montigny, B.A. Testard. *Colonization Région Labelle*. Montréal: C.O. Beauchemin et Fils, 1895.

Delâge, Denys. *Le Pays Renversé: Amérindiens et Européens En Amérique Du Nord-Est, 1600 - 1664*. Boréal Compact 25. Montréal: Boréal, 1991.

Deslandres, Dominique, John Alexander Dickinson, Ollivier Hubert, and Jacques Des Rochers, eds. *Les Sulpiciens de Montréal: Une Histoire de Pouvoir et de Discrétion, 1657-2007*. Saint-Laurent, Québec: Fides, 2007.

DeVries, Laura. *Conflict in Caledonia: Aboriginal Land Rights and the Rule of Law*. Law and Society Series. Vancouver: UBC Press, 2011.

Dickason, Olive Patricia. *Louisborug and the Indians*. 1971. Reprint, Ottawa: University of Ottawa, 2012.

Palmer, William R. *Why the North Star Stands Still, and Other Indian Legends*. Borodino Books, n.d.

Family Histories. *1856 Arundel 2006*. Arundel, QC: Municipality of Arundel, 2006.

Fenton, William N. *The Great Law and the Longhouse: A Political History of the Iroquois Confederacy*. The Civilization of the American Indian Series, vol. 223. Norman: University of Oklahoma Press, 1998.

Fischer, David Hackett. *Champlain's Dream: The Visionary Adventurer Who Made a New World in Canada*. Toronto: Vintage Canada, 2009.

Freud, Sigmund, and James Strachey. *Moses and Monotheism: Three Essays; Translated and Edited by James Strachey*. London: Hogarth Press: Institute of Psycho-Analysis, 1974.

Friedman, Richard Elliott. *Who Wrote the Bible?* Englewood Cliffs, NJ: Prentice Hall, 1987.

Froude, James Anthony. *The Spanish Story of the Armada and Other Essays*. London: Longmans, Green, and Co., 1892.

Gabriel-Doxtater, Brenda Katlatont, Arlette Kawanatatie Van den Hende, and Kanesatake Education Center. *At the Woods' Edge: An Anthology of the History of the People of Kanehsatà:Ke*. Kanesatake, QC: Kanesatake Education Center, 1995.

Garneau, François-Xavier. *Histoire du Canada français*. vols. 1–6. Montréal Les amis de l'histoire. 1845–1848. Reprint, Montreal: François Beauval, 1969.

Garrad, Charles. *Petun to Wyandot: The Ontario Petun from the Sixteenth Century*. Edited by William Fox and J.-L. Pilon. Mercury Series 174. Gatineau, Queebec: Ottawa: Canadian Museum of History; University of Ottawa Press, 2014.

Gatti, Maurizio. *Littérature amérindienne du Québec: écrits de langue française*, Montréal : Hurtubise HMH, 2004.

Gehl, Lynn. *Claiming Anishinaabe: Decolonizing the Human Spirit.* Regina, SK: University of Regina Press, 2017.

———. *The Truth That Wampum Tells: My Debwewin on the Algonquin Land Claims Process.* Halifax: Fernwood Publishing, 2014.

Gespe'gewa'gi Mi'gmawei Mawiomi, ed. *Nta'tugwaqanminen: Our Story: The Evolution of the Gespe'gewa'gi Mi'gmaq.* Black Point, NS: Fernwood Publishing, 2016.

Goeman, Mishuana. *Mark My Words: Native Women Mapping Our Nations.* First Peoples: New Directions in Indigenous Studies. Minneapolis: University of Minnesota Press, 2013.

Goldfarb, Ben. *Eager: The Surprising, Secret Life of Beavers and Why They Matter.* White River Junction, VT: Chelsea Green Publishing, 2018.

Graham, Joseph. *Naming the Laurentians: A History of Place Names "Up North."* Lachute, QC: Main Street, 2005.

Grand Council of the Crees (of Quebec), ed. *Sovereign Injustice: Forcible Inclusion of the James Bay Crees and Cree Territory into a Sovereign Québec.* Nemaska, Québec: Grand Council of the Crees, 1995.

Guinard, Joseph E. *Les noms indiens de mon pays.* Montréal: Rayonnement, 1960.

Henrich, Joseph Patrick. *The Weirdest People in the World: How the West Became Psychologically Peculiar and Particularly Prosperous.* New York: Farrar, Straus and Giroux, 2020.

Henty, G. A. *Saint Bartholomew's Eve.* 1894. Reprint, London: Blackie and Sons Ltd.

Houston, James. *Confessions of an Igloo Dweller.* Toronto, ON: McClelland & Stewart, 1995.

Hudon, Théophile. *L'Institut Canadien de Montréal.* Montréal: Librairie Beauchemin Limitée, 1938.

Hughes, Robert. *The Fatal Shore.* 1st American ed., New York: Knopf, 1987.

Hughson, John W. Bond, Courtney C.J. Bond, *Hurling Down the Pine: The Story of the Wright, Gilmour and Hughson Families, Timber and Lumber Manufacturers in the Hull and Ottawa Region and on the Gatineau River, 1800–1920.* Old Chelsea, QC: The Historical Society of the Gatineau. 2nd ed., Revised, 1965.

Jacobsen, Thorkild. *The Treasures of Darkness: A History of Mesopotamian Religion.* New Haven: Yale University Press, 1976.

Jacoby, Russell. *Bloodlust: On the Roots of Violence from Cain and Abel to the Present.* New York: Free Press, 2011.

Jenkinson, Charles. *A Collection of All the Treaties of Peace, Alliance and Commerce Between Great Britain and Other Powers.* vol. 3. London: J. Debrett, 1785.

Jenness, Eileen. *The Indian Tribes of Canada.* Toronto: Ryerson Press, 1966.

Jennings, Francis. *The Ambiguous Iroquois Empire: The Covenant Chain Confederation of Indian Tribes with English Colonies from Its Beginnings to the Lancaster Treaty of 1744.* New York: Norton, 1984.

Jiles, Paulette. *North Spirit: Travels among the Cree and Ojibway Nations and Their Star Maps.* Toronto: Doubleday Canada, 1995.

Keller, Werner, and Joachim Rehork. *The Bible as History.* 2nd rev. ed., 1st U.S. ed.

New York: Morrow, 1981.

Kimmerer, Robin Wall. *Braiding Sweetgrass: Indigenous Wisdom, Scientific Knowledge and the Teachings of Plants*. Minneapolis, MN: Milkweed Editions, 2013.

King, Thomas. *The Truth about Stories: A Native Narrative*. The Massey Lectures Series. Toronto: House of Anansi Press, 2003.

Kirsch, Jonathan. *The Woman Who Laughed at God: The Untold History of the Jewish People*. New York: Viking, 2001.

Lahontan, Baron de. *Dialogues avec un sauvage*. Collection ni-t'chawama/mon ami mon frère. 1690. Reprint, Montréal: éditions sociales/éditions Leméac, 1973.

Lapierre, André. *Toponymie française en Ontario*. Collection l'Ontario Français. Montréal: Éd. Études Vivantes, 1981.

Larin, Robert. *Brève Histoire des Protestants en Nouvelle-France et au Québec, XVIe-XIXe Siècles*. Collection Patrimoine, n° 2. Saint-Alphonse-de-Granby, Québec: Editions de la Paix, 1998.

Laubin, Reginald and Gladys. *The Indian Tipi*. 1971. Reprint, New York: Ballantine Books Inc., 1973.

Laurin, Serge. *Histoire des Laurentides*. Collection Les Régions du Québec 3. Québec: Institut québécois de recherche sur la culture, 1989.

Lee, Robert C. *The Canada Company and the Huron Tract, 1826-1853: Personalities, Profits and Politics*. Toronto: Natural Heritage Books, 2004.

Lerner, Gerda. *The Creation of Patriarchy*. Women and History, vol. 1. New York: Oxford University Press, 1986.

Li, Shenwen. *Stratégies missionnaires des jésuites français en Nouvelle-France et en Chine au XVIIe siècle*. Collection Intercultures. Sainte-Foy, Québec: Paris: Presses de l'UniversitéLaval; L'Harmattan, 2001.

Linebaugh, Peter, and Marcus Rediker. *The Many-Headed Hydra: Sailors, Slaves, Commoners, and the Hidden History of the Revolutionary Atlantic*. 2nd ed. Boston: Beacon Press, 2013.

Lovelock, James. *Healing Gaia: Practical Medicine for the Planet*. 1st American ed. New York: Harmony Books, 1991.

Lower, Arthur R. M. *Great Britain's Woodyard: British America and the Timber Trade, 1763-1867*. Montreal: McGill-Queen's University Press, 1973.

MacCaffrey, James. *History of the Catholic Church from the Renaissance to the French Revolution*. vols. 1 & 2. Dublin, Ireland: Guilielmus, Archiep. Dublinen., Hiberniæ Primas., 1914.

MacDonald, Robert. *The Romance of Canadian History*. vol. 2. Calgary, Alberta: The Ballantrae Foundation, 1974.

Maltais, André. *Le Réveil de l'aigle: Les Peuples Autochtones, des Sociétés en Mutation*. Rosemère, Québec: Éditions Pierre Tisseyre, 2013.

Mann, Barbara Alice. *Iroquoian Women: The Gantowisas*. New York: P. Lang, 2000.

Mann, Charles C. *1491: New Revelations of the Americas before Columbus*. 1st ed. New York: Knopf, 2005.

Mann, Barbara Alice, Editor. North American Speakers of the Eastern Woodlands,

Selected Speeches and Critical Analysis, Greenwood Press, 2001.

———. *Spirits of Blood, Spirits of Breath: The Twinned Cosmos of Indigenous America.* New York: Oxford University Press, 2016.

Marsh, James H., ed. *The Canadian Encyclopedia.* Edmonton: Hurtig Publishers, 1985.

———. *The Canadian Encyclopedia.* Toronto: McClelland & Stewart, 2000.

Mika, Nick, Helma Mika, and Nick Mika. *Places in Ontario: Their Name Origins and History.* Encyclopedia of Ontario; vol. 2. Belleville, ON: Mika Publishing Co, 1977.

Miller, Dorcas S. *Stars of the First People: Native American Star Myths and Constellations.* Boulder, CO: Pruett Pub. Co, 1997.

Moodie, Suzanna. *Roughing It in the Bush.* 1871. Reprint, Toronto: Maclear & Co., 2011.

Motley, Timothy J., ed. *Darwin's Harvest: New Approaches to the Origins, Evolution, and Conservation of Crops.* New York: Columbia University Press, 2006.

National Centre for Truth and Reconciliation. *Truth and Reconciliation.* Manitoba: University of Manitoba, n.d.

Palmer, William R. *Why the North Star Stands Still.* 1946. Reprint, Springdale, UT: Zion Natural History Association, 1978.

Paquin, Jean-Guy. *Au pays des Weskarinis: récit.* Chénéville, QC: Collection Outaouais éditeur, 2014.

Parkman, Francis. *France and England in North America. Part First - Pioneers of France in the New World.* New York: Library of America.

———. *Montcalm and Wolfe.* Markham, ON: Viking, 1984.

———. *The Conspiracy of Pontiac and the Indian War after the Conquest of Canada.* Lincoln: University of Nebraska Press, 1994.

Parr Traill, Catharine. *The Backwoods of Canada.* 1836.

Pasternak, Shiri. *Grounded Authority: The Algonquins of Barriere Lake against the State.* Minneapolis: University of Minnesota Press, 2017.

Paxton, James W. *Joseph Brant and His World: Eighteenth-Century Mohawk Warrior and Statesman.* Toronto: J. Lorimer & Co., 2008.

Perkins, Bradford, ed. *The Causes of the War of 1812: National Honor or National Interest?* New York: Holt, Rinehart and Winston, 1965.

Perrin, Jean Paul. *History of the Ancient Christians.* 1618. Reprint, Rapidan, VA: Hartland Publications, 1997.

Philbrick, Nathaniel. *Mayflower: A Voyage to War.* London: HarperPress, 2006.

Poirier, Jean. *Regards sur les Noms de Lieux.* Études et Recherches Toponymiques 3. Québec: Commission de toponymie, Gouvernement, 1982.

Pound, Arthur. *Johnson of the Mohawks.* New York: The MacMillan Company, 1930.

Prechtel, Martín. *The Unlikely Peace at Cuchumaquic: The Parallel Lives of People as Plants, Keeping the Seeds Alive.* Berkeley, CA: North Atlantic Books, 2012.

Quimby, George I. *Indian Life in the Upper Great Lakes: 11,000 B.C. to A.D. 1800.* Chicago: Chicago University Press, 1974.

Raver, Miki. *Listen to Her Voice: Women of the Hebrew Bible.* San Francisco, CA:

Chronicle Books, 1998.

Reséndez, Andrés. *A Land so Strange: The Epic Journey of Cabeza de Vaca: The Extra-ordinary Tale of a Shipwrecked Spaniard Who Walked across America in the Six-teenth Century*. New York: Basic Books, 2007.

Royal Ontario Museum and McCord Museum, eds. *Quillwork by Native Peoples in Canada: Royal Ontario Museum, from October 1977 to January 1978 = Travaux En Piquants de Porc-Épic Exécutés Par Les Autochtones Au Canada: Musée McCord Museum de Février À Mai 1978*. Toronto, ON: Royal Ontario Museum, 1977.

Saul, John Ralston. *A Fair Country: Telling Truths about Canada*. Toronto: Viking Ca-nada, 2008.

Schele, Linda, and David A. Freidel. *A Forest of Kings: The Untold Story of the Ancient Maya*. New York: Quill/W. Morrow, 1992.

Schmalz, Peter S. *The Ojibwa of Southern Ontario*. Toronto; Buffalo: University of To-ronto Press, 1991.

Schneider, Paul. *The Adirondacks: A History of America's First Wilderness*. 1st ed. New York: H. Holt and Co, 1997.

Scott, David. *Ontario Place Names*. 5th ed. Allanburg, ON: Despub, 2007.

Seeman, Erik R. *The Huron-Wendat Feast of the Dead: Indian-European Encounters in Early North America*. Witness to History. Baltimore: Johns Hopkins University Press, 2011.

Shemie, Bonnie. *Houses of Bark: Tipi, Wigwam and Longhouse: Native Dwellings: Woodland Indians*. Montreal, QC; Plattsburgh, NY: Tundra Books, 1990.

Shorto, Russell. *The Island at the Center of the World: The Untold Story of Dutch Man-hattan and the Founding of New York*. London; New York: Doubleday, 2004.

Simpson, Audra. *Mohawk Interruptus: Political Life across the Borders of Settler States*. Durham, NC: Duke University Press, 2014.

Sioui, Georges E., and Dalie Giroux. *Histoires de Kanatha: vues et contées; essais et dis-cours, 1991-2008: seen and told; essays and discourses, 1991-2008 = Histories of Ka-natha*. Ottawa: Presses de l'Université d'Ottawa, 2008.

Stephens, Hiram B. *Jacques Cartier and His Four Voyages to Canada*. 1890. Montreal: W. Drysdale & Co.

Stone, William L. *The Life and Times of Sir William Johnson, Bart*. vol. 2. 1865. Re-print, Albany, NY: J. Munsell, 2008.

———. *The Life and Times of Sir William Johnson, Bart*. vol. 1. 1865. Reprint, Albany, NY: J. Munsell, 2010.

Talaga, Tanya. *All Our Relations: Finding the Path Forward*. The CBC Massey Lectures Series. Toronto: Anansi, 2018.

Taylor, Alan. *The Divided Ground: Indians, Settlers and the Northern Borderland of the American Revolution*. New York: Vintage, 2007.

Teilhard de Chardin, Pierre. *Hymn of the Universe*. William Collins Sons & Co. Ltd. Fontana Religious Books. 1965. Reprint, Glasgow: William Collins Sons & Co. Ltd and Harper and Rowe, New York, 1981.

———. *The Phenomenon of Man.* Fontana Books. 1959. Reprint, London: William Collins Sons and Co. Ltd and New York: Harper Brothers, 1966.

The Torah The Five Books of Moses: A New Translation of the Holy Scriptures According to the Masoretic Text. Philadelphia: The Jewish Publication Society of America, 1962.

Thomas, Cyrus. *History of the Counties of Argenteuil, Quebec & Prescott, Ontario.* Milton, ON: Global, 1999.

Thomas, Earle. *The Three Faces of Molly Brant: A Biography.* Kingston, ON: Quarry Press, 1996.

Treuer, David. *The Heartbeat of Wounded Knee: Native America from 1890 to the Present.* New York: Riverhead Books, 2019.

Trigger, Bruce G. *The Children of Aataentsic: A History of the Huron People to 1660.* Reprint with a new preface, 1st paperback ed. Kingston: McGill-Queen's University Press, 1987.

Van Ruymbeke, Bertrand, and Randy J Sparks, eds. *Memory and Identity: The Huguenots in France and the Atlantic Diaspora.* Columbia, SC: University of South Carolina Press, 2008.

Vaugeois, Denis, Käthe Roth, and Louise Côté. *America's Gift: What the World Owes to the Americas and Their First Inhabitants.* Montreal; Sillery: Baraka Books; Septentrion, 2009.

Veyssière, Laurent, and Bertrand Fonck, eds. *La Guerre de Sept Ans en Nouvelle-France.* Montréal: Septentrion, 2012.

Waldman, Carl. *Atlas of the North American Indian.* 12. print. New York: Facts on File, 1985.

Weatherford, Jack McIver. *Indian Givers: How the Indians of the Americas Transformed the World.* 1. Ballantine Books ed. New York: Fawcett Columbine, 1990.

White, Henry. *The Massacre of St. Bartholomew.* 1868. London: John Murray.

Whitehead, A.W. *Gaspard de Coligny.* 1896. Reprint, London: Methuen & Co.

Woolley, Charles Leonard. *The Sumerians.* New York: Norton, 2004.

Woolley, Sir Leonard. *Ur.* London; New York: Penguin Books, 1946.

Wright, J. V. *Quebec Prehistory.* Toronto: Van Nostrand Reinhold, 1979.

Wright, Ronald. *Stolen Continents: The "New World" through Indian Eyes.* Toronto: Penguin Books, 1993.

Zinn, Howard. *A People's History of the United States.* 1st ed. New York: Harper Perennial, 1990.

Bibliography
Online Sources and Inspirations
Available with live links at InsatiableHunger.ca

Al Jazeera News Agency November 22, 2018, *US missionary killed by endangered Andaman island tribesmen*, https://www.aljazeera.com/news/southasia/2018/11/tourist-killed-arrow-shooting-andaman-island-tribesmen-181121074347304.html

Alesina, Alberto F, Paola Giuliano, and Nathan Nunn. *On the Origins of Gender Roles: Women and the Plough*. https://www.nber.org/papers/w17098.pdf

Algonquins of Ontario. *Our Proud History*. http://www.tanakiwin.com/algonquins-of-ontario/our-proud-history/

Alexander, Chris. *A Wretched and Motley Crew, The Struggle that Defined Two Nations*, Literary Review of Canada, November 2020 also viewable at https://reviewcanada.ca/magazine/2020/11/a-wretched-motley-crew/

Amos, Christopher J. *Ganatsekwyagon, The Seneca! and Other Observations*. http://www.rivernen.ca/g_proj_0.htm

Ancient World History. *Visigoth Kingdom of Spain*. http://earlyworldhistory.blogspot.com/2012/01/visigoth-kingdom-of-spain.html

Andre, Jacki. *Contagious disease and Huron Women, 1630-1650*. https://harvest.usask.ca/handle/10388/etd-10122007-133351

Arthur, Stephen. *An Anarchist Study of the Rotinonshón:ni Polity*. http://nefac.net/anarchiststudyofiroquois

Ashley, Maurice, and John S. Morrill. *Oliver Cromwell*. https://www.britannica.com/biography/Oliver-Cromwell

Atikamekw Nehirowisiw, *Déclaration de Souveraineté d'Atikamekw Nehirowisiw*. https://www.cerp.gouv.qc.ca/fileadmin/Fichiers_clients/Documents_deposes_a_la_Commission/P-034.pdf

Awashish, Philip, Richard Saunders, and Robert Kanatewat. *Cree-Nascapi Commission 1998 report*. http://www.creenaskapicommission.net/1998/rep98.htm

Bakker, Peter. *A Basque Etymology for the Amerindian Tribal Name Iroquois*. www.ehu.eus/ojs/index.php/ASJU/article/download/9275/8503

Bangs, Jeremy Dupertuis. *The Pilgrims and Other English in Leiden Records*. https://jhowell.com/tng/histories/PilgrimsAndOtherEnglishinLeidenRecordsByJeremy-Bangs.pdf

———. *Who Were the Pilgrims*. http://www.leidenamericanpilgrimmuseum.org/Page31K.htm

Basseterre. *Basseterre, St. Kitt's*. https://potbs.fandom.com/wiki/Basseterre

BBC History. *Henry VIII*. http://www.bbc.co.uk/history/people/henry_viii/

Becker, Anke. *Herding and Male Dominance (Preliminary Version)*. https://ssrn.com/abstract=3069684

———. *On the Economic Origins of Female Genital Cutting*. https://papers.ssrn.com/sol3/papers.cfm?abstract_id=3069684

Bélanger, Claude. *Henri de Lévis, Duc de Ventador (short description)*. http://faculty.marianopolis.edu/c.belanger/quebechistory/encyclopedia/HenrideLevisducdeVentadour-QuebecHistory.htm

———. *Huron Indians*. http://faculty.marianopolis.edu/c.belanger/quebechistory/encyclopedia/HuronIndians.htm

———. *Huron Indians: The Quebec Encyclopedia*. http://faculty.marianopolis.edu/c.belanger/quebechistory/encyclopedia/HuronIndians.htm

———. *Pontiac's War*. http://faculty.marianopolis.edu/c.belanger/quebechistory/encyclopedia/Pontiacwar.htm

Béliveau, Jean Claude «Sa'n». *Nations des Ameriques.* http://www.astrosante.com/NationsDesAmeriques.html

Belleau, Irène. *Les Filles du Roy par nom de famille (nom de fille).* http://lesfillesduroy-quebec.org/images/Les_filles_du_Roy_par_nom_de_famille.140212.pdf

———. *Filles du Roy protestantes.* http://lesfillesduroy-quebec.org/publications/articles/de-la-shfr/104-filles-du-roy-protestantes

Betros, Gemma. *The French Revolution and the Catholic Church.* https://www.historytoday.com/archive/french-revolution-and-catholic-church

Biography Newsletter. *Anne Boleyn Biography.* https://www.biography.com/people/anne-boleyn-9218155

———. *Daniel Boone Biography.* http://www.biography.com/people/daniel-boone-9219543

———. *Henry IV Biography (1553–1610).* https://www.biography.com/royalty/henry-iv

———. *Henri IV Biography Synopsis.* http://www.biography.com/people/henry-iv-9335199#synopsis

———. *John Calvin Theologian, Journalist (1509–1564) synopsis.* http://www.biography.com/people/john-calvin-9235788#synopsis

Birch, Jennifer. *Coalescence and Conflict in Iroquoian Ontario.* http://anthropology.uga.edu/

Birch, Jennifer, and Ronald F Williamson. *Navigating ancestral landscapes in the Northern Iroquoian world.* https://asiheritage.ca/publication/navigating-ancestral-landscapes-in-the-northern-iroquoian-world/

Blair, Peggy. *Iroquoian Torture.* https://peggyblair.wordpress.com/2013/12/31/iroquois-torture-canadian-history-part-ii/

Bonaparte, Darren. *The Seven Nations of Canada: The Other Iroquois Confederacy.* http://www.wampumchronicles.com/sevennations.html

Booth, Hannah. *The Kingdom of Women: The Society where a Man is Never the Boss.* https://www.theguardian.com/lifeandstyle/2017/apr/01/the-kingdom-of-women-the-tibetan-tribe-where-a-man-is-never-the-boss

Boswell, Randy. *Asian Link found with Dene, Navaho, Apache Languages.* http://www.montrealgazette.com/life/Asian+link+found+with+Dene+Navaho+Apache+languages/3244436/story.html#ixzz0typhvOvG

Brackney, William H. *Birthing a Principle: Baptists and Separation of Church and State.* http://www.txbc.org/2004Journals/April%202004/Apr04BirthingaPrinciple.htm

Bradley, Harriett. *The Enclosures in England an Economic Reconstruction.* https://socialsciences.mcmaster.ca/econ/ugcm/3ll3/bradley/Enclosure.pdf

Bremer, Francis J. *The American Puritans: Christian History Timeline.* http://www.christianitytoday.com/history/issues/issue-41/american-puritans-christian-history-timeline.html

Britannica. *Peace of Augsburg.* https://www.britannica.com/event/Peace-of-Augsburg

———. *Peace of Augsburg.* https://www.britannica.com/print/article/42767

———. *Peter Minuit, Dutch Colonial Governor.* https://www.britannica.com/biography/Peter-Minuit

———. *Pilgrimage of Grace.* https://www.britannica.com/event/Pilgrimage-of-Grace

———. *Puritanism.* https://www.britannica.com/topic/Puritanism

———. *Religion Germany: Religious Affiliation.* https://www.britannica.com/place/Germany/Religion#ref296841

Burke, A. E., *Jacques Cartier's First Voyage and the Landing at Cascumpec,* The Prince Edward Island Magazine, October 1899 Vol 1 No. 8, 294 to 299 https://www.islandimagined.ca/articles

Bycroft, Clare, Ceres Fernandez-Rozadilla, Clara Ruiz-Ponte, Inés Quintela, Angel Carracedo, Peter Donnelly, and Simon Myers. *Patterns of Genetic Differentiation and the Footprints of Historical Migrations in the Iberian Peninsula.* https://www.nature.com/articles/s41467-018-08272-w

Canada, Indian Act 74 (1) *Elections of Chiefs and Band Councils.* https://laws-lois.justice.gc.ca/PDF/I-5.pdf

Canadian Genealogy. *The Recollet Friars.* http://www.canadiangenealogy.net/chronicles/rocollet_friars.htm

Carroll, Sean B. *History of Corn.* https://www.nytimes.com/2010/05/25/science/25creature.html

Cartwright, Mark. *Dissolution of the Monasteries.* https://www.ancient.eu/Dissolution_of_the_Monasteries/

Casavant, James W. *Henri IV et l'Edit de Nantes.* https://sites.google.com/site/casavaniajwm/trivial-importance/henri-quatre-et-l-edit-de-nantes

Castelow, Ellen. *Lady Jane Grey.* http://www.historic-uk.com/HistoryUK/HistoryofEngland/Lady-Jane-Grey/

Cavendish, Richard. *New Amsterdam Surrendered to the English.* www.historytoday.com/archive/history-today/volume-64-issue-9-september-2014

Cebert, Hermann H. *Le Vrai Discours Actuel de Hermann Cebert.* https://levraidiscoursactuel.com/2014/09/09/declaration-de-souverainete-datikamekw-nehirowisiw-un-precedent-de-souverainete-et-dindependance-dans-lhistoire-du-canada-et-du-quebec/

Chadwick, Ian. *Henry Hudson, The Aftermath of Hudson's Voyages and Related Notes, 1611-on.* http://www.ianchadwick.com/hudson/hudson_05.htm

Chaney, Eric. *Institutional Inertia: Political Legitimacy in Muslim Iberia.* http://economics.stanford.edu/files/Theses/Theses_2003/Chaney.pdf

Charles, Jean-Léon. *Alessandro Farnese, Duke of Parma and Piacenza.* https://www.britannica.com/biography/Alessandro-Farnese-duke-of-Parma-and-Piacenza

Cheng, Selina. *DNA Evidence Proves a Maternal Dynasty Existed in North America 1,200 Years Ago.* https://qz.com/916728/dna-evidence-proves-a-maternal-dynasty-existed-in-north-america-1200-years-ago/

Cheung, Iva. *10 Ancient Methods of Birth Control.* http://listverse.com/2010/11/14/10-ancient-methods-of-birth-control/

Choi, Charles Q., *Hunters and Herders: Ancient Civilization Made Rapid Switch, Live Science,* https://www.livescience.com/45188-neolithic-transition-hunting-herding.html

Christian History. *John Calvin Father of the Reformed Faith.* http://www.christianitytoday.com/history/people/theologians/john-calvin.html

Clark, Jessica. *Timucua Indians of the Southeast.* https://www.manataka.org/page1232.html

Clifford, Cassandra. *Rape as a Weapon of War and Its Long-Term Effects on Victims and Society.* https://www.peacewomen.org/sites/default/files/vaw_rapeasaweaponofwar_stopmodern-slavery_may2008_0.pdf

Columbia Encyclopedia, 6th ed. *Antoine de Bourbon.* https://www.encyclopedia.com/people/history/french-history-biographies/antoine-de-bourbon

Colonial Williamsburg Foundation. *Neolin's Vision.* http://www.ouramericanrevolution.org/index.cfm/page/view/m0168

Come, Penny. *First Nations to be Stewards of the Land.* http://rabble.ca/blogs/bloggers/otherhand/2018/03/first-nations-be-stewards-land

Congregation Kehillat Israel. *History of the Jews in Spain.* http://kehillatisrael.net/docs/learning/sephardim.html

Cortez, Jan. *1881 History of Northern Wisconsin Illustrated.* http://www.jansdigs.com/Winnebago/1881indianhistory.html

Cruikshank, E.A., Coll. *Records of Niagara 1784-1787.* www.nhsm.ca/media/NHS39.pdf

Cryer, A. B. *Indian Barrier State Explained.* https://everything.explained.today/Indian_barrier_state/

Cummins, Joseph. *Algonquin Beliefs in Spirits & Nature.* http://classroom.synonym.com/algonquin-beliefs-spirits-nature-8407.html

Daschuk, James. *CBC podcast Secret Life of Canada 'Why some folks feel weird about Hudson's Bay blankets'* https://www.cbc.ca/radio/secretlifeofcanada/why-some-folks-feel-weird-about-hudson-s-bay-blankets-1.4846059

Day Translations Team. *Ancient Wari Civilization.* https://www.daytranslations.com/blog/2014/07/ancient-wari-civilization-surprising-secrets-revealed-recent-discovery-5215

Delors, Catherine. *14th of May 1610: Assassination of King Henri IV.* http://blog.catherinedelors.com/14th-of-may-1610-assassination-of-king-henri-iv/

Doré, José. *Mademoiselle Baboche, héroïne oubliée du quartier Saint-Roch.* https://monsaintroch.com/2018/mademoiselle-baboche-heroine-oubliee-saint-roch/

Drake, Nadia. *Prehistoric Women Had Stronger Arms Than Modern Athletes.* https://news.nationalgeographic.com/2017/11/prehistoric-women-manual-labor-stronger-athletes-science/?em_pos=large&ref=headline

Droulers-Tsiionhiakwatha Archeological Site Interpretation Center. *Iroquoiens Saint-Laurent, Un portrait des descendants.* http://www.virtualmuseum.ca/sgc-cms/expositions-exhibitions/iroquoiens-iroquoians/descendants_contact-story_continues_contact-fra.html

Dubois, François. *The Saint Bartholomew's Day Massacre.* http://www.reformation.org/bart.html

Dunn, Susan. *An Icy Conquest.* https://getpocket.com/explore/item/an-icy-conquest?utm_source=pocket-newtab

El Kenz, David. *Massacres During the Wars of Religion.* http://www.massviolence.org/Massacres-during-the-Wars-of-Religion?cs=print

Economist. *Geomythology: An Australian Legend May Be the World's Oldest Datable Story.* https://www.economist.com/science-and-technology/2020/02/27/an-australian-legend-may-be-the-worlds-oldest-datable-story

Eccles W.J. *Brisay De Denonville, Jacques-René De, Marquis de Denonville*, Dictionary of Canadian Biography http://www.biographi.ca.

Encyclopedia Britannica 1911. *Lamoral, Count of Egmont.* https://theodora.com/encyclopedia/e/lamoral_count_of_egmont.html

Encyclopedia of World Biography. *Mary (Molly) Brant.* http://www.encyclopedia.com/people/history/historians-miscellaneous-biographies/molly-brant

Engelbrecht, William. *Factors Maintaining Low Population Density Among the Prehistoric New York Iroquois.* https://www.jstor.org/stable/281057 & https://www.academia.edu/12753626/Factors_Maintaining_Low_Population_Density_among_the_Prehistoric_New_York_Iroquois?email_work_card=view-paper

Engelbrecht, William, and Bruce Jamieson. *Stone-Tipped versus Bone- and Antler-tipped Arrows and the Movement of the St. Lawrence Iroquoians from Their Homeland.* https://www.ontarioarchaeology.org/resources/Publications/OA96-8%20Engelbrecht%20Jamieson.pdf

Famous People. *Louis XIII of France.* http://www.thefamouspeople.com/profiles/louis-xiii-of-france-6768.php

Farley, William P. *Thomas Cartwright And English Presbyterianism.* http://enrichmentjournal.ag.org/200501/200501_120_cartwright.cfm

Ferguson, Rich. *Spur's Defeat by Shawnee in 1812.* http://www.warof1812.ca/spurdefeat.htm

Find a Grave. *Chief "Hokolewskwa" Cornstalk.* http://www.findagrave.com/cgi-bin/fg.cgi?page=gr&GRid=5782

Flores, Bartolomé de. *La felice victoria.* http://common-place.org/book/la-felice-victoria/

Gairdner, James. *Queen Mary I (1516-1558).* http://www.luminarium.org/encyclopedia/queen-mary.htm

Garner, Dwight. *The Real-Life story of 'The Last Whalers' Reads Like a First-Rate Novel.* https://www.nytimes.com/2019/01/14/books/review-last-whalers-doug-bock-clark.html?emc=edit_th_190115&nl=todaysheadlines&nlid=383056670115

Garrad, Charles. *The Recollects and the Petun.* http://www.wyandot.org/PETUN/RB%2021%20to%2030/PRI24.pdf

———. *Ekarenniondi and Oscotarach.* http://www.wyandot.org/PETUN/RB%201%20to%2020/PRI20.pdf

Gascoigne, Bamber. *History of the Spanish Empire.* http://www.historyworld.net/wrldhis/PlainTextHistories.asp?groupid=1734&HistoryID=ab49&gtrack=pthc

———. *The Punic Wars.* http://www.historyworld.net/wrldhis/PlainTextHistories.asp?historyid=ac53

Genetic Science Learning Centre. *The Evolution of Corn.* http://learn.genetics.utah.edu/content/variation/corn/

Gerulaityte, Egle. *Guna Yala: The Island Where Women Make the Rules.* http://www.bbc.com/travel/story/20180813-guna-yala-the-islands-where-women-make-the-rules

Gilder Lehrman Collection. *The Doctrine of Discovery, 1493.* https://www.gilderlehrman.org/content/doctrine-discovery-1493

Godfrey, Kate. *Early Visions of Florida, Pedro Menéndez de Avilés, Letter to King Philip II.* http://earlyfloridalit.net/?page_id=647

Goettner-Abendroth, Heide. *Matriarchal Society and the Gift Paradigm.* http://www.gift-economy.com/womenand/womenand_matriarchal.html

Gottheil, Richard, and Meyer Kayserling. *Nagdela, Abu usain Joseph Ibn.* http://www.jewish-encyclopedia.com/articles/11271-nagdela-nagrela-abu-husainjoseph-ibn

Greenwood, Frederick, *Greenwood Gemeologies, 1154-1914, Chapter 5: The Execution of John Greenwood.* http://www.rootsweb.ancestry.com/~genepool/grnwd5.htm

Greshko, Michael. *Famous Viking Warrior was a Woman, DNA Reveals.* https://www.reddit.com/r/SpaceFeminists/comments/706z99/famous_viking_warrior_was_a_woman_dna_reveals_by/

Guizot, Francois Pierre Guillaume. *A Popular History of France Vol 5 XXXVIII. Louis XIII., Cardinal Richelieu, and the Court, 1622-42.* http://www.hellenicaworld.com/France/Literature/FPGuizot/en/APopularHistoryOfFrance5.html#2HCH6

Gustavus Adolphus College. *Terra Nullius.* http://homepages.gac.edu/~lwren/AmericanIdentititesArt%20folder/AmericanIdentititesArt/Terra%20Nullius.html

Guttinger, Christiane *La Place des Huguenots dans l'Établissement de la Nouvelle France.* http://www.huguenots.fr/2010/09/la-place-des-huguenots-dans-letablissement-de-la-nouvelle-france/

Guy, John. *The Economy under Henry VIII.* https://tudorteacher.wordpress.com/economyhenryviii/

Hannan, Angela A. *A Chapter in the History of Huronia.* http://www.umanitoba.ca/colleges/st_pauls/ccha/Back%20Issues/CCHA1944-45/Hannan.html

Hanson, Marilee. *Mary, Queen of Scots: Biography, Facts, Portraits & Information.* https://englishhistory.net/tudor/relative/mary-queen-of-scots/

Hat Shapers. *Information on How to Felt and Felting.* http://web.archive.org/web/20100708043049/http://www.hatshapers.com/Felting%20Info.htm

Hazard, Ebenezer. *Dutch Minister Describes the Iroquois (1644).* http://www.swarthmore.edu/SocSci/bdorsey1/41docs/07-dut.html

Heal, Felicity. *Cuius Regio, Eius Religio? The Churches, Politics, and Religious Identities, 1558-1600.* https://www.oxfordscholarship.com/view/10.1093/0198269242.001.0001/acprof-9780198269243-chapter-10

Hickerson, Harold. *The Feast of the Dead Among the Seventeenth Century Algonkians of the Upper Great Lakes.* http://onlinelibrary.wiley.com/doi/10.1525/aa.1960.62.1.02a00050/pdf

Hickman, Kennedy. *French & Indian War: Field Marshal Jeffery Amherst.* https://www.thoughtco.com/french-indian-war-field-marshal-jeffery-amherst-2360684

L'histoire de France et du Monde. *Chronologie des rois de France.* http://www.histoire-pour-tous.fr/chronologies/3302-chronologie-des-rois-de-france.html

Historie Normandie. *Les Guerres de religion.* http://www.histoire-normandie.fr/la-normandie-de-1469-a-1789/les-guerres-de-religion

History Newsletter. *Thirty Years' War.* http://www.history.com/topics/thirty-years-war

History of the Netherlands. *(Timeline) Exploring America's Dutch Heritage.* https://www.newnetherlandinstitute.org/education/for-students/fun-re/going-dutch-a-visit-to-new-netherland/timeline/

History World. *History of the Netherlands.* http://www.historyworld.net/wrldhis/PlainTextHistories.asp?groupid=3102&HistoryID=ac90&gtrack=pthc

History.com. *Roger Williams.* https://www.history.com/topics/reformation/roger-williams

Holinshed, Raphael. *The First Book of the Historie of England.* http://www.gutenberg.org/files/16496/16496-8.txt

Holmes, Joan. *Algonquins of Golden Lake Claim.* http://www.joanholmes.ca/Execsum.pdf

Holy Roman Empire Association. *The Complete List of Holy Roman Emperors.* http://www.holyromanempireassociation.com/list-of-holy-roman-emperors.html

Horn-Miller, Kahente *The Integral Role of Indigenous Women's Knowledge".* http://rabble.ca/books/reviews/2016/07/integral-role-indigenous-womens-knowledge

Hunter, James. *History of the Huron People until 1614.* http://www.wyandot.org/wn_early.htm

Hutchinson, Robert. *How the Spanish Armada Was Really Defeated.* http://www.thehistoryreader.com/modern-history/spanish-armada-really-defeated/

d'Huy, Julien. "The Evolution of Myths," *Scientific American Vol* 315, no. 6 (December 2016) p.64: ISSN: 00368733.

Hyper History On-line. *War of Spanish Succession.* http://www.hyperhistory.com/online_n2/civil_n2/histscript6_n2/span_succ.html

Illing, Sean. *Why a leading political theorist thinks civilization is overrated,* interview with Vox https://www.vox.com/conversations/2017/11/22/16649038/civilization-progress-humanity-history-technology?wpisrc=nl_todayworld&wpmm=1

Indigenous and Northern Affairs Canada. *Algonquins of Barriere Lake.* https://www.aincinac.gc.ca/eng/1100100016352/1100100016353

International Relations and Security Network. *Treaty of Westphalia; October 24, 1648.* https://is.muni.cz/el/1423/podzim2008/MVZ430/um/Treaty-of-Westphalia.pdf

Jackson, Victoria. *Mortuary Customs.* http://www.jps.library.utoronto.ca/index.php/prandium/article/download/16209/13243

Jacoby, Russell. *Bloodlust.* https://books.google.com/

Jaenen, Cornelius. *Les Huguenots de la Nouvelle France.* http://www.erq.qc.ca/stmarc/huguenots.html

Jean, Lionel. *La colonie française de la Louisiane.* http://www.axl.cefan.ulaval.ca/francophonie/Nlle-France-Louisiane.htm

Jesuit Relations and Allied Documents *Volume X, Hurons 1636.* http://moses.creighton.edu/kripke/jesuitrelations/relations_10.html

———. *Volume XLVIII, Lower Canada, Ottawas 1662-1664.* http://moses.creighton.edu/kripke/jesuitrelations/relations_48.html

Johnson, Ben, ed. *Kings and Queens of England & Britain.* http://www.historic-uk.com/HistoryUK/KingsQueensofBritain/

———. *Kings and Queens of Scotland.* https://www.historic-uk.com/HistoryUK/HistoryofScotland/Kings-Queens-of-Scotland/

Johnson, Caleb. *The Mayflower.* http://mayflowerhistory.com/pilgrim-history

———. *Tisquantum ("Squanto").* http://mayflowerhistory.com/tisquantum/

Kelly, Martin. *The Great Awakening of the Early 18th Century.* https://www.thoughtco.com/great-awakening-of-early-18th-century-104594

———. *Jonathan Edwards, Colonial Clergyman of the Great Awakening.* *https://www.thoughtco.com/jonathan-edwards-4003804*

Khalaf, Salim George. *History of the Phoenician Canaanites.* http://www.phoenicia.org/history.html

Kidd, Kenneth, and Jim Coyle. *Crucible of Flames: Canada's War of 1812.* http://stardispatches.com/2012/12/crucible.pdf

Kimmerer, Robin Wall. *The Serviceberry: An Economy of Abundance.* https://emergencemagazine.org/story/the-serviceberry/?utm_source=pocket-newtab

King George III. *Royal Proclamation of October 7, 1763.* http://www.canadianlawsite.ca/royalproclamation.htm

Kingswood, Elizabeth Ellis. *"Gantowisas: The Role of Woman within the Haudenosaunee (Iroquois) Confederacy and Her Influence on the Early Suffrage Movement.* https://www.academia.edu/28940304/Gantowisas_The_Role_of_Woman_within_the_Haudenosaunee_Iroquois_Confederacy_and_Her_Influence_on_the_Early_Suffrage_Movement

Kirkpatrick, Nick. *Kingdom of Girls.* https://www.washingtonpost.com/news/insight/wp/2015/04/17/kingdom-of-girls-women-hold-power-in-this-remote-indian-village/

Kleen, Michael. *Colonial Intimacies.* https://michaelkleen.com/2016/11/14/colonial-intimacies-a-revealing-look-at-american-indian-marriage-in-new-england/

Klüppel, Karolin. *Inside a Fading Culture Ruled by Women.* https://www.washingtonpost.com/news/in-sight/wp/2017/07/12/for-hundreds-of-years-women-ruled-this-chinese-ethnic-minority-but-today-the-matriarchy-is-at-risk/?wpisrc=nl_todayworld&wpmm=1%20https://muse.jhu.edu/article/512043

Knoji. *What is the Origin of the Semitic People.* http://spirituality.knoji.com/what-is-the-origin-of-the-semitic-people/

Koch, Alexander. Chris Brierley, Mark M. Maslin, Simon L. Lewis. *Earth system impacts of the European arrival and Great Dying in the Americas after 1492*, Quaternary Science Reviews 207 (2019) 13e36, https://www.sciencedirect.com/science/article/pii/S0277379118307261/pdfft?md5=7640a392ed3d133a81e194f56b244627&pid=1-s2.0-S0277379118307261-main.pdf

Kratzer, Gary D. *Native American Mythology Cylinder.* https://starlab.com/wp-content/uploads/2017/04/D.-9.-Native-American-Myth-v616.pdf

La Roque de Roquebrune, R. *La Rocque de Roberval, Jean-François de,* Dictionary of Canadian Biography, http://www.biographi.ca.

LaDuke, Winona. *The Long and Honorable Battle of the Ojibwe to Keep Their Wild Rice Wild.* https://indiancountrymedianetwork.com/news/the-long-and-honorable-battle-of-the-ojibwe-to-keep-their-wild-rice-wild/

———. *'Minobimaatisiiwin: The Good Life'.* Accessed 21 January 2021. http://www.culturalsurvival.org/publications/cultural-survival-quarterly/minobimaatisiiwin-good-life.

Laframboise, Sandra, and Michael Anhorn. *The Way of the Two-Spirited People.* http://www.dancingtoeaglespiritsociety.org/twospirit.php

Lanham, Valerie, ed. *Early Visions of Florida, Jacques Le Moyne Narrative.* http://earlyfloridalit.net/?page_id=164

———. *Early Visions of Florida, Jean Ribaut, The Whole & True Discouerye of Terra Florida.*

http://earlyfloridalit.net/?page_id=122

———. *Early Visions of Florida, John Sparke, The Voyage Made by M. John Hawkins.* http://earlyfloridalit.net/?page_id=143

———. *Widow's Petition.* http://earlyfloridalit.net/?page_id=57

Leaving France. *LaRochelle.* http://www.apointinhistory.net/larochelle.php

Le Challeux, Nicholas. *Early Visions of Florida, Octet and Discours.* http://earlyfloridalit.net/?page_id=151

Lebanon 2000. *Canaanite & Phoenician History & Culture.* http://www.lebanon2000.com/ph.htm

Lefebvre, Melanie, and Alicia Elliott. *We Didn't Choose to Be Called Indigenous.* https://thewalrus.ca/we-didnt-choose-to-be-called-indigenous/

Lévesque, Carole, and Bruno Sioui. *Parlons de l'éducation des Autochtones au Québec.* http://www.reseaudialog.qc.ca/docs/CahierDIALOG-201102.pdf

Lipovsky, Dr. Igor P. *Where Did the Ancient Semites Come From?* http://biblicaltheology.com/Research/Lipovsky101.pdf

Lizotte, Marjorie. *Leaving France... (Hugenots Larochelle).* http://www.apointinhistory.net/larochelle.php

The Louisiana Purchase. http://www.monticello.org/site/jefferson/louisiana-purchase

Lowensteyn, Peter. *The Role of the Dutch in the Iroquois Wars.* http://www.lowensteyn.com/iroquois/

———. *The Role of Chief Canagueese in the Iroquois Wars.* http://www.lowensteyn.com/iroquois/canaqueese.html

Lytwyn, Victor P. *A Dish with One Spoon.* https://ojs3.library.carleton.ca/index.php/ALGQP/article/viewFile/262/249

George MacBeath, *Dugua de Mons, Pierre,* Dictionary of Canadian Biography http://www.biographi.ca

MacCaffrey, James. *History of the Catholic Church, From the Renaissance to the French Revolution Vol.1 Ch.5&7.* http://catholicity.elcore.net/MacCaffrey/HCCRFR_TOC.html

MacCulloch, Diarmaid, and Mark D'Arcy. *Thomas Cromwell – a very modern politician?* http://www.bbc.co.uk/history/0/22450966

MacDonald, David. *'Clearing the Plains' Continues with the Acquittal of Gerald Stanley.* https://www.nationalnewswatch.com/2018/02/12/clearing-the-plains-continues-with-the-acquittal-of-gerald-stanley/#.WoHZUejwaUm

Mann, Barbara A., and Jerry L. Fields. *A Sign in the Sky: Dating the League of the Haudenosaunee.* https://meridian.allenpress.com/aicrj/article-abstract/21/2/105/211735/A-Sign-in-the-Sky-Dating-the-League-of-the?redirectedFrom=fulltext

———. Spirits of Blood, Spirits of Breath: The Twinned Cosmos of Indigenous America. New York: Oxford University Press, 2016.

Mann, Charles C. *How Humankind Conquered the World.* https://www.wsj.com/articles/book-review-sapiens-a-brief-history-of-humankind-by-yuval-noah-harari-1423261230

Marche, Stephen. *The Unexamined Brutality of the Male Libido.* https://www.nytimes.com/2017/11/25/opinion/sunday/harassment-men-libido-masculinity.html?emc=edit_th_20171126&nl=todaysheadlines&nlid=38305667&_r=0

Marx, Karl. *The German Ideology: Part I.* https://www.marxists.org/archive/marx/works/1845/german-ideology/ch01b.htm

McGrath J.I. *The Code of Handsome Lake.* http://www.philtar.ac.uk/encyclopedia/nam/handsome.html

McIntosh, Emma *As Ottawa agrees to land talks with Six Nations, Ford pledges to 'protect' police.* https://www.nationalobserver.com/2020/08/21/news/ottawa-agrees-land-talks-six-nations-ford-pledges-protect-police

McIvor, Sharon, Pamela Palmater, and Shelagh Day. *Equality delayed is Equality Denied for Indigenous Women*. http://policyoptions.irpp.org/magazines/december-2017/equality-delayed-is-equality-denied-for-indigenous-women/

McLean, Ruth. *Our God Is Stronger' - Can Biodiverse Bijagós Fend Off Evangelical Threat?* https://www.theguardian.com/global-development/2018/nov/06/our-god-is-stronger-can-biodiverse-bijagos-fend-off-evangelical-threat

McLeod, D. Peter. *New Friends and Allies*. http://www3.sympatico.ca/donald.macleod2/jaenen.html

Mees, Mary C. *Teach Them the Moral Way of Living*. http://www.loyno.edu/~history/journal/1997-8/Mees.html

Melançon, R.P. ed. *Que Penser des Frères Kirke ?* http://collections.banq.qc.ca/jrn03/dn2087/src/1938/11/164865_1938-11.pdf

Mi'kma'ki. *Nations des Amériques*. http://www.astrosante.com/NationsDesAmeriques.html

Milanich, Dr. Jerald T. *What Happened to the Timucua?* https://www.aaanativearts.com/extinct-native-american-tribes-t-v-2/what-happened-to-the-timucua.html

Miller, Hunter, ed. *British-American Diplomacy, Preliminary Articles of Peace; November 30, 1782*. https://avalon.law.yale.edu/18th_century/prel1782.asp

———. *Declaration Signed by the American Commissioners*. http://avalon.law.yale.edu/18th_century/dec783.asp

Miller, Mark. *4,500-Year-Old Burial Suggests Norte Chico People of Peru Practiced Gender Equality*. https://www.ancient-origins.net/news-history-archaeology/4500-year-old-burial-suggests-norte-chico-people-peru-practiced-gender?nopaging=1

Monteil, Pierre. *La huitième guerre de religion sous le règne d'Henri IV*. http://www.histoire-fr.com/bourbons_henri4_2.htm

Moore, Amanda. *Edward VI and Vagrancy Act 1547 Poor Laws*. https://intriguing-history.com/edward-vi-enacts-harsh-statute-against-vagabonds/

Morrison, James. *Algonquin History in the Ottawa River Watershed*. http://ottawariver.org/pdf/05-ch2-3.pdf

———. *L'histoire des Algonquins sur la rivière des Outaouais*. http://www.comte-argenteuil.com/ha.pdf

Mosby, Ian. *Administering Colonial Science: Nutrition Research and Human Biomedical Experimentation in Aboriginal Communities and Residential Schools, 1942–1952*. https://muse.jhu.edu/article/512043

Murphy. Gerald *The Constitution of the Iroquois Nations: The Great Binding Law, Gayanashagowa* http://web.pdx.edu/~caskeym/iroquois_web/html/greatlaw.html#:~:text=If%20any%20man%20or%20any,Confederate%20Council%2C%20they%20shall%20be

National Aboriginal Health Organization. *Terminology*. http://www.naho.ca/publications/topics/terminology/

National Huguenot Society. *Who Were the Huguenots?* http://www.huguenot.netnation.com/general/huguenot.htm

National Parks Service, U.S. Department of the Interior. *U.S. National Park Service*. https://www.nps.gov/fost/learn/historyculture/1768-boundary-line-treaty.htm

Native Heritage Project. *Tecumseh – Die Like a Hero Going Home*. https://nativeheritageproject.com/2013/11/17/tecumseh-die-like-a-hero-going-home/

Native Languages of the Americas: Preserving and Promoting American Indian Languages. *Native American Tribes of Florida*. http://www.native-languages.org/florida.htm

Native Languages of the Americas. http://www.native-languages.org/wyandot-legends.htm

Native American Tribes of Florida. http://www.native-languages.org/florida.htm

Neuenschwander, René. *Valdès de Lyon (1140-1217)*. https://www.universdelabible.net/bible-et-histoire/les-reformateurs/133-valdes-de-lyon-1140-1217

New Netherland Institute. *A Tour of New Netherland, Albany.* http://www.newnetherlandinstitute.org/history-and-heritage/digital-exhibitions/a-tour-of-new-netherland/albany/fort-nassau/

Newhouse, David. *Indigenous Peoples, Canada and the Possibility of Reconciliation.* http://irpp.org/research-studies/insight-no11/?mc_cid=82a1f6c591&mc_eid=e135bb5a73

———. *A Nineteenth Century Indian Act for 21st Century Objectives?* http://policyoptions.irpp.org/magazines/october-2017/a-19th-century-indian-act-for-21st-century-objectives/

Newitz, Annalee. *What New Science Technique Tell us about Ancient Women Warriors.* https://www.nytimes.com/2021/01/01/opinion/women-hunter-leader.html?campaign_id=2&emc=edit_th_20210102&instance_id=25588&nl=todaysheadlines&regi_id=38305667&segment_id=48210

Norcliffe, G.B., and C.E. Heindrich. *The Preferred Orientation of Iroquoian Longhouses in Ontario.* https://www.ontarioarchaeology.org/Resources/Publications/oa23-1-norcliffe.pdf

O'Brien, Greg. *Mississippi History Now.* http://www.mshistorynow.mdah.ms.gov/index.php?id=8

Ohio University. *Stalagmite reveals carbon footprint of early Native Americans.* https://phys.org/news/2010-04-stalagmite-reveals-carbon-footprint-early.html

Old and Sold, Turn of the Century Wisdom for Today. *Paris - The Marais (originally published 1921).* http://www.oldandsold.com/articles08/paris-travel-23.shtml

The Old Farmer's Almanac. http://www.almanac.com/astronomy/moon/names/index.php

Omand, Gordon. *Study Explores How Ancient First Nations Gardened the Ocean on B.C.'s Coast.* http://www.nationalobserver.com/2016/12/21/news/study-explores-how-ancient-first-nations-gardened-ocean-bcs-coast

Ouellet Fernand. *Bédard, Pierre-Stanislas*, Dictionary of Canadian Biography http://www.biographi.ca/en/index.php

Parker, Geoffrey. *The Spanish Road to the Netherlands.* http://www.historynet.com/the-spanish-road-to-the-netherlands.htm

Parmenter, Jon. *The Meaning of Kaswentha.* http://honorthetworow.org/wp-content/uploads/2012/01/The-Meaning-of-Kaswentha-and-the-Two-Row.pdf

Pitt, Steven. *Windigo.* https://www.thecanadianencyclopedia.ca/en/article/windigo

Pomedli, Michael. *Different approaches to the 17th century Jesuit Mission.* https://www.brandonu.ca/arts/files/2011/01/panelistLecture20101206.pdf

Population of the State of Ohio. *Historical Population.* https://population.us/oh/

Pouliot-Thisdale, Eric. lecture, Laval Historical Society, March 6, 2018.

Preston, Douglas. *An Ancient City Emerges in a Remote Rain Forest.* http://www.newyorker.com/tech/elements/an-ancient-city-emerges-in-a-remote-rain-forest

Proceedings of the Massachusetts Historical Society. *Menéndez de Avilés August 1565 Letter 2.* https://thenewworld.us/the-letters-of-pedro-menendez-aviles/

Pryor, Cathy. *Rethinking Indigenous Australia's Agricultural Past.* http://www.abc.net.au/radionational/programs/bushtelegraph/rethinking-indigenous-australias-agricultural-past/5452454

Publius Historicus sur le XVIe siècle. *Le massacre de la Saint-Barthélemy 24 août 1572.* http://www.publius-historicus.com/st-bart2.htm

Puritan New England. https://www.khanacademy.org/humanities/ap-us-history/period-2/apush-colonial-north-america/a/puritan-new-england-massachusetts-bay

Rafferty, John P. Stephen T. Jackson, *Little Ice Age Geochronology,* https://www.britannica.com/science/Little-Ice-Age

Raynor, John. *Who Were Iroquet's "People?".* http://www.oashuroniachapter.com/2010/02/who-wereiroquetspeople.html

Redish, Laura. *Pukwudgie*. http://www.native-languages.org/pukwudgie.htm

Renaissance and Reformation 1500-1620: A Biographical Dictionary. *Albret, Jeanne D'.*
https://renaissance_and_reformation.enacademic.com/8/ALBRET%2C_Jeanne_D%27

Rioux, Christian. *Des Amérindiens si proches.* http://www.ledevoir.com/non-classe/478483/la-fondation-de-montreal-3-4-des-amerindiens-si-proches

Rosencranz, Hermanda. *Hidden People.* http://nativeamericanencyclopedia.com/native-american-beliefs-in-little-people

Ruizinowitz, Pablo Djankowicz. *Native Americans: Why Didn't the Mesoamerican Civilisations Spread Further North.* https://www.quora.com/Native-Americans-Why-didnt-the-Mesoamerican-civilisations-spread-further-north

Sampson, Anastacia. *Sweden, Religion.* http://www.sweden.org.za/sweden-religion.html

Sanderson, Douglas. *The Indian Act and the Subsidization of the South.*
http://policyoptions.irpp.org/magazines/september-2017/the-indian-act-and-indigenous-subsidization-of-the-south/

Sandhu, Sukhdev. *Revolution at the Docks.*
https://www.theguardian.com/books/2001/jan/27/historybooks

Sault Naturalists and Friends of Gros Cap. *Gros Cap, A Gem at Risk.*
http://soonats.pbworks.com/w/file/fetch/49812847/Sault%20Naturalists%202001%20Gros%20Cap%20Bluffs%20-%20A%20Gem%20at%20Risk.pdf

Savard, Rémi. *L'algonquin Tessouat et la fondation de Montréal.*
http://classiques.uqac.ca/contemporains/savard_remi/algonquin_tessouat/algonquin_tessouat_tdm.html

Sayenqueraghta. http://www.galafilm.com/chiefs/htmlen/mohawk/sp_sayenqueraghta.html

Schneider, Robert C. *Louis XIII, King of France Biography* https://galeapps.gale.com/apps/

Seven Nations of Canada. *Seven Nations of The Iroquois Confederacy.*
https://www.revolvy.com/topic/Seven%20Nations%20of%20Canada&item_type=topic

Shanahan, David. *Land for Goods: The Crawford Purchases.*
http://anishinabeknews.ca/2018/11/18/land-for-goods-the-crawford-purchases/

Shrubsole, Nocholas. *The Impossibility of Indigenous Religious Freedom.*
http://policyoptions.irpp.org/magazines/november-2017/the-impossibility-of-indigenous-religious-freedom/?mc_cid=5c4deb3a67&mc_eid=e135bb5a73

Simkin, John. *Was Henry VIII as Bad as Adolf Hitler and Joseph Stalin?* https://spartacus-educational.com/spartacus-blogURL48.htm

Simpson, Leanne. *Looking after Gdoo-naaganinaa: Precolonial Nishnaabeg Diplomatic and Treaty Relationships.* https://nandogikendan.com/wp-content/uploads/2018/04/69b9f-23-2-simpson.pdf

Sisson, Johnathan. *A Conceptual Framework for Dealing with the Past.* https://www.kairoscanada.org/wp-content/uploads/2015/06/UN-Joinet-Orentlicher-Principles.pdf

Six Nations Legacy Consortium. *1764 Treaty of Fort Niagara Wampum Belts.* https://www.canadiancrown.com/uploads/3/8/4/1/3841927/treaty_of_fort_niagara_wampum_belts.pdf

Smith, George H. *Immanuel Kant on Property Rights.*
https://www.libertarianism.org/columns/immanuel-kant-property-rights

Social Networks and Archival Context cooperative. *Loudoun, John Campbell, Earl of, 1705-1782.* http://snaccooperative.org/ark:/99166/w6k65b23

Soylent Communications. *Wives of Henri IV.* http://www.nndb.com/people/178/000092899/

St. Augustine Lighthouse and Maritime Museum. *Timeline of the French Colonization Attempts in Florida and the Loss of the 1565 French Fleet.*
http://www.staugustinelighthouse.com/LAMP/Research/FrenchFleet/frenchfleettimeline

Stanford University. *New World Post-Pandemic Reforestation Helped Start Little Ice Age, Say Stanford Scientists.* https://phys.org/news/2008-12-world-post-pandemic-reforestation-ice-age.html

Steen-Mcintyre, Virginia, Roald Fryxell, and Harold E. Malde. *Geologic Evidence for Age of Deposits at Hueyatlaco Archeological Site, Valsequillo, Mexico.* http://pleistocenecoalition.com/steen-mcintyre/Quat.Research_1981.pdf

Steingrad, Elena. *The Sun King Louis XIV Timeline.* http://www.louis-xiv.de/index.php?id=41

Sultzman, Lee. *Abenaki History.* http://www.tolatsga.org/aben.html

———. *Algonkin History.* http://www.tolatsga.org/alg.html

———. *Catawba History.* http://www.dickshovel.com/Catawba.html

———. *Chitimacha History.* http://www.dickshovel.com/chi.html

———. *Erie History.* http://www.dickshovel.com/erie.html

———. *Huron History.* http://www.tolatsga.org/hur.html

———. *Iroquois History.* http://www.tolatsga.org/iro.html

———. *Massachuset History.* http://www.dickshovel.com/massa.html

———. *Montagnais History.* http://www.dickshovel.com/mon.html

———. *Nipmuc History.* http://www.dickshovel.com/nipmuc.html

———. *Narragansett History.* http://www.dickshovel.com/Narra.html

———. *Neutral History.* www.dickshovel.com/neutral.html

———. *Pennacook History.* http://www.dickshovel.com/penna.html

———. *Pequot History.* http://www.dickshovel.com/peq.html

———. *Potawatomi History.* http://www.tolatsga.org/pota.html

———. *Wampanoag History.* http://www.tolatsga.org/wampa.html

Surtees, R. *Indian Land Surrenders of Land in Ontario, 1763-1867.* http://publications.gc.ca/collections/collection_2017/aanc-inac/R5-350-1983-eng.pdf

Susquehanna Indian Tribe History. http://www.accessgenealogy.com/native/tribes/susquehanna/susquehannahist.htm

Swedish Colonial Society. *A Brief History of New Sweden in America.* http://colonialswedes.net/History/History.html

This Day in History. *1588 Spanish Armada Defeated.* https://www.history.com/this-day-in-history/spanish-armada-defeated

Thomas Jefferson Foundation, Monticello Catalogue. *The Louisiana Purchase.* http://www.monticello.org/site/jefferson/louisiana-purchase

Thomas, Katsithawi Ashley. *Gender Roles Among the Iroquois.* http:///modules/locker/files/get_group_file.phtml?fid=16248953&gid=4640073

Thompson, Gary D. *Episodic Survey of the History of the Constellations.* http://members.westnet.com.au/gary-david-thompson/page11-2.html

Thornhill, Randy, and Craig T. Palmer. *Why Men Rape.* http://www.csus.edu/indiv/m/merlinos/thornhill.html

Tremblay, Roland. *La mission de la Montagne et le fort des Messieurs.* https://ville.montreal.qc.ca/memoiresdesmontrealais/la-mission-de-la-montagne-et-le-fort-des-messieurs

Trudel, Marcel. *Champlain, Samuel de; Caën, Guillaume de; Caën, Émery de* Dictionary of Canadian Biography http://www.biographi.ca

Trueman, C N. *Henry VII and the Economy.* https://www.historylearningsite.co.uk/tudor-england/henry-vii-and-the-economy/

———. *John Calvin.* http://www.historylearningsite.co.uk/john-calvin/

Truth and Reconciliation Commission of Canada. *Truth and Reconciliation Commission of Canada: Calls to Action.* http://nctr.ca/assets/reports/Calls_to_Action_English2.pdf

Tulloch, Hugh. *Early Visions of Florida, René Goulaine de Laudonnière.* http://earlyfloridalit.net/?p=588

University of Utah GSLC. *Evolution of Corn.* http://learn.genetics.utah.edu/content/selection/corn/

Vågene, Åshild. *500 Years Later, Scientists Discover What Probably Killed the Aztecs.* https://www.apdnews.com/science-military/816438.html

Van Doren, C, and J.R. Boyd, eds. *A Treaty with the Indian Six Nations, 1744* (1938). http://treatiesportal.unl.edu/earlytreaties/treaty.00003.html

Van Popta, J. L. *John Calvin: A Man of Compassion.* http://spindleworks.com/library/van-popta/calvin.htm

Velde, François. *The Holy Roman Empire.* http://www.heraldica.org/topics/national/hre.htm#Name

Venables, Robert W. *Polishing of the Silver Covenant Chain.* http://honorthetworow.org/wp-content/uploads/2013/03/Venables-on-the-Covenant-Chain-of-Treaties.pdf

Vigne, Randolph. *Field Marshal Earl Ligonier (1680-1770).* http://www.rdgmuseum.org.uk/ligonier.htm

Le Vrai Discours Actuel de Hermann Cebert. *Déclaration de Souveraineté d'Atikamekw Nehirowisiw.* https://levraidiscoursactuel.com/2014/09/09/declaration-de-souverainete-datikamekw-nehirowisiw-un-precedent-de-souverainete-et-dindependance-dans-lhistoire-du-canada-et-du-quebec/

Welcome to Dutch Dikes. *(Dutch) Dike History.* http://dutchdikes.net/history/

Welker, Glenn, coll. *Constitution of the Iroquois Nations.* http://www.indigenouspeople.net/iroqcon.htm

What-When-How. *Birth Control, Native Americans of California.* http://what-when-how.com/birth-control/native-americans-of-california-birth-control

White, Craig. *Three Versions of the Iroquois Creation Story.* http://coursesite.uhcl.edu/HSH/Whitec/texts/Amerind/origins/AmindorsIroquois.htm

Whittall, James P. *The Inscribed Stones of Sherbrooke, Quebec,* Transcription, CBC Ideas May 6, 1977.

Widmer, Ted. *Carter Roger Williams Initiative.* http://www.findingrogerwilliams.com/essays/native-americans

Wilde, Robert. *The Rulers of France: From 840 Until 2017.* https://www.thoughtco.com/rulers-of-france-840-until-2015-3861418

Wilensky, Gabriel. *Six Million Crucifixions.* http://sixmillioncrucifixions.com/

Winterhaze13. *The English Navy 1649-1815.* http://allempires.com/article/index.php?q=english_navy_1649-1815

World Heritage Encyclopedia. *Philip de Montmorency, Count of Horn.* http://self.gutenberg.org/articles/eng/Philip_de_Montmorency,_Count_of_Horn

World Heritage Encyclopedia. *Northwest Territory.* http://self.gutenberg.org/articles/Northwest_Territory

World History. *King Philip's War.* https://www.worldhistory.biz/modern-history/85511-king-philipps-war.html

Wright, Ronald. *Into the Heart of Empire.* http://reviewcanada.ca/magazine/2017/01/into-the-heart-of-empire/

Wright, Roy. *Ontario Iroquois Languages.* http://www.ontarioarchaeology.on.ca/Resources/ArchNotes/an74-7.pdf

Wroth, David. *Japingka Aboriginal Art.* https://japingkaaboriginalart.com/articles/songlines-important-aboriginal-art/

Yirka, Bob. *Research Team Suggests European Little Ice Age Came About Due to Reforestation in the New World.* https://phys.org/news/2011-10-team-european-ice-age-due.html#jCp

Yudkowsky, Eliezer. *The Tragedy of Group Selectionism.* https://www.lesswrong.com/posts/QsMJQSFj7WfoTMNgW/the-tragedy-of-group-selectionism#comments

Yumpu. *Swidden Agriculture.* https://www.yumpu.com/en/document/read/6252433/swidden-agriculture-ancient-systems-in-transition-sustaining-food

Illustrations

Page 14. Image inspired by and adapted from a map illustrated by Molly Braun in Waldman, Carl, and Molly Braun, 1985. Atlas of the North American Indian. Facts on File, New York.

Page 22. Greyscale rendering of "Corncobs" https://en.wikipedia.org/wiki/File:Corncobs.jpg. Author: Sam Fentress, https://creativecommons.org/licenses/by-sa/2.0/deed.en

Page 27. Map depicting Jacques Cartier's first trip to North America inspired by Hiram B. Stephens, Jacques Cartier and His Four Voyages to Canada Montreal, Canada: W. Drysdale & Co., 1890.

Page 29. Reproduced in greyscale with permission from the artist, Bonnie Shemie Taken from Houses of Bark: Tipi, Wigwam and Longhouse. Montreal, Quebec: Tundra Books, 1998.

Page 44. Map of the Holy Roman Empire prepared by the author in collaboration with Rita Bauer.

Page 46. Overview of the Rhine and Meuse deltas: Wikimedia Commons. It is a greyscale of a screenshot from NASA World Wind.

Page 51. Natives worshipping erected column. 1562. State Archives of Florida, Florida Memory. https://www.floridamemory.com/items/show/4352.

Page 74. Leiden pilgrims on the deck of the Speedwell: Wikimedia Commons, greyscale from painting by Robert Walter Weir, 1803-1889. https://commons.wikimedia.org/wiki/File:Embarkation_of_the_Pilgrims.jpg.

Page 83. The Old Mill Inn
https://en.wikipedia.org/wiki/File:%C3%89tienne_Br%C3%Bbl%C3%A9_-_The_Old_Mill_Inn,_Toronto.JPG>, Author: PFHLai,
https://creativecommons.org/licenses/by-sa/3.0/deed.en

Page 88. Assassination of Henri IV. Wikimedia Commons:
https://commons.wikimedia.org/wiki/File:The_assassination_of_Henry_IV,_King_of_France,_1610;_a_tumul_Wellcome_V0041777.jpg

Page 91. Eve tastes the forbidden fruit. This file is made available under the Creative Commons CC0 1.0 Universal Public Domain Dedication.

https://commons.wikimedia.org/wiki/File:Temptation_Adam_Eva.jpg

Page 93. Three Sisters garden, photo by author..

Page 97. Half Moon on the Hudson. Wikimedia Commons. No source information found. https://commons.wikimedia.org/wiki/File:Half_Moon_in_Hudson.jpg

Page 98. The last voyage of Henry Hudson. Greyscale. Wikimedia Commons. Artist John Collier, 1850 – 1934. https://commons.wikimedia.org/wiki/File:Last_Voyage_Of_Henry_Hudson.jpg

Page 108. 1605 map drawn by Samuel de Champlain of Plymouth Harbour. Wikimedia Commons, United States National Park service.
https://en.wikipedia.org/wiki/Squanto#/media/File:Champlain's_Map_of_Plymouth_Harbor.jpg

Page 113. Line drawing by Sheila Eskenazi, annotation Rita Bauer.

Page 117. Greyscale. Cardinal Richelieu at the Siege of La Rochelle. Henri-Paul Motte, 1846 – 1922, painting completed Paris, 1881. Wikimedia Commons,
https://wiki2.org/en/File:RichelieuRochelle_jpg#/media/File:Siege_of_La_Rochelle_1881_Henri_Motte.png

Page 118. Surrender of Quebec to the Huguenot Captain David Kirke. Original black and white sketch made by Richard Caton Woodville Jr. (1856 -1927) for an Oilette postcard. Wikimedia Commons https://commons.wikimedia.org/wiki/File:OUR_FIRST_FOOT-ING_IN_CANADA._CHAMPLAIN_SURRENDERING_QUEBEC_TO_ADMIRAL_KIRK E._JULY_20_1629.jpg

Page 134. Jérôme Le Royer de La Dauversière. Oil on canvas, Adèle-Joséphine Grosjean, 1836, Archives et collection des hospitalières de Saint-Joseph de Montréal. Wikimedia Commons. https://fr.wikipedia.org/wiki/J%C3%A9r%C3%B4me_Le_Royer_de_La_Dauversi%C3%A8 re#/media/Fichier:Jerome_Le_Royer_de_la_Dauversiere.JPG

Page 136. Fort Ville Marie on Montreal Island, 1645. Wikimedia Commons, sketch by Pierre-Louis Morin, 1884. https://upload.wikimedia.org/wikipedia/commons/c/c4/Fort_Mon-treal_1645.jpg

Page 145. Line drawing by Sheila Eskenazi, annotation Rita Bauer.

Page 154. King Philip. Wikimedia Commons, by Paul Revere 1735-1818. https://commons.wikimedia.org/wiki/File:Philip_King_of_Mount_Hope_by_Paul_Revere.j peg

Page 154. The Kawentha, Two Row Wampum belt. Wikimedia Commons under Creative Commons Attribution-ShareAlike 4.0 International Public License. Credit: Wikipedia con-tributor Nativemedia.

https://commons.wikimedia.org/wiki/File:The_Two_Row_Wampum_is_one_of_the_oldest_tr eaty_relationships_between_the_Onkwehonweh_original_people_of_Turtle_Island_North _America_and_European_immigrants._The_treaty_was_made_in_1613.jpg

Page 157. The Great Swamp Fight. Wikimedia Commons, engraver unknown, published 1857. https://upload.wikimedia.org/wikipedia/commons/2/21/CaptureOfKingPhillipsFort.jpg

Page 165. La Grande Paix de Montréal. Wikimedia Commons. https://commons.wikimedia.org/wiki/File:Grande_Paix_Montreal.jpg

Page 167. Seven Fires (Nations) map. Modified version of Wikipedia contributor Peterseji's NASA base map. Wikipedia Commons. https://en.wikipedia.org/wiki/Seven_Nations_of_Canada#/media/File:Seven_Nations_copy .jpg

Page 170. Nooherooka Tuscarora stronghold. National Register of Historic Places in the United States of America. Reference number is 9000529. Wikipedia contributor Roskera. Wikimedia Commons. https://commons.wikimedia.org/wiki/File:Fort_Neoheroka_His-torical_Marker.jpg

Page 177. Sir William Johnson. Old New York Frontier by Francis Whiting Halsey (1851–1919) for Charles Scribner's sons, 1901. Wikimedia Commons https://commons.wiki-media.org/wiki/File:Sir_William_Johnson.png

Page 179. Seven Years' War. Greyscale of Wikipedia contributor Gabagool. Wikimedia Com-mons https://commons.wikimedia.org/wiki/File:SevenYearsWar.png

License: https://creativecommons.org/licenses/by/3.0/deed.en

Page 182. Fort DuQuesne and Fort Necessity. Map drawn by Joshua Fry & Peter Jefferson in 1751, published by Thos. Jefferys, London, 1755. Wikimedia Commons. https://com-mons.wikimedia.org/wiki/File:Kitfry-1-.jpg

Page 186. Line drawing by Sheila Eskenazi, annotation Rita Bauer.

Page 194. Crown Point. United States Library of Congress Prints and Photographs division Digital ID cph.3a49136. Wikimedia Commons. Artist: Thomas Davies, 1737 -1812. https://commons.wikimedia.org/wiki/File:South_view_of_crown_point_1760.jpg

Page 197. Seven Years' War map. Wikipedia contributor Hoodinski CC BY-SA 3.0 https://creativecommons.org/licenses/by-sa/3.0/

Wikimedia Commons.
https://commons.wikimedia.org/wiki/File:French_and_indian_war_map.svg

Page 200. Pontiac Conspiracy. Wikimedia Commons. Artist Alfred Bobbett, 1840-1888.
https://commons.wikimedia.org/wiki/File:Pontiac_conspiracy.jpg

Page 201. British territorial assumption. New borders drawn by the Royal Proclamation of 1763. Wikipedia contributor Jon Playtek, 2008. CC BY-SA 3.0
https://creativecommons.org/licenses/by-sa/3.0/ Wikimedia Commons. https://en.wikipedia.org/wiki/Royal_Proclamation_of_1763#/media/File:NorthAmerica1762-83.png

Page 203. U.S. postage 6-cent-stamp from 1968.

Page 204. Seven Years' War British warships. Greyscale reproduction of Clarkson Frederick Stanfield (1793-1867) painting the Battle of Trafalgar. 1836. Wikimedia Commons.
https://commons.wikimedia.org/wiki/File:The_Battle_of_Trafalgar_by_William_Clarkson_Stanfield.jpg

Page 205. The Proclamation of 1763 and 1768 Treaty of Fort Stanwix. Greyscale with modification. NationalAtlas.gov | 1970 print edition: Library of Congress, Perry-Castañeda Library. Wikimedia Commons.
https://commons.wikimedia.org/wiki/File:Map_of_territorial_growth_1775.jpg

Page 207. Johnson Hall. Greyscale reproduction of artist Edward Lawson Henry (1841–1919) in 1903. Wikimedia Commons.
https://commons.wikimedia.org/wiki/File:Johnson_Hall_by_Henry.jpg

Page 211. Buffer State. Greyscale with annotations added. Wikipedia contributor Drdpw, 2013. CC BY-SA 4.0 https://creativecommons.org/licenses/by-sa/4.0/

Wikimedia Commons.
https://en.wikipedia.org/wiki/Indian_barrier_state#/media/File:NW_Native_Tribes,_1792.png

Page 217. British divided Quebec. Greyscale annotated. Originally created by Wikipedia contributor Astrokey44. CC BY-SA 3.0 https://creativecommons.org/licenses/by-sa/3.0/

Wikimedia Commons.
https://commons.wikimedia.org/wiki/File:Canada_upper_lower_map.PNG

Page 222. Louisiana Purchase. Greyscale with added annotations from Wikipedia contributor RaviC, 2007. Wikimedia Commons.
https://commons.wikimedia.org/wiki/File:Aquired_Lands_of_the_US.svg

Page 227. Fort at Michilimackinac. The Pictorial Field Book of the War of 1812 Benson J. Lossing, 1896, University of California, p 267.

Page 230. Manifest Destiny. Greyscale copy of American Progress (1872) by John Gast. Wikimedia Commons.
https://commons.wikimedia.org/wiki/File:American_Progress_(John_Gast_painting).jpg

Index

ABOUT THE AUTHOR

PHOTO: MICHAEL AVERILL

Joseph Graham, a historian from the Laurentian mountains north of Montreal, is the author of the best-selling *Naming the Laurentians*.

He has worked for decades to encourage people to know and value their history.

Together, he and his partner grow their own food, inspired by Indigenous farming methods.

InsatiableHunger.ca